D0916817

Classic Knitted Cotton Edgings

Towels, curtains and doll's bed—featuring antique knitting.

Classic Knitted Cotton Edgings

Furze Hewitt and Billie Daley

Dryad Press Ltd   London

To
Geoffrey Charles Campbell Daley
for his help and encouragement.
Vale.

Acknowledgment

Our grateful thanks to our families and friends. To the many antique dealers who willingly searched through their stock for old needlework publications, especially John Cummin of Queanbeyan Books and Prints, Millhouse Gallery.

A special thanks to Robyn Healy of the Australian National Gallery who gave us her time and expertise.

Also thanks to the Power House Museum, Ultimo, Sydney, for their help in providing access to their patterns.

To Robert Roach, our photographer, for his calm approach to a mammoth task, completed with dedication.

To Neville Pannowitz for his help with the photographic sets.

To Martin Daley for his appropriate illustrations and to his wife Sue for her understanding.

To Gillian Colquhoun who volunteered to type our patterns and managed to create order from chaos. Our appreciation to the following for their help in various ways: Digby Wilson, James & Patsy Ranger, Carol Davey, Lisa Brown, Leigh Taumoefolau, Clare Harris, Lexi Greig, Marie White, Eileen Smith, Jane Carmichael, and to everyone who made this work possible.

Cover: Hand knitted curtains—antique. Teatray with knitted lace edging.

© F. Hewitt & B. Daley 1987

Published simultaneously in Great Britain and Australia in 1987 by Dryad Press Ltd 8 Cavendish Square London WIM OAJ and Kangaroo Press Pty Ltd 3 Whitehall Road (P.O. Box 75) Kenthurst 2156 Typeset by G.T. Setters Pty Limited Kenthurst 2156 Printed in Singapore by Kyodo-Shing Loong Printing Industries Pte Ltd

ISBN 0 8521 9740 3

Contents

'If you can do, or think you can, begin it.'

Anon.

Victorian tea cloth.

Introduction

There is a tranquil beauty about white cotton lace knitting which the Victorians used to edge white on white embroidery and trapunto quilting. Samples of fine Victorian knitting are still to be found in antique shops, especially those dealing in fine linen. These knitted edgings are sometimes confused with crochet work, and one can but marvel at the delicacy that can be achieved in knitting.

We have collected many examples of these exquisite items, but were frustrated to find a dearth of patterns for the knitted edgings and insertions. This book is the result of our search for such patterns.

The majority of these patterns were found in old needlework books of the nineteenth century, and we are indebted to people who have shared their patterns with us. We enjoyed researching, amending and knitting the samples, and found ourselves more and more engrossed in the endless variations and intricacy of the craft. Perhaps we should warn you—white cotton lace knitting is addictive!

There are distinct advantages to our craft. The durability of cotton knitting is assured. The materials are portable: all that is needed is a pair of needles, a ball of cotton and we found it useful to have a notebook and pencil to record the row being worked.

Cotton can be worked during the summer months, when most other knitting has been set aside, and there is no worry about colour combinations.

The edgings and insertions have many uses. Apart from the trimming of household linens, they can provide a decorative trim for clothing and furnishings.

In this book we have included simple beginner's patterns (marked with an asterisk), others are more complicated to satisfy the experienced knitter.

Each pattern is illustrated and has the full instructions. Abbreviations are given on page 19.

There is a section on the origins of the names of the patterns. These names differ in various regions. For this reason we have decided to dispense with the nomenclature, and have relied on a numerical system.

The patterns in this book were knitted on size 2mm (14) needles, and No. 8, or 4 ply cotton. However, they can be worked on larger or smaller needles.

Needles

Knitting needles must be cared for, especially when using white cotton. The old steel needles respond to the occasional rub with beeswax. We rub our spare needles with a coating of wax before storing in tissue. Plastic film for storing old metal needles is to be avoided. The film can cause a moisture build up, which will rust the metal. These sets of needles are becoming increasingly difficult to find, and should be well cared for. A slight stickiness of the needle whilst knitting is annoying. An old remedy for this is to rub the needle through your hair—it works!

The edgings, especially the narrow ones, need to be knitted on short needles. Try looking through the antique shops in your area. You may be lucky enough to find a set of glove needles. These are the ideal length for lace edgings.

Purchasing Your Cotton

Quantity will depend on the article being trimmed. It is wise to purchase your cotton from the same dye lot, as you can get an optical variation in white cotton. Left over yarn can be used to trim or make smaller articles. Other fibres can be used such as silk, wool, linen or even fine metallic thread.

Knitting Notes

Always read the instructions before casting on. The patterns are there to guide you, only you can decide whether to use the edging to trim a pair of sheets, or a thick towel.

No measurements are given in this book, your use of yarn, needles and tension will determine the width of the edging. We suggest a sample be knitted to determine the width you require.

The use of a notebook and pencil to record the row being worked is essential in lace knitting.

Should you drop a stitch whilst knitting an edging it is easier to undo the work, row by row, than to try and retrieve the stitch.

Avoid joining yarn in the middle of your work, join and leave a piece of thread on the straight edge of the edging. You can use this to sew the edging to the article being trimmed.

Turning. When turning in a row, slip the first stitch on each return row to make a neater turn.

Right side. First row of the edging is always the right side, unless otherwise stated.

Asterisks. Take care to repeat *—* the number of times stated.

Parenthesis. The instructions inside the brackets must be worked the number of times stated immediately after the brackets.

Allowing for fullness. When the edging is used to trim an article with corners, allow ample and even fullness at each corner.

Knitted collars.

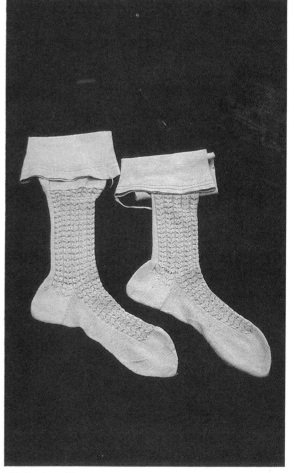

Knitted stockings—antique.

Casting On

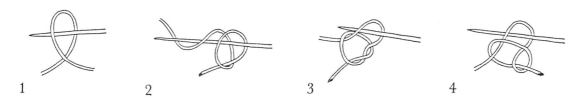

1   2   3   4

Thumb Method

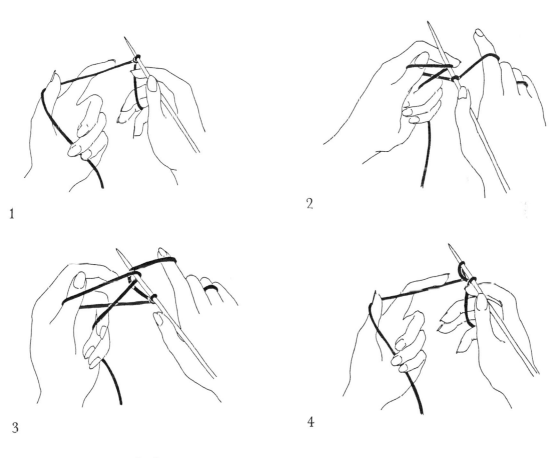

1   2

3   4

Invisible cast on method.
1. With contrasting thread, cast on the number of stitches required, work two rows in stocking stitch.
2. With main thread, continue edging until length required.
3. When edging is completed remove contrasting thread. Either graft, or sew together open stitches from both ends of work.

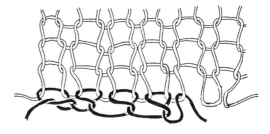

How to Knit

How to Purl

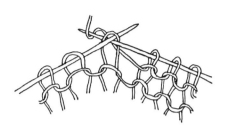
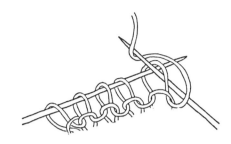

Garter Stitch

Knit each row.

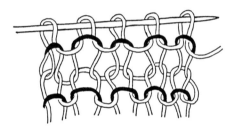

Stocking Stitch

One row knit, one row purl.

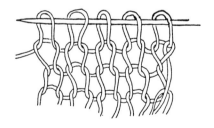

Right side—smooth side.

Wrong side showing loops or ridges.

Increasing in lace knitting. There are three methods of increasing the number of stitches on a row. One way is to knit twice into a stitch (= inc 1 in this book). This can be done k-wise, p-wise or both ways, and it can be done into the front or the back of the stitch. Read the pattern carefully to see which way to work the stitch.

A second method is to pick up a stitch from the previous row (i.e. the thread running between the needles) and knit into that loop. Again, read the instructions carefully. This prevents a hole and is suitable for darts and for shaping.

The third method (= ml, yon, yfwd or yrn in this book) produces the holes in lace patterns. The way it is worked depends on whether the extra stitch is to be made between two knit stitches, a knit and a purl, or two purl stitches. Between knit stitches the yarn is brought forward, and over the needle as you knit the next stitch, thus forming a new stitch. Between two purl stitches, take the yarn over, and round the needle, purl the next stitch and your new stitch is formed. Between a knit and a purl stitch, wrap the yarn round the needle before working the next stitch.

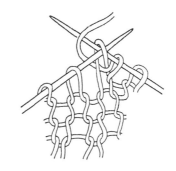

1. Increase one in next stitch.

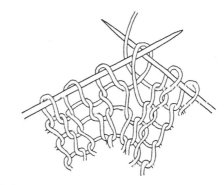

2. Pick up a stitch.

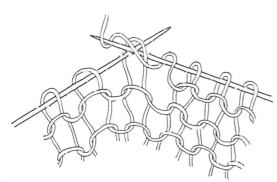

3(a). Make one between two knit stitches.

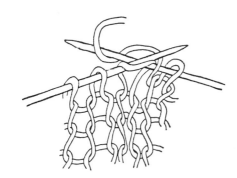

3(b). Make one between two purl stitches.

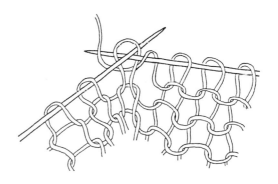

3(c). Make one between a knit and a purl stitch.

Decreasing in lace knitting. Again there are several methods. One way is to knit or purl two stitches together. A second method is to pass the next but one stitch previously worked over the latter.

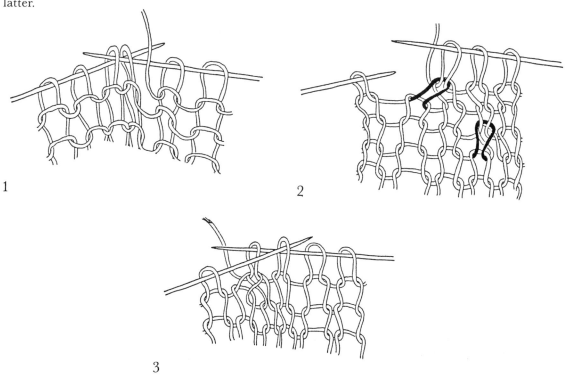

1

2

3

Casting off. If you are inclined to cast off tightly, use a needle a size larger.

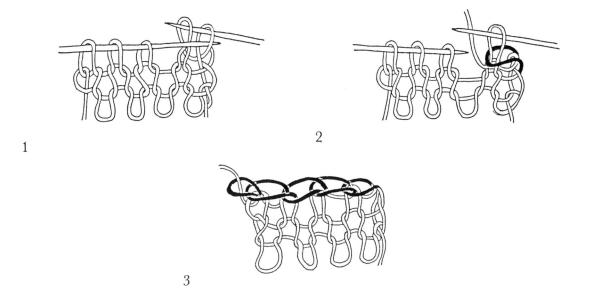

1

2

3

Attaching Edging

Use a flat seam to attach your edging. Hold work right sides together, do not pull the thread too tight, or your seam will not lie flat. Aim for a neat even join.

Caring for Your Work

Always wrap your white cotton knitting in a soft white cloth before putting it away. Spread the cloth over your lap whilst knitting. The constant pulling of the thread over a rough fabric skirt can damage the yarn.

Hands play an important role in producing all crafts. They need to be cared for too. See that they are clean, and kept smooth with a good hand cream. In hot sticky weather a little talcum powder helps to keep them dry.

The old magazines gave detailed washing instructions. One publication even suggests leaving the articles in the moonlight to bleach the cotton. Here is an updated version, which we have found reliable.

Wash your knitting frequently. Dirt and grit can cause deterioration of the fibres. Articles can be safely washed in a machine with care. Cotton absorbs moisture, so large articles will need support when drying so that they do not sag. Remove as much moisture as possible before hanging over a sheet stretched across two lines. Small articles can be dried flat. Avoid exposing washing to strong sunlight, which can yellow the thread, and if possible choose a windy day. Edgings respond to pressing with a light iron. Use a towel underneath the work to prevent the design being flattened.

When you think of the time spent creating the beauty of white cotton knitting, it is worth a little extra time spent caring for it.

Finally, enjoy using the patterns in this book. We have both learnt a lot about this fascinating craft since we started collecting our edgings. We even discovered St Fiacre, the patron saint of all knitters.

Sheets—knitted edge.

Towels with knitted edgings.

Antique bedspread with deep leaf and fluted edging.

Swirl bedspread with fringed edging.

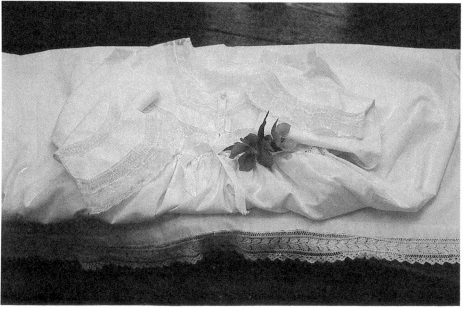

Antique nightgown—knitted edging.

Pattern Names

Some of the oldest lace knitting patterns are to be found on edgings. The early knitters in rural or island communities named their patterns after familiar articles, and the knitting patterns were given different names in different regions. Collecting patterns for our samples we found a wealth of names, some of which we have recorded.

In fishing areas you find names connected with the fishing industry. Examples in this book include Pattern 1: Sea Urchin, Pattern 2: Cable and Fishbone, Pattern 26: Rope Edging, Pattern 27: Shell Insertion, Pattern 51: Cockle Shell, Pattern 62: Shale Border, Pattern 73: Shale Variation, Pattern 74: Small Scallop, Pattern 121: Shark's tooth, Pattern 144: Restless Wave, Pattern 192: Crab, Pattern 168: Twisted Rope and Faggot Insertion, and Pattern 199: Fishbone. Old Shale was named after the stratified stone which forms the beaches.

Feather patterns abound, one of the earliest being Feather and Fan (Pattern 62). Pattern 192 is also known as Feather and Faggot Border. Feathers played a role in rural communities. The feathers of sea birds and domestic fowl were carefully saved and washed to provide feather ticks or mattresses and pillows. We found a quilled pattern, Pattern 47, and wondered if it received its name from a writing quill, or the goffering so fashionable in the nineteenth century.

Plants too played their part in providing names for the early patterns. Leaf patterns include the popular Raised Leaf in many designs, also known as Lily Pond (Patterns 78 and 99), and the much favoured Twin Leaf or Double Rose Leaf Pattern (Patterns 127 and 66). We came across this pattern frequently and have many knitted examples in our collection. Examples in this book include Pattern 11: Leaves, Pattern 70: Oak Leaves, Pattern 161: Oak, Pattern 100: Feathered Leaves, Pattern 127: Miniature Twin Leaf, Pattern 145: Travelling Vine, Pattern 150: Rose Leaf, Pattern 153: Fern, Pattern 164: Palm or Palmate, Pattern 165: Sheaves of Wheat, Pattern 176: Marching Leaves, Pattern 189: Falling Leaves, and Pattern 190: Beech Leaves.

We found bobble patterns of all sizes, both single and clustered, in rows, diamonds, and squares. Some are incorporated with fluted edgings. The Victorians must have enjoyed knitting them. Pattern 123 is Flute and Bobble, Pattern 130: Clustered Bobble and Lace, Pattern 134: Open Bobble and Leaf, Pattern 139: Clustered Bobble and Leaf, and Pattern 140: Blistered Bobble Insertion.

The welt family of patterns, made up of raised lines, are effective for creating geometric designs of great complexity. Quaker's Welt is well known. It probably owes its name to its simplistic beauty, and because of its plain welt it was used by the Quakers. Pattern 194 is an example of this, and is also known as Diagonal Welted Square Insertion. The welts are an ancient family of patterns and could easily have received their name from the footwear industry. Some examples in this book are Pattern 18: Pleated Welt, Pattern 37: Fluted, Pattern 84: Narrow Pleated, and Pattern 182: Zigzag Welt.

The triangles also have several names. The Flag or Pennant is so called because the rows of triangles appear like little flags. Used horizontally the triangles are known as Wedge Pattern. Pattern 42 is a Small Flag Edging, Pattern 162 is a Double Wedge Insertion, and Pattern 198 a Wedge Insertion.

Antique cloths—knitted lace.

Victorian tea cloth.

The White Cotton Knitting Mania

Many exquisite examples of knitted lace were produced in the Victorian era.

This craft was enjoyed all over Europe, but in Britain it was of particular importance. Tariffs were imposed on the importation of lace into Britain, so the knitting of white cotton lace became a worthy substitute.

The invention of new machinery in the industrial revolution, plus the improved trade with India, saw vast quantities of raw cotton (which became known as 'tree wool') imported into the country.

The period also saw rapid economic expansion. Knitting cotton became freely available: early publications of women's magazines advertised quality cotton yarns at one penny a ball. This proved suitable for knitting the household items the Victorians loved, and encouraged a spate of white cotton knitting. Women's magazines became popular in the mid-nineteenth century, and they provided, for the first time, written information on dozens of different knitted articles.

Each issue contained new stitches and intricate combinations of purl and plain emerged.

White cotton knitting swept the land. Yards of finely knitted lace were made to trim pillow shams, sheets, valances, petticoats, and other articles of clothing. The work was executed with fine cotton on metal needles. The needles ranged from size 16 to a tiny size 24—almost the size of a fine darning needle.

Examples of this work are numerous, and warrant every respect. We have included a few illustrations of Victorian knitting in this book.

Unfortunately in the mid-twentieth century the vogue for Victorian artifacts was at an ebb. Consequently, much of the early work has disappeared. Hopefully we have contributed to the preservation of their patterns.

There is an emerging interest in the gentle craft of white cotton knitting, which we fully support, and are trying to foster with the patterns in this book.

Handkerchief—knitted edging.

Knitted cloth.

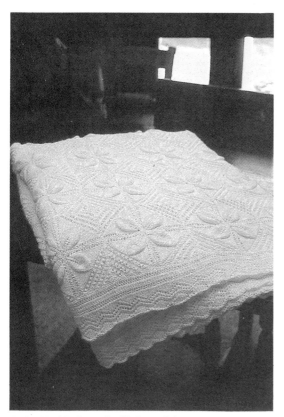

Raised leaf bedspread with lace edging.

Antique edging.

Some Helpful Abbreviations

k	knit
p	purl
st	stitch
sts	stitches
b	back
f	front
sl	slip
wyib	with yarn in back
wyif	with yarn in front
tog	together
inc 1	knit twice into following stitch
m1	make one stitch by winding yarn round needle
turn	work is turned before end of row
dpn	double pointed needle
motif	design unit
panel	narrow insertion

st.st	stocking stitch—knit right side, purl wrong side
garter st	knit all rows
mb	make bobble
beg	beginning
psso	pass slipped stitch over
p2sso	pass 2 slipped stitches over
p-wise	purlwise
k-wise	knitwise
tbl	through back of loops
ybk	yarn back
yfwd	yarn forward
yon	yarn over needle
yrn	yarn around needle
R.H.	right hand
L.H.	left hand

Comparative Terms

British	American
cast off	bind off
shape cap	shape top
alternate rows	every other row
tension	gauge
miss	skip
work straight	work even
stocking stitch	stockinette stitch

Bedspread—lace edging.

Patterns

Pattern 1

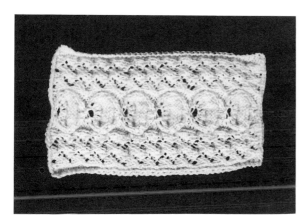

Cast on 34 sts

Row 1: P.

Row 2: Sl 1, p3, k1, m1, k2 tog, k2, m1, k2 tog, k2, p3, *k next but one st behind the 1st st, m5, then k 1st st*, p3, k1, m1, k2 tog, k2, m1, k2 tog, k2, k1 tbl.

Row 3: Sl 1, k3, p1, p2 tog, m1, p2, p2 tog, m1, p2, k3, p1, k5 tbl, p1, k3, p1, p2 tog, m1, p2, p2 tog, m1, p2, k3, k1 tbl.

Row 4: Sl 1, p3, k3, m1, k2 tog, k2, m1, k2 tog, p3 (k1, m1) 6 times, k1, p3, k3, m1, k2 tog, k2, m1, k2 tog, p3, k1 tbl.

Row 5: Sl 1, k3, p1, m1, p2 tog, p2, m1, p2 tog, p2, k3, p13, k3, p1, m1, p2 tog, p2, m1, p2 tog, p2, k3, k1 tbl.

Row 6: Sl 1, p3, k1, k2 tog, m1, k2, k2 tog, m1, k2, p3, k13, p3, k1, k2 tog, m1, k2, k2 tog, m1, k2, p3, k1 tbl.

Row 7: Sl 1, k3, p3, m1, p2 tog, p2, m1, p2 tog, k3, p13, k3, p3, m1, p2 tog, p2, m1, p2 tog, k3, k1 tbl.

Row 8: Sl 1, p3, k1, m1, k2 tog, k2, m1, k2 tog, k2, p3, k1, p11, k1, p3, k1, m1, k2 tog, k2, m1, k2 tog, k2, p3, k1 tbl.

Row 9: Sl 1, k3, p1, p2 tog, m1, p2, p2 tog, m1, p2, k3, p1, k11, p1, k3, p1, p2 tog, m1, p2, p2 tog, m1, p2, k3, k1 tbl.

Row 10: Sl 1, p3, k3, m1, k2 tog, k2, m1, k2 tog, p3, sl 1, k1, psso, p9, k2 tog, p3, k3, m1, k2 tog, m1, k2 tog, p3, k1 tbl.

Row 11: Sl 1, k3, p1, m1, p2 tog, p2, m1, p2 tog, p2, k3, p2 tog, p7, p2 tog, k3, p1, m1, p2 tog, p2, m1, p2 tog, p2, k3, k1 tbl.

Row 12: Sl 1, p3, k1, k2 tog, m1, k2, k2 tog, m1, k2, p3, sl 1, k1, psso, k5, k2 tog, p3, k1, k2 tog, m1, k2, k2 tog, m1, k2, p3, k1 tbl.

Row 13: Sl 1, k3, p3, m1, p2 tog, p2, m1, p2 tog, k3, p2 tog, p3, p2 tog, k3, p3, m1, p2 tog, p2, m1, p2 tog, k3, k1 tbl.

Row 14: Sl 1, p3, k1, m1, k2 tog, k2, m1, k2 tog, k2, p3, k3 tog, k2 tog, p3, k1, m1, k2 tog, k2, m1, k2 tog, k2, p3, k1 tbl.

Row 15: Sl 1, k3, p1, p2 tog, m1, p2, p2 tog, m1, p2, k3, repeat*—*row 2, k3, p1, p2 tog, m1, p2, p2 tog, m1, p2, k3, k1 tbl.

Row 16: Sl 1, p3, k3, m1, k2 tog, k2, m1, k2 tog, p3, k1, k5 tbl, k1, p3, k3, m1, k2 tog, k2, m1, k2 tog, p3, k1 tbl.

Row 17: Sl 1, k3, p1, m1, p2 tog, p2, m1, p2 tog, p2, k3, (p1, m1) 6 times, p1, k3, p1, m1, p2 tog, p2, m1, p2 tog, p2, k3, k1 tbl.

Row 18: Sl 1, p3, k1, k2 tog, m1, k2, k2 tog, m1, k2, p3, k13, p3, k1, k2 tog, m1, k2, k2 tog, m1, k2, p3, k1 tbl.

Row 19: Sl 1, k3, p3, m1, p2 tog, p2, m1, p2 tog, k3, p13, k3, p3, m1, p2 tog, p2, m1, p2 tog, k3, k1 tbl.

Row 20: Sl 1, p3, k1, m1, k2 tog, k2, m1, k2 tog, k2, p3, k13, p3, k1, m1, k2 tog, k2, m1, k2 tog, k2, p3, k1 tbl.

Row 21: Sl 1, k3, p1, p2 tog, m1, p2, p2 tog, m1, p2, k3, p1, k11, p1, k3, p1, p2 tog, m1, p2, p2 tog, m1, p2, k3, k1 tbl.

Row 22: Sl 1, p3, k3, m1, k2 tog, k2, m1, k2 tog, p3, k1, p11, k1, p3, k3, m1, k2 tog, k2, m1, k2 tog, p3, k1 tbl.

Row 23: Sl 1, k3, p1, m1, p2 tog, p2, m1, p2 tog, p2, k3, p2 tog, k9, p2 tog, k3, p1, m1, p2 tog, p2, m1, p2 tog, p2, k3, k1 tbl.

Row 24: Sl 1, p3, k1, k2 tog, m1, k2, k2 tog, m1, k2,

p3, sl 1, k1, psso, k7, k2 tog, p3, k1, k2 tog, m1, k2, k2 tog, m1, k2, p3, k1 tbl.

Row 25: Sl 1, k3, p3, m1, p2 tog, p2, m1, p2 tog, k3, p2 tog, p5, p2 tog, k3, p3, m1, p2 tog, p2, m1, p2 tog, k3, k1 tbl.

Row 26: Sl 1, p3, k1, m1, k2 tog, k2, m1, k2 tog, k2, p3, sl 1, k1, psso, k3, k2 tog, p3, k1, m1, k2 tog, k2, m1, k2 tog, k2, p3, k1 tbl.

Row 27: Sl 1, k3, p1, p2 tog, m1, p2, p2 tog, m1, p2, k3, p2 tog, p3 tog, k3, p1, p2 tog, m1, p2, p2 tog, m1, p2, k3, k1 tbl.

Repeat rows 2–27 until desired length. Cast off.

Pattern 3

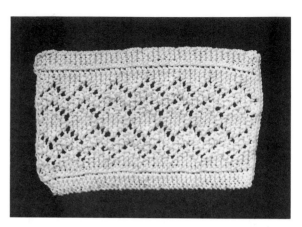

Pattern 2

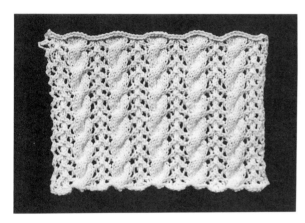

Cast on a multiple of 11 sts, plus 7.

Row 1: P.

Row 2: K1, *m1, k1, sl 1, psso, k1, k2 tog, m1, k6*, repeat *—* to last 6 sts, m1, sl 1, k1, psso, k1, k2 tog, m1, k1.

Row 3: P.

Row 4: K2, *m1, sl 1, k2 tog, psso, m1, k1, sl next 3 sts to dpn leave at b of work, k3, k3 from dpn, k1*, repeat *—* to last 5 sts, m1, sl 1, k2 tog, psso, m1, k2.

Row 5: P.

Row 6: Repeat row 2.

Row 7: P.

Row 8: K2, *m1, sl 1, k2 tog, psso, m1, k8*, repeat *—* to last 5 sts, m1, sl 1, k2 tog, psso, m1, k2.

Repeat rows 1–8 until desired length. Cast off.

Cast on 33 sts.

Row 1: K.

Row 2: Sl 1, k3, m1, sl 1, k1, psso, k2, k2 tog, m2, (sl 1, k1, psso) twice, m2, k2 tog, k1, sl 1, k1, psso, m2, (sl 1, k1, psso) twice, m2, sl 1, k1, psso, k3, m1, sl 1, k1, psso, k3.

Row 3: K10, p1, k3, p1, k4, p1, k3, p1, k9.

Row 4: Sl 1, k3, m1, sl 1, k1, psso, k1, k2 tog, m2, (sl 1, k1, psso) twice, m2, k2 tog, k3, sl 1, k1, psso, m2, (sl 1, k1, psso) twice, m2, sl 1, k1, psso, k2, m1, sl 1, k1, psso, k3.

Row 5: K9, p1, k3, p1, k6, p1, k3, p1, k8.

Row 6: Sl 1, k3, m1, sl 1, k1, psso, k2 tog, m2 (sl 1, k1, psso) twice, m2, k2 tog, k5, sl 1, k1, psso, m2 (sl 1, k1, psso) twice, m2, sl 1, k1, psso, k1, m1, sl 1, k1, psso, k3.

Row 7: K8, p1, k3, p1, k8, p1, k3, p1, k7.

Row 8: Sl 1, k3, m1, sl 1, k1, psso, k1, sl 1, k1, psso, m2, (sl 1, k1, psso) twice, m2, sl 1, k1, psso, k3, k2 tog, m2, (sl 1, k1, psso) twice, m2, sl 1, k1, psso, k2, m1, sl 1, k1, psso, k3.

Row 9: K9, p1, k3, p1, k6, p1, k3, p1, k8.

Row 10: Sl 1, k3, m1, sl 1, k1, psso, k2, sl 1, k1, psso, m2, (sl 1, k1, psso) twice, m2, sl 1, k1, psso, k1, k2 tog, m2, (sl 1, k1, psso) twice, m2, sl 1, k1, psso, k3, m1, sl 1, k1, psso, k3.

Row 11: K10, p1, k3, p1, k4, p1, k3, p1, k9.

Row 12: Sl 1, k3, m1, sl 1, k1, psso, k3, sl 1, k1, psso, m2, (sl 1, k1, psso) twice, m2, sl 1, k2 tog, psso, m2, (sl 1, k1, psso) twice, m2, sl 1, k1, psso, k4, m1, sl 1, k1, psso, k3.

Row 13: K11, p1, k3, p1, k2, p1, k3, p1, k10.

Repeat rows 2–13 until desired length. Cast off.

Pattern 4

Cast on 34 sts.

Row 1: K2, (*k2 tog [*see below*]*, k10, repeat *—*, k2) twice.

Row 2: K2, (p2, k2, p6, k2, p2, k2) twice.

Row 3: Repeat row 1.

Row 4: Repeat row 2.

Row 5: K2, (repeat *—* row 1, k2, sl next 3 sts on dpn, leave at b of work, k3, k3 from dpn, k2, repeat *—* row 1, k2) twice.

Row 6: K2, (p2, k2, p6, k2, p2, k2) twice.

Repeat rows 1–6 until desired length. Cast off.

K2 tog thus: Sl R.H. needle through 2 sts k-wise on L.H. needle, pass cotton over as normal for k st, when withdrawing R.H. needle do so by bringing point of R.H. needle between the 2 sts being knitted together, sl the 2 loops off L.H. needle leaving 2 loops on R.H. needle. These form the p2 of the next row.

Pattern 5

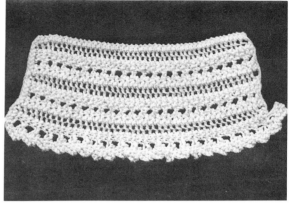

Cast on 25 sts.

Row 1: K6, m1, k2 tog, k6, m1, k2 tog, k6, m1, k2 tog, k1.

Row 2: Sl 1, k2, m1, k2 tog, k2 tog, m2, sl 1, k1, psso, k2, m1, (k2 tog) twice, m2, sl 1, k1, psso, k2, m1, k2 tog, k1, m3, k3.

Row 3: K4, p1, k4, m1, k2 tog, k2, p1, k3, m1, k2 tog, k2, p1, k3, m1, k2 tog, k1.

Row 4: Sl 1, k2, m1, k2 tog, k6, m1, k2 tog, k6, m1, k2 tog, k7.

Row 5: Cast off 3 sts, k5, m1, k2 tog, k6, m1, k2 tog, k6, m1, k2 tog, k1.

Repeat rows 2–5 until desired length. Cast off.

Pattern 6

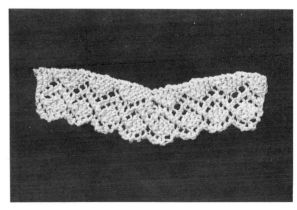

Cast on 9 sts.
Row 1: K.

Row 2: K3, k2 tog, m1, k2 tog, m1, k1, m1, k1.
Row 3: K.
Row 4: K2, k2 tog, m1, k2 tog, m1, k3, m1, k1.
Row 5: K.
Row 6: K1, k2 tog, m1, k2 tog, m1, k5, m1, k1.
Row 7: K.
Row 8: K3, m1, k2 tog, m1, k2 tog, k1, k2 tog, m1, k2 tog.
Row 9: K.
Row 10: K4, m1, k2 tog, m1, k3 tog, m1, k2 tog.
Row 11: K.
Row 12: K5, m1, k3 tog, m1, k2 tog.
Repeat rows 1–12 until a corner is desired. To start corner work rows 1–6, then:

Corner
Row 13: K10, turn.
Row 14: Sl 1, m1, k2 tog, m1, k2 tog, k1, k2 tog, m1, k2 tog.
Row 15: K8, turn.
Row 16: Sl 1, m1, k2 tog, m1, k3 tog, m1, k2 tog.
Row 17: K6, turn.
Row 18: Sl 1, m1, k3 tog, m1, k2 tog.
Row 19: K6, turn.
Row 20: K2 tog, m1, k2 tog, m1, k1, m1, k1.
Row 21: K8, turn.
Row 22: K2 tog, m1, k2 tog, m1, k3, m1, k1.
Row 23: K10, turn.
Row 24: K2 tog, m1, k2 tog, m1, k5, m1, k1.
Row 25: K to end.
This completes corner shaping. Continue from row 8 of pattern and repeat rows 1–12 until desired length. Cast off.

*Pattern 7

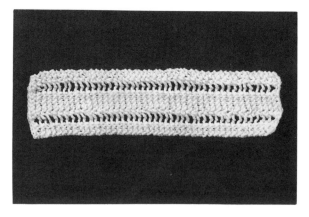

Cast on 15 sts.
Row 1: K.
Row 2: Sl 1, k1, k2 tog, m2, k2 tog, k3 tbl, k2 tog, m2, k2 tog, k2.
Row 3: K4, p1, k6, p1, k3.
Repeat rows 2–3 until desired length. Cast off.

Pattern 8

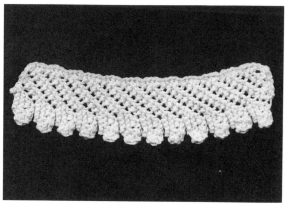

Cast on 8 sts loosely.
Row 1: K to last 2 sts, inc 1 k-wise, yfwd, leave at f of work, sl 1 p-wise. (9 sts on needle.)
Row 2: K1 tbl, k1, (m1, sl 1, k1, psso, k1) twice, yfwd, sl 1 p-wise.
Row 3: K1 tbl, k to end, turn, cast on 3 sts.
Row 4: K1, inc 1 k-wise, k2, (m1, sl 1, k1, psso, k1) twice, m1, k1, yfwd, sl 1 p-wise.
Row 5: K1 tbl, k to last 2 sts, inc 1 k-wise, yfwd, sl 1 p-wise.
Row 6: K1 tbl, inc 1 k-wise, k2, (m1, sl 1, k1, psso, k1) 3 times, k1, yfwd, sl 1 p-wise.
Row 7: K1 tbl, k to last 2 sts, k2 tog.
Row 8: Sl 1 p-wise, ybk, k1, psso, sl 1, k1, psso, k4, (m1, sl 1, k1, psso, k1) twice yfwd, sl 1 p-wise.
Row 9: K1 tbl, k to last 2 sts, k2 tog.
Row 10: Cast off 3 sts, k2, m1, sl 1, k1, psso, k1, m1, sl 1, k1, psso, yfwd, sl 1 p-wise. [9 sts on needle.]
Repeat rows 3–10 until desired length. Cast off.

*Pattern 9

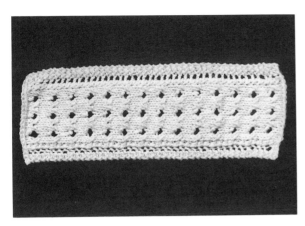

Cast on 22 sts.
Row 1: P.
Row 2. Sl 1, k2, m1, sl 1, k1, psso, k14, m1, sl 1, k1, psso, k1.
Row 3: Sl 1, k2, m1, sl 1, k1, psso, p14, m1, sl 1, k1, psso, k1.
Row 4: Sl 1, k2, m1, (sl 1, k1, psso, k2 tog, m2) 3 times, sl 1, k1, psso, k2, m1, sl 1, k1, psso, k1.
Row 5: Sl 1, k2, m1, sl 1, k1, psso, p2, k1, p3, k1, p3, k1, p3, m1, sl 1, k1, psso, k1.
Row 6: Repeat row 2.
Row 7: Repeat row 3.
Repeat rows 2–7 until desired length. Cast off

*Pattern 10

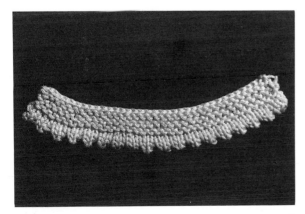

Cast on an even number of sts for desired length of edging.

Row 1: K.
Row 2: P.
Row 3: K2, *yfwd, k2 tog*, repeat *–* to end.
Row 4: P.
Row 5: K.
Row 6: P.
Row 7: Fold work at row 3 to make hem by knitting tog one st from needle and one loop from cast on edge.
Rows 8–12: K.
Cast off.

Pattern 11

Cast on 8 sts.
Row 1: K5, yon, k1, yon, k2.
Row 2: P6, k into f and b of next st [= inc 1 for this pattern only], k3.
Row 3: K4, p1, k2, yon, k1, yon, k3.
Row 4: P8, inc 1, k4.
Row 5: K4, p2, k3, yon, k1, yon, k4.
Row 6: P10, inc 1, k5.
Row 7: K4, p3, k4, yon, k1, yon, k5.
Row 8: P12, inc 1, k6.
Row 9: K4, p4, sl 1, k1, psso, k7, k2 tog, k1.
Row 10: P10, inc 1, k7.
Row 11: K4, p5, sl 1, k1, psso, k5, k2 tog, k1.
Row 12: P8, inc 1, k2, p1, k5.
Row 13: K4, p1, k1, p4, sl 1, k1, psso, k3, k2 tog, k1.
Row 14: P6, inc 1, k3, p1, k5.
Row 15: K4, p1, k1, p5, sl 1, k1, psso, k1, k2 tog, k1.
Row 16: P4, inc 1, k4, p1, k5.
Row 17: K4, p1, k1, p6, sl 1, k2 tog, psso, k1.
Row 18: P2 tog, cast off next 5 sts starting with the 'p2 tog', st just worked to cast off first st, p3, k4.
Repeat rows 1–18 until desired length. Cast off.

Pattern 12

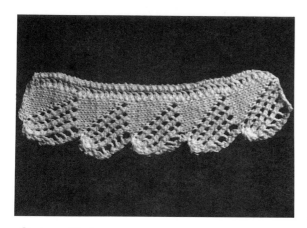

Cast on 13 sts.

Row 1: P.

Row 2: Sl 1, k1, yrn, p2 tog, k1, (yfwd, sl 1, k1, psso) 3 times, y2rn, k2 tog.

Row 3: M1, k2 tog, p9, yrn, p2 tog, k1.

Row 4: Sl 1, k1, yrn, p2 tog, k2, (yfwd, sl 1, k1, psso) 3 times, y2rn, k2 tog.

Row 5: Yfwd, k2 tog, p10, yrn, p2 tog, k1.

Row 6: Sl 1, k1, yrn, p2 tog, k3, (yfwd, sl 1, k1, psso) 3 times, y2rn, k2 tog.

Row 7: Yfwd, k2 tog, p11, yrn, p2 tog, k1.

Row 8: Sl 1, k1, yrn, p2 tog, k4, (yfwd, sl 1, k1, psso) 3 times, y2rn, k2 tog.

Row 9: Yfwd, k2 tog, p12, yrn, p2 tog, k1.

Row 10: Sl 1, k1, yrn, p2 tog, k5, (yfwd, sl 1, k1, psso) 3 times, y2rn, k2 tog.

Row 11: Yfwd, k2 tog, p13, yrn, p2 tog, k1.

Row 12: Sl 1, k1, yrn, p2 tog, k6, (yfwd, sl 1, k1, psso) 3 times, y2rn, k2 tog.

Row 13: Yfwd, k2 tog, p14, yrn, p2 tog, k1.

Row 14: Sl 1, k1, yrn, p2 tog, k7, (yfwd, sl 1, k1, psso) 3 times, y2rn, k2 tog.

Row 15: Yfwd, k2 tog, p15, yrn, p2 tog, k1.

Row 16: Sl 1, k1, yrn, p2 tog, k8, yfwd, k1, return last st to L.H. needle and with point of R.H. needle pass the next 7 sts one at a time over this st and off needle, then sl st back onto R.H. needle.

Row 17: P2 tog, p9, yrn, p2 tog, k1.

Repeat rows 2–17 until desired length. Cast off.

Pattern 13

Cast on 31 sts.

Row 1: K, working into b of all sts.

Row 2: K.

Row 3: K3, p20, yon, k2 tog, (yfwd, k2 tog) twice, yfwd, k2.

Row 4: K29, turn.

Row 5: P21, yon, k2 tog, (yfwd, k2 tog) twice, yfwd, k2.

Row 6: K30, turn.

Row 7: P22, yon, k2 tog, (yfwd, k2 tog) twice, yfwd, k2.

Row 8: K31, turn.

Row 9: Sl 1, (yfwd, k2 tog) 14 times, yfwd, k2.

Row 10: K9, p23, k3.

Row 11: K 35.

Row 12: Cast off 4 sts, k to end.

Repeat rows 3–12 until desired length. Cast off.

Pattern 14

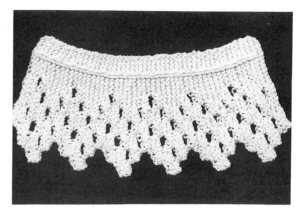

Cast on 21 sts.

Row 1: K.

Row 2: K4, p1, k to end.

Row 3: K.

Row 4: K4, p1, k4, (cast off 3 sts, k3) twice.

Row 5: Cast on 3 sts, k7, cast on 3 sts [=eyelet], k4, cast on 3 sts [=eyelet], k to end.

Row 6: K4, p1, k to end.

Row 7: K.

Row 8: K4, p1, k7, (cast off 3 sts, k3) twice.

Row 9: Cast on 3 sts, k7, cast on 3 sts, k4, cast on 3 sts, k to end.

Row 10: K4, p1, k to end.

Row 11: K.

Row 12: K4, p1, k10, cast off 3 sts, k3, cast off 3 sts, k to end.

Row 13: Cast off 3 sts, cast on 3 sts, k4, cast on 3 sts, k to end.

Row 14: K4, p1, k to end.

Row 15: K.

Row 16: K4, p1, k7, (cast off 3 sts, k3) twice.

Row 17: Cast off 3 sts, cast on 3 sts, k4, cast on 3 sts, k to end.

Row 18: K4, p1, k to end.

Row 19: K.

Row 20: K4, p1, k4, cast off 3 sts, k3, cast off 3 sts, k to end.

Repeat rows 5–20 until desired length. Cast off.

Row 3 and alternate rows: Sl 1, k to end.

Row 4: Yfwd, k6, (k2 tog, yfwd) twice, k8, (k2 tog, yfwd) twice, k5, yfwd, k2 tog, k13, yfwd, k2 tog, k2.

Row 6: Yfwd, k6 (k2 tog, yfwd) twice, k8, (k2 tog, yfwd) twice, (k6, yfwd, k2 tog) twice, k5, yfwd, k2 tog, k2.

Row 8: Yfwd, k6, (k2 tog, yfwd) 8 times, k7, yfwd, k2 tog, k4, k2 tog, yfwd, k1, yfwd, k2 tog, k4, yfwd, k2 tog, k2.

Row 10: Yfwd, (k2 tog) twice, k5 (yfwd, k2 tog) twice, k8, (yfwd, k2 tog) twice, k5, yfwd, k2 tog, k6, yfwd, k2 tog, k5, yfwd, k2 tog, k2.

Row 12: Yfwd, (k2 tog) twice, k5, (yfwd, k2 tog) twice, k8, (yfwd, k2 tog) twice, k4, yfwd, k2 tog, k13, yfwd, k2 tog, k2.

Row 14: Yfwd, (k2 tog) twice, k5, (yfwd, k2 tog) twice, (k3, yfwd, k2 tog) twice, yfwd, k2 tog, k3, yfwd, k2 tog, k2, yfwd, k2 tog, k6, yfwd, k2 tog, k1, yfwd, k2 tog, k2.

Row 16: Yfwd, (k2 tog) twice, k5, (yfwd, k2 tog) twice, k2 tog, yfwd, k1, yfwd, k2 tog, k3, (yfwd, k2 tog) 4 times, k2 tog, yfwd, k2 tog, k3, k2 tog, yfwd, k1, (yfwd, k2 tog) twice, k2.

Row 17: Sl 1, k to end.

Repeat rows 2–17 until desired length. Cast off.

Pattern 16

Pattern 15

Cast on 45 sts.

Row 1: K.

Row 2: Yfwd, k6, (k2 tog, yfwd) twice, yfwd, k2 tog, k6, yfwd, k2 tog, k1, yfwd, k2 tog, k2.

Cast on 11 sts.

Row 1: M1, k2 tog, k to last 6 sts, p3, k3.

Row 2: Sl 1, k2, m1, p3 tog, m1, k2 tog, m1, k2 tog, k1.

Row 3: Repeat row 1.

Row 4: Sl 1, k7, m1, k2.

Row 5: Repeat row 1.
Row 6: Sl 1, k8, m1, k2.
Row 7: Repeat row 1.
Row 8: Sl 1, k9, m1, k2.
Row 9: Repeat row 1.
Row 10: Sl 1, k10, m1, k2.
Row 11: Repeat row 1.
Row 12: Sl 1, k2, m1, p3 tog, m1, k6, m1, k2.
Row 13: Repeat row 1.
Row 14: Sl 1, k9, k2 tog, m1, k2 tog, k1.
Row 15: Repeat row 1.
Row 16: Sl 1, k8, k2 tog, m1, k2 tog, k1.
Row 17: Repeat row 1.
Row 18: Sl 1, k7, k2 tog, m1, k2 tog, k1.
Row 19: Repeat row 1.
Row 20: Sl 1, k6, k2 tog, m1, k2 tog, k1.
Repeat these 20 rows until a corner is required.

Corner

Work rows 1–12 of pattern.
Row 21: M1, k2 tog, k7, p3, k2, turn.
Row 22: Sl 1, k8, k2 tog, m1, k2 tog, k1.
Row 23: M1, k2 tog, k6, p3, k1, turn.
Row 24: Sl 1, k6, k2 tog, m1, k2 tog, k1, turn.
Row 25: M1, k2 tog, k5, p3, turn.
Row 26: Sl 1, k4, k2 tog, m1, k2 tog, k1.
Row 27: M1, k2 tog, k4, p2, turn.
Row 28: Sl 1, k2, k2 tog, m1, k2 tog, k1.
Row 29: M1, k2 tog, k3, p1, turn.
Row 30: Sl 1, k2 tog, m1, k2 tog, k1.
Row 31: M1, k2 tog, k2, p1, turn.
Row 32: Sl 1, k2, m1, k2.
Row 33: M1, k2 tog, k3, p2, turn.
Row 34: Sl 1, k4, m1, k2.
Row 35: M1, k2 tog, k4, p3, turn.
Row 36: Sl 1, k6, m1, k2.
Row 37: M1, k2 tog, k5, p3, k1, turn.
Row 38: Sl 1, k8, m1, k2.
Row 39: M1, k2 tog, k6, p3, k2, turn.
Row 40: Sl 1, k1, m1, p3 tog, m1, k6, m1, k2.
Row 41: M1, k2 tog, k7, p3, k3.
Continue from row 14 of pattern, repeating rows 1–20 until desired length. Cast off.

*Pattern 17

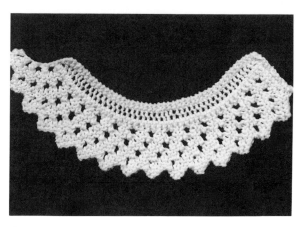

Cast on 14 sts.
Row 1: Sl 1, k2, m1, k2 tog, k1, m2, k2 tog, m2, k2 tog, m2, k2 tog, m2, k2 tog.
Row 2: K2, p1, k2, p1, k2, p1, k2, p1, k3, m1, k2 tog, k1.
Row 3: Sl 1, k2, m1, k2 tog, k13.
Row 4: K15, m1, k2 tog, k1.
Row 5: Sl 1, k2, m1, k2 tog, k13.
Row 6: Cast off 4 sts, k10, m1, k2 tog, k1.
Repeat rows 1–6 until desired length. Cast off.

Pattern 18

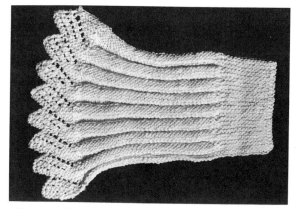

Cast on 60 sts.
Row 1: K.
Row 2: Sl 1, k53, (yfwd, k2 tog) twice, yfwd, k2.
Row 3: Sl 1, k8, p36, leave 16 sts on L.H. needle, turn.

Row 4: Sl 1, k38, (yfwd, k2 tog) twice, yfwd, k2.
Row 5: Sl 1, k9, p36, k16.
Row 6: Sl 1, k55, (yfwd, k2 tog) twice, yfwd, k2.
Row 7: Sl 1, k10, p36, leave 16 sts on L.H. needle, turn.
Row 8: Sl 1, p35, k5, (yfwd, k2 tog) twice, yfwd, k2.
Row 9: Sl 1, k63.
Row 10: Sl 1, k15, p36, k6, (yfwd, k2 tog) twice, yfwd, k2.
Row 11: Sl 1, k48, leave 16 sts on L.H. needle, turn.
Row 12: Sl 1, p35, k7, (yfwd, k2 tog) twice, yfwd, k2.
Row 13: Cast off 6 sts, k to end.
Repeat rows 1–13 until desired length. Cast off.

*Pattern 19

Cast on 9 sts.
Row 1: K.
Row 2: K4, m1, k2 tog, m1, k2 tog, m1, k1.
Row 3: K.
Row 4: K5, m1, k2 tog, m1, k2 tog, m1, k1.
Row 5: K.
Row 6: K6, m1, k2 tog, m1, k2 tog, m1, k1.
Row 7: K.
Row 8: K7, m1, k2 tog, m1, k2 tog, m1, k1.
Row 9: K.
Row 10: K8, m1, k2 tog, m1, k2 tog, m1, k1.
Row 11: K.
Row 12: K9, m1, k2 tog, m1, k2 tog, m1, k1.
Row 13: Cast off 6 sts, k8. [9 sts on needle.]
Repeat rows 2–13 until desired length. Cast off.

Pattern 20

Cast on 34 sts.
Row 1: K.
Row 2: Sl 1, k3, k2 tog, m2, k2 tog, k5, k2 tog, m2, (k2 tog) twice, m2, k2 tog, k4, k2 tog, m2, (k2 tog) twice, m2, k2 tog, k1.
Row 3: M1, k3, p1, k3, p1, k7, p1, k3, p1, k8, p1, k5.
Row 4: Sl 1, k1, k2 tog, m2, k2 tog, k5, k2 tog, m2, (k2 tog) twice, m2, k2 tog, k8, k2 tog, m2, k2 tog, k4.
Row 5: M1, k6, p1, k11, p1, k3, p1, k8, p8, k3.
Row 6: Sl 1, k3, k2 tog, m2, k2 tog, k5, k2 tog, m2, (k2 tog) twice, m2, k2 tog, k4, k2 tog, m2, k2 tog, k7.
Row 7: M1, k9, p1, k7, p1, k3, p1, k8, p1, k5.
Row 8: Sl 1, k1, k2 tog, m2, (k2 tog) twice, m2, k2 tog, k5, k2 tog, m2, (k2 tog) twice, m2, (k2 tog) twice, m2, k2 tog, k10.
Row 9: M1, k12, p1, k3, p1, k3, p1, k8, (p1, k3) twice.
Row 10: Sl 1, k3, k2 tog, m2, (k2 tog) twice, m2, k2 tog, k5, k2 tog, m2, (k2 tog) twice, m2, k2 tog, k13.
Row 11: M1, k15, p1, k3, p1, k8, p1, k3, p1, k5.
Row 12: Sl 1, k1, k2 tog, m2, (k2 tog) twice, m2, (k2 tog) twice, m2, k2 tog, k5, k2 tog, m2, k2 tog, k16.
Row 13: K2 tog, k16, p1, k8, (p1, k3) 3 times.
Row 14: Sl 1, k3, k2 tog, m2, (k2 tog) twice, m2, k2 tog, k5, k2 tog, m2, (k2 tog) twice, m2, k2 tog, k13.
Row 15: K2 tog, k13, p1, k3, p1, k8, p1, k3, p1, k5.
Row 16: Sl 1, k1, k2 tog, m2, (k2 tog) twice, m2, k2 tog, k5, k2 tog, m2, (k2 tog) twice, m2, (k2 tog) twice, m2, k2 tog, k10.
Row 17: K2 tog, k10, p1, k3, p1, k3, p1, k8, (p1, k3) twice.

Row 18: Sl 1, k3, k2 tog, m2, k2 tog, k5, k2 tog, m2, (k2 tog) twice, m2, k2 tog, k4, k2 tog, m2, k2 tog, k7.
Row 19: K2 tog, k7, p1, k7, p1, k3, p1, k8, p1, k5.
Row 20: Sl 1, k1, k2 tog, m2, k2 tog, k5, k2 tog, m2, (k2 tog) twice, m2, k2 tog, k8, k2 tog, m2, k2 tog, k4.
Row 21: K2 tog, k4, p1, k11, p1, k3, p1, k8, p1, k3.
Row 22: Sl 1, k3, k2 tog, m2, k2 tog, k5, k2 tog, m2, (k2 tog) twice, m2, k2 tog, k4, k2 tog, m2, (k2 tog) twice, m2, k2 tog, k1.
Row 23: M1, k3, p1, k3, p1, k7, p1, k3, p1, k8, p1, k5.
Row 24: Sl 1, k1, k2 tog, m2, (k2 tog) twice, m2, k2 tog, k5, k2 tog, m2, k2 tog, k8, k2 tog, m2, k2 tog, k4.
Row 25: M1, k6, p1, k11, p1, k8, (p1, k3) twice.
Row 26: Sl 1, k3, k2 tog, m2, (k2 tog) twice, m2, k2 tog, k5, k2 tog, m2, k2 tog, k4, k2 tog, m2, k2 tog, k7.
Row 27: M1, k9, p1, k7, p1, k8, p1, k3, p1, k5.
Row 28: Sl 1, k1, k2 tog, m2, (k2 tog) twice, m2, (k2 tog) twice, m2, k2 tog, k5, k2 tog, m2, (k2 tog) twice, m2, k2 tog, k10.
Row 29: M1, k12, p1, k3, p1, k8, (p1, k3) 3 times.
Row 30: Sl 1, k3, k2 tog, m2, (k2 tog) twice, m2, (k2 tog) twice, m2, k2 tog, k5, k2 tog, m2, k2 tog, k13.
Row 31: M1, k15, p1, k8, (p1, k3) twice, p1, k5.
Row 32: Sl 1, k1, k2 tog, m2, (k2 tog) twice, m2, (k2 tog) twice, m2, (k2 tog) twice, m2, k2 tog, k21.
Row 33: K2 tog, k21, (p1, k3) 4 times.
Row 34: Sl 1, k3, k2 tog, m2, (k2 tog) twice, m2, (k2 tog) twice, m2, k2 tog, k5, k2 tog, m2, k2 tog, k13.
Row 35: K2 tog, k13, p1, k8, (p1, k3) twice, p1, k5.
Row 36: Sl 1, k1, k2 tog, m2, (k2 tog) twice, m2, (k2 tog) twice, m2, k2 tog, k5, k2 tog, m2, (k2 tog) twice, m2, k2 tog, k10.
Row 37: K2 tog, k10, p1, k3, p1, k8, p1, k3, p1, k3, p1, k3.
Row 38: Sl 1, k3, k2 tog, m2, (k2 tog) twice, m2, k2 tog, k5, k2 tog, m2, k2 tog, k4, k2 tog, m2, k2 tog, k7.
Row 39: K2 tog, k7, p1, k7, p1, k8, p1, k3, p1, k5.
Row 40: Sl 1, k1, k2 tog, m2, (k2 tog) twice, m2, k2 tog, k5, k2 tog, m2, k2 tog, k8, k2 tog, m2, k2 tog, k4.
Row 41: K2 tog, k4, p1, k11, p1, k8, (p1, k3) twice.
Repeat rows 2–41 until desired length. Cast off.

Pattern 21

Cast on 30 sts.
Row 1: K.
Row 2: K.
Row 3: K6, (yfwd, k2 tog) 11 times, yfwd, k2.
Row 4: K.
Row 5: K9, (yfwd, k2 tog) 10 times, yfwd, k2.
Row 6: K.
Row 7: K12, (yfwd, k2 tog) 9 times, yfwd, k2.
Row 8: K.
Row 9: K15, (yfwd, k2 tog) 8 times, yfwd, k2.
Row 10: K.
Row 11: K18, (yfwd, k2 tog) 7 times, yfwd, k2.
Row 12: K.
Row 13: K15, (yfwd, k2 tog) 9 times, yfwd, k2.
Row 14: K.
Row 15: K12, (yfwd, k2 tog) 11 times, yfwd, k2.
Row 16: K.
Row 17: K9, (yfwd, k2 tog) 13 times, yfwd, k2.
Row 18: K.
Row 19: K6, (yfwd, k2 tog) 15 times, yfwd, k2. [39 sts on needle.]
Row 20: K.
Row 21: K.
Row 22: Cast off 9 sts loosely, k to end.
Repeat rows 1–22 until desired length. Cast off.

*Pattern 22

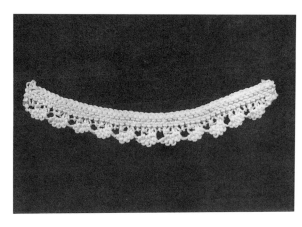

Cast on a multiple of 5 sts, plus 2, for required length of edging.

Row 1: K1, yfwd and over needle to make one st, *K5, turn, lift 2nd, 3rd, 4th & 5th sts over the first st and off the needle, turn, yfwd*, repeat *—* to last st, k1.

Row 2: K1, *(p1, yon to make one st, k1 tbl) all into next st, p1, repeat *—* to end.

Row 3: K2, k1 tbl, *k3, k1 tbl*, repeat *—* to last 2 sts, k2.

Work 3 rows garter st. Cast off.

Pattern 23

Cast on 9 sts.

Row 1: Sl 1, k2, m1, k2 tog, k1, m2, k2 tog, k1.
Row 2: K3, p1, k3, m1, k2 tog, k1.
Row 3: Sl 1, k2, m1, k2 tog, k5.

Row 4: K7, m1, k2 tog, k1.
Row 5: Sl 1, k2, m1, k2 tog, k1, m2, k2 tog, m2, k2.
Row 6: K3, p1, k2, p1, k3, m1, k2 tog, k1.
Row 7: Sl 1, k2, m1, k2 tog, k8.
Row 8: K10, m1, k2 tog, k1.
Row 9: Sl 1, k2, m1, k2 tog, k1, m2, k2 tog, m2, k2 tog, m2, k2 tog, k1.
Row 10: K3, p1, k2, p1, k2, p1, k3, m1, k2 tog, k1.
Row 11: Sl 1, k2, m1, k2 tog, k11.
Row 12: Cast off 7 sts, k5, m1, k2 tog, k1.
Repeat rows 1–12 until desired length. Cast off.

Pattern 24

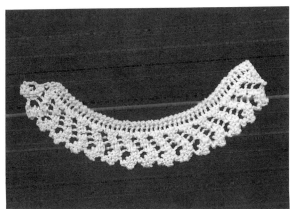

Cast on 8 sts.

Row 1: Sl 1, k1, m1, k2 tog, m1, k2 tog, k1, m3, k1.
Row 2: K2, p1, k8.
Row 3: Sl 1, k1, m1, k2 tog, k1, m1, k2 tog, k4.
Row 4: K11.
Row 5: Sl 1, k1, m1, k2 tog, k2, m1, k2 tog, k3.
Row 6: Cast off 3 sts, k7.
Repeat rows 1–6 until desired length. Cast off.

Pattern 25

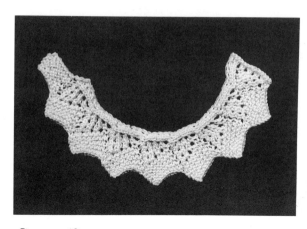

Cast on 13 sts.

Row 1: Sl 1, p1, p2 tog, m1, k9.
Row 2: Sl 1, k8, m1, k2, k1 tbl, k1.
Row 3: Sl 1, p2, m1, p2 tog, m1, k9.
Row 4: Sl 1, k8, m1, k2 tog, m1, k2 k1 tbl, k1.
Row 5: Sl 1, p2, (m1, p2 tog) twice, m1, k9.
Row 6: Sl 1, k8, (m1, k2 tog) twice, m1, k2, k1 tbl, k1.
Row 7: Sl 1, p2, (m1, p2 tog) 3 times, m1, k9.
Row 8: Sl 1, k8, (m1, k2 tog) 3 times, m1, k2, k1 tbl, k1.
Row 9: Sl 1, p2 (m1, p2 tog) 4 times, m1, k9.
Row 10: Cast off 8 sts, k10, k1 tbl, k1.
Repeat rows 1–10 until desired length. Cast off.

*Pattern 26

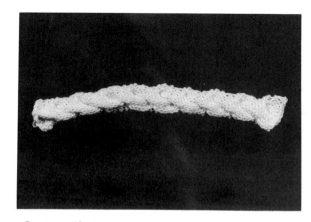

Cast on 10 sts.

Row 1: K1, p8, k1.
Row 2: P1, k8, p1.
Row 3: K1, p8, k1.
Row 4: P1, k8, p1.
Row 5: K1, p8, k1.
Row 6: P1, sl next 4 sts onto a dpn, leave at b of work, k4, k the 4 sts on dpn, p1.
Row 7: K1, p8, k1.
Repeat rows 1–7 until desired length. Cast off.

Pattern 27

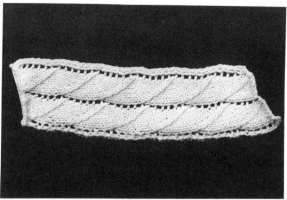

Cast on a multiple of 7 sts, plus 4, for required width of edging.

Row 1: K2, *yon, sl 1, k1, psso, k5*, repeat *—* to last 2 sts, yon, k2 tog.
Row 2 and all even rows: P.
Row 3: K2, *yon, k1, sl 1, k1, psso, k4*, repeat *—* to last 2 sts, yon, k2 tog.
Row 5: K2, *yon, k2, sl 1, k1, psso, k3*, repeat *—* to last 2 sts, yon, k2 tog.
Row 7: K2, *yon, k3, sl 1, k1, psso, k2*, repeat *—* to last 2 sts, yon, k2 tog.
Row 9: K2, *yon, k4, sl 1, k1, psso, k1*, repeat *—* to last 2 sts, yon, k2 tog.
Row 11: K2, *yon, k5, sl 1, k1, psso*, repeat *—* to last 2 sts, yon, k2 tog.
Row 12: P.
Repeat rows 1–12 until desired length. Cast off.

Pattern 28

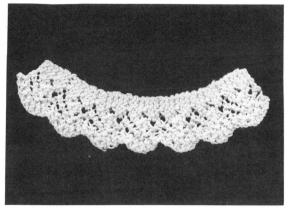

Cast on 9 sts.
Row 1: K4, yfwd, k2 tog, yfwd, k3.
Row 2: Yrn, k2 tog, k1, yfwd, k2 tog, yfwd, k5.
Row 3: K6, yfwd, k2 tog, yfwd, k3.
Row 4: Yrn, k2 tog, k1, yfwd, k2 tog, yfwd, k1, yfwd, k2 tog, k4.
Row 5: K3, k2 tog, yfwd, k3, yfwd, k2 tog, yfwd, k3.
Row 6: Yrn, k2 tog, k1, yfwd, k2 tog, yfwd, k5, yfwd, k2 tog, k2.
Row 7: K4, yfwd, k2 tog, k1, k2 tog, (yfwd, k2 tog) twice, k2.
Row 8: Yrn, (k2 tog) twice, yfwd, k2 tog, yfwd, sl 1, k2 tog, psso, yfwd, k5.
Row 9: K5, (k2 tog, yfwd) twice, k2 tog, k2.
Row 10: Yrn, (k2 tog) twice, (yfwd, k2 tog) twice, k4.
Row 11: K3. (k2 tog, yfwd) twice, k2 tog, k2.
Row 12: Yrn, (k2 tog) twice, (yfwd, k2 tog) twice, k2.
Repeat rows 1–12 until desired length. Cast off.

Pattern 29

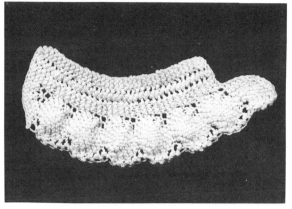

Cast on 20 sts.
Row 1: K.
Row 2: K3, yon, p2 tog, k3, yon, k10, yon, p2 tog.
Row 3: Yon, p2 tog, k14, yon, p2 tog, k3.
Row 4: K3, yon, p2 tog, k3, yon, k1, yon, k10, yon, p2 tog.
Row 5: Yon, p2 tog, k16, yon, p2 tog, k3.
Row 6: K3, yon, p2 tog, k3, (yon, k1) 3 times, yon, k10, yon, p2 tog.
Row 7: Yon, p2 tog, k20, yon, p2 tog, k3.
Row 8: K3, yon, p2 tog, k6, yon, k1, yon, k13, yon, p2 tog.
Row 9: Yon, p2 tog, k22, yon, p2 tog, k3.
Row 10: K3, yon, p2 tog, k13, then pass 2nd st on L.H. needle over 1st st until 2 sts remain, yon, p2 tog.
Row 11: Yon, p2 tog, k13, yon, p2 tog, k3.
Repeat rows 2–11 until desired length. Cast off.

Pattern 30

Cast on 20 sts.

Row 1: Sl 1, k2, m1, k2 tog, k2, m1, k2 tog, k5, k2 tog, m1, k3, inc 1 k-wise in last st.

Row 2: K6, m1, sl 1, k1, psso, k3, k2 tog, m1, k4, m1, k2 tog, k2.

Row 3: Sl 1, k2, m1, k2 tog, k4, m1, sl 1, k1, psso, k1, k2 tog, m1, k6, inc 1 k-wise in last st.

Row 4: K9, m1, sl 1, k2 tog, psso, m1, k6, m1, k2 tog, k2.

Row 5: Sl 1, k2, m1, k2 tog, k4, k2 tog, m1, k1, m1, k2 tog, k4, m2, k3, inc 1 k-wise in last st.

Row 6: K6, p1, k3, k2 tog, m1, k3, m1, sl 1, k1, psso, k4, m1, k2 tog, k2.

Row 7: Sl 1, k2, m1, k2 tog, k2, k2 tog, m1, k5, m1, sl 1, k1, psso, k9.

Row 8: Cast off 5 sts, k2, k2 tog, m1, k7, m1, sl 1, k1, psso, k2, m1, k2 tog, k2. (20 sts on needle.)

Repeat rows 1–8 until desired length. Cast off.

Pattern 32

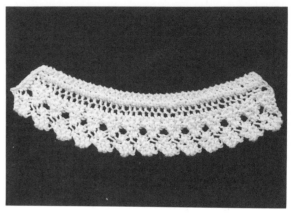

Cast on 11 sts.

Row 1: K4, yrn, p2 tog, k4, yfwd, (k1, p1) into last st.

Row 2: K3, yrn, p2 tog, k4, yrn, p2 tog, k1, sl 1.

Row 3: K4, yrn, p2 tog, k1, p2 tog, yon, k4.

Row 4: K5, yrn, p2 tog, k2, yrn, p2 tog, k1, sl 1.

Row 5: K4, yrn, p2 tog, k2, yrn, p2 tog, k3.

Row 6: Cast off 3 sts, yfwd, k5, yrn, p2 tog, k1, sl 1.

These 6 rows form the pattern. Cast off.

Pattern 31

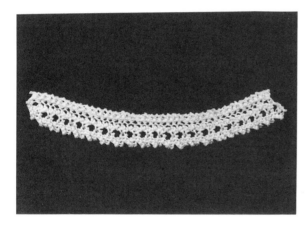

Cast on 7 sts.

Row 1: K3, yfwd, k2 tog tbl, m2, k2.

Row 2: K3, p1, k2, yfwd, k2 tog tbl, k1 tbl.

Row 3: K3, yfwd, k2 tog tbl, k4.

Row 4: Cast off 2 sts, k4, yfwd, k2 tog tbl, k1 tbl..

Repeat rows 1–4 until desired length. Cast off.

Pattern 33

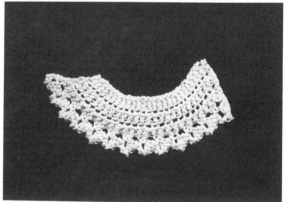

Cast on 11 sts.

Row 1: K.

Row 2: K3, k2 tog, yfwd, k1, k2 tog, yfwd, k3.

Row 3: K9, (yfwd, yrn, k1) twice. [15 sts on needle.]

Row 4: (K2, k1 tbl) twice, (k1, k2 tog, yfwd) twice, k3.

Row 5: K15.

Row 6: Cast off 4 sts, k2, k2 tog, yfwd, k1, k2 tog, yfwd, k3. [11 sts on needle.]

Repeat rows 3–6 until desired length, ending with row 5. Cast off.

*Pattern 34

Cast on 4 sts.

Row 1: K1, yfwd, k1, yfwd, k2.

Rows 2 & 4: K.

Row 3: K2, yfwd, k2 tog, yfwd, k2.

Row 5: K3, yfwd, k2 tog, yfwd, k2.

Row 6: Cast off 4 sts, k to end.

Repeat rows 1–6 until desired length. Cast off.

Cast on 18 sts.

Row 1: K3, yfwd, k2 tog, k1, (yfwd, k2 tog) twice, k1, (yfwd, k2 tog) twice, (yon) twice, k2 tog, k1.

Row 2: K3, p1, k9, yfwd, k2 tog, k1, yfwd, k2 tog, k1.

Row 3: K3, yfwd, k2 tog, k1, (yfwd, k2 tog) twice, k2, (yfwd, k2 tog) twice, yon, twice, k2 tog, k1.

Row 4: K3, p1, k10, yfwd, k2 tog, k1, yfwd, k2 tog, k1.

Row 5: K3, yfwd, k2 tog, k1, (yfwd, k2 tog) twice, k3, (yfwd, k2 tog) twice, (yon) twice, k2 tog, k1.

Row 6: K3, p1, k11, yfwd, k2 tog, k1, yfwd, k2 tog, k1.

Row 7: K3, yfwd, k2 tog, k1, (yfwd, k2 tog) twice, k4, (yfwd, k2 tog) twice, (yon) twice, k2 tog, k1.

Row 8: K3, p1, k12, yfwd, k2 tog, k1, yfwd, k2 tog, k1.

Row 9: K3, yfwd, k2 tog, k1, (yfwd, k2 tog) twice, k5, (yfwd, k2 tog) twice, (yon) twice, k2 tog, k1.

Row 10: K3, p1, k13, yfwd, k2 tog, k1, yfwd, k2 tog, k1.

Row 11: K3, yfwd, k2 tog, k1, (yfwd, k2 tog) twice, k6, (yfwd, k2 tog) twice, (yon) twice, k2 tog, k1.

Row 12: K3, p1, k14, yfwd, k2 tog, k1, yfwd, k2 tog, k1.

Row 13: K3, yfwd, k2 tog, k1 (yfwd, k2 tog) twice, k7, (yfwd, k2 tog) twice, (yon) twice, k2 tog, k1.

Row 14: K3, p1, k15, yfwd, k2 tog, k1, yfwd, k2 tog, k1.

Row 15: K3, yfwd, k2 tog, k1, (yfwd, k2 tog) twice, k15.

Row 16: Cast off 7 sts, k11, yfwd, k2 tog, k1, yfwd, k2 tog, k1.

Repeat rows 1–16 until desired length. Cast off.

Pattern 35

*Pattern 36

Cast on 7 sts.

Row 1: K.
Row 2: K2, p5.
Row 3: K5, p2.
Row 4: K6, turn, k1, p5.
Row 5: P5, k2.
Row 6: K.
Row 7: P5, turn, k5.
Row 8: P5, k1, turn, k6.

Repeat rows 2–8 until desired length. Cast off.

Pattern 37

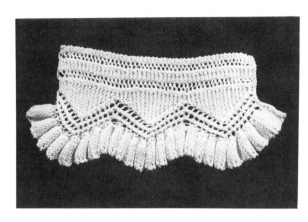

Cast on 25 sts.

Row 1: (K3, m1, k2 tog) 3 times, m1, k2 tog, m1, *k8, turn, sl 1, p7, turn*, repeat *—*, k8, turn, sl 1, p7, k10, m1, k2 tog, k3, m1, k2 tog, k1.
Row 2: (K3, m1, k2 tog) twice, k4, m1, k2 tog, m1, k2 tog, m1, *p8, turn, sl 1, k7, turn*, repeat *—*, p8, turn, sl 1, k18, m1, k2 tog, k3, m1, k2 tog, k1.
Row 3: (K3, m1, k2 tog) twice, k5, (m1, k2 tog) twice, m1, k8, turn, *sl 1, p7, turn, k8, turn*, repeat *—*, sl 1, p7, k12, m1, k2 tog, k3, m1, k2 tog, k1.
Row 4: (K3, m1, k2 tog) twice, k6, (m1, k2 tog) twice, m1, p8, *turn, sl 1, k7, turn, p8*, repeat *—*, turn, sl 1, k20, m1, k2 tog, k3, m1, k2 tog, k1.
Row 5: (K3, m1, k2 tog) twice, k7 (m1, k2 tog) twice, m1, k8, *turn, sl 1, p7, turn, k8*, repeat *—*, turn, sl 1, p7, k14, m1, k2 tog, k3, m1, k2 tog, k1.
Row 6: (K3, m1, k2 tog) twice, k8, (m1, k2 tog) twice, m1, p8, *turn, sl 1, k7, turn, p8*, repeat *—*, turn, sl 1, k22, m1, k2 tog, k3, m1, k2 tog, k1.
Row 7: (K3, m1, k2 tog) twice, k9, (m1, k2 tog) twice, m1, k8, *turn, sl 1, p7, turn, k8*, repeat *—*, turn, sl 1, p7, k16, m1, k2 tog, k3, m1, k2 tog, k1.
Row 8: (K3, m1, k2 tog) twice, k10, (m1, k2 tog) twice, m1, p8, *turn, sl 1, k7, turn, p8*, repeat *—*, turn, sl 1, k24, m1, k2 tog, k3, m1, k2 tog, k1.
Row 9: (K3, m1, k2 tog) twice, k8, k2 tog, (m1, k2 tog) twice, m1, k2 tog, k7, *turn, sl 1, p7, turn, k8*, repeat *—*, turn, sl 1, p7, k16, m1, k2 tog, k3, m1, k2 tog, k1.
Row 10: (K3, m1, k2 tog) twice, k7, k2 tog, (m1, k2 tog) twice, m1, p2 tog, p7, *turn, sl 1, k7, turn, p8*, repeat *—*, turn, sl 1, k22, m1, k2 tog, k3, m1, k2 tog, k1.
Row 11: (K3, m1, k2 tog) twice, k6, k2 tog, m1, k2 tog, m1, k2 tog, m1, k2 tog, k7, *turn, sl 1, p7, turn, k8*, repeat *—*, turn, sl 1, p7, k14, m1, k2 tog, k3, m1, k2 tog, k1.
Row 12: (K3, m1, k2 tog) twice, k5, k2 tog, (m1, k2 tog) twice, m1, p2 tog, p7, *turn, sl 1, k7, turn, p8*, repeat *—*, turn, sl 1, k20, m1, k2 tog, k3, m1, k2 tog, k1.
Row 13: (K3, m1, k2 tog) twice, k4, k2 tog, (m1, k2 tog) twice, m1, k2 tog, k7, *turn, sl 1, p7, turn, k8*, repeat *—*, turn, sl 1, p7, k12, m1, k2 tog, k3, m1, k2 tog, k1.
Row 14: (K3, m1, k2 tog) twice, k3, k2 tog, (m1, k2 tog) twice, m1, p2 tog, p7, *turn, sl 1, k7, turn, p8*, repeat *—*, turn, sl 1, k18, m1, k2 tog, k3, m1, k2 tog, k1.
Row 15: (K3, m1, k2 tog) twice, k2, k2 tog, (m1, k2 tog) twice, m1, k2 tog, k7, *turn, sl 1, p7, turn, k8*, repeat *—*, turn, sl 1, p7, k10, m1, k2 tog, k3, m1, k2 tog, k1.
Row 16: (K3, m1, k2 tog) twice, k1, k2 tog, (m1, k2 tog) twice, m1, p2 tog, p7, turn, *sl 1, k7, turn, p8*, repeat *—*, turn, sl 1, k16, m1, k2 tog, k3, m1, k2 tog, k1.

Repeat rows 1–16 until desired length. Cast off.

Pattern 38

Cast on 11 sts.

Row 1: K1, (k2 tog, yfwd) twice, (k2 tog) twice, yfwd, k2.

Row 2 and alternate rows: K.

Row 3: K2, yfwd, (k2 tog, yfwd, k2) twice.

Row 5: K2, yfwd, k2 tog, yfwd, k3, k2 tog, yfwd, k2.

Row 7: K2, yfwd, k2 tog, yfwd, k4, k2 tog, yfwd, k2.

Row 9: K2, yfwd, k2 tog, yfwd, k5, k2 tog, yfwd, k2.

Row 11. K2, yfwd, k2 tog, yfwd, k6, k2 tog, yfwd, k2.

Row 13: K1, (k2 tog, yfwd) twice, k2 tog, k4, k2 tog, yfwd, k2.

Row 15: K1, (k2 tog, yfwd) twice, k2 tog, k3, k2 tog, yfwd, k2.

Row 17: K1, (k2 tog, yfwd) twice, k2 tog, k2, k2 tog, yfwd, k2.

Row 19: K1, (k2 tog, yfwd) twice, k2 tog, k1, k2 tog, yfwd, k2.

Row 20: K.

Repeat rows 1–20 until desired length. Cast off.

Pattern 39

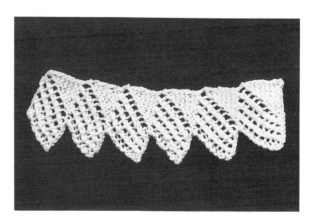

Cast on 17 sts.

Row 1: K to end.

Row 2. K3, (yrn, p2 tog) twice, yon, k1 tbl, k2 tog, p1, sl 1, k1, psso, k1 tbl, yfwd, k3.

Row 3: K3, p3, k1, p3, k2 (yrn, p2 tog) twice, k1.

Row 4: Repeat row 2.

Row 5: Repeat row 3.

Row 6: K3, (yrn, p2 tog) twice, yon, k1 tbl, yfwd, k2 tog, p1, sl 1, k1, psso, yfwd, k4.

Row 7: K4, p2, k1, p4, k2, (yrn, p2 tog) twice, k1.

Row 8: K3, (yrn, p2 tog) twice, yon, k1 tbl, k1, k1 tbl, yfwd, sl 1, k2 tog, psso, yfwd, k5.

Row 9: K5, p7, k2, (yrn, p2 tog) twice, k1.

Row 10: K3, (yrn, p2 tog) twice, yon, k1 tbl, k3, k1 tbl, yfwd, k7.

Row 11: Cast off 4 sts, k2, p7, k2, (yrn, p2 tog) twice, k1.

Repeat rows 2–11 until desired length. Cast off.

Pattern 40

Cast on 9 sts.
Row 1: K1, (m1, k2 tog) 3 times.
Row 2 and all even rows: K1, inc 1, k to end.
Row 3: K2, (m1, k2 tog) to end.
Row 5: K3, (m1, k2 tog) to end.
Row 7: K4, (m1, k2 tog) to end.
Row 9: K5, (m1, k2 tog) to end.
Row 11: K6, (m1, k2 tog) to end.
Row 13: K7, (m1, k2 tog) to end.
Row 14: Repeat row 2. [16 sts on needle.]
Row 15: K8, (m1, k2 tog) to end.
Row 16: Cast off 7 sts, k to end.
Repeat rows 1–16 until desired length. Cast off.

*Pattern 42

Cast on 11 sts.
Row 1: K2, inc 1, k4, p1, k3.
Row 2: K.
Row 3: K2, inc 1, k4, p2, k3.
Row 4: K.
Row 5: K2, inc 1, k4, p3, k3.
Row 6: K.
Row 7: K2, inc 1, k4, p4, k3.
Row 8: K.
Row 9: K2, inc 1, k4, p5, k3.
Row 10: K.
Row 11: Cast off 5 sts, k1, inc 1, k4, p1, k3.
Repeat rows 2–11 until desired length. Cast off.

Pattern 41

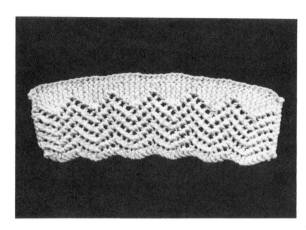

Cast on 15 sts.
Row 1: K.
Row 2: Sl 1, k4, (m1, k2 tog) 4 times, m1, k2.
Row 3: K.
Row 4: Sl 1, k5, (m1, k2 tog) 4 times, m1, k2.
Row 5: K.
Row 6: Sl 1, k6, (m1, k2 tog) 4 times, m1, k2.
Row 7: K.
Row 8: Sl 1, k7, (m1, k2 tog) 4 times, m1, k2.
Row 9: K.
Row 10: Sl 1, k5, k2 tog, (m1, k2 tog) 5 times, k1.
Row 11: K.
Row 12: Sl 1, k4, k2 tog, (m1, k2 tog) 5 times, k1.
Row 13: K.
Row 14: Sl 1, k3, k2 tog, (m1, k2 tog) 5 times, k1.
Row 15: K.
Row 16: Sl 1, k2, k2 tog, (m1, k2 tog) 5 times, k1.
Row 17: K.
Repeat rows 2–17 until desired length. Cast off.

*Pattern 43

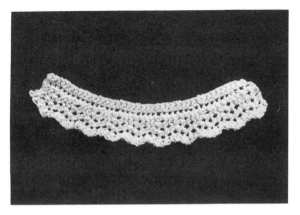

Cast on 9 sts.
Row 1: K2, m1, k2 tog, k1, m1, k2 tog, m1, k2.

Row 2: M1, k2 tog, k to end.
Row 3: K2, (m1, k2 tog) 3 times, m1, k2.
Row 4: M1, k2 tog, k to end.
Row 5: K2, m1, (k2 tog) twice, (m1, k2 tog) twice, k1.
Row 6: M1, k2 tog, k to end.
Row 7: K2, m1, k2 tog, k1, k2 tog, m1, k2 tog, k1.
Row 8: M1, k2 tog, k to end.
Repeat rows 1–8 until desired length. Cast off.

Pattern 45

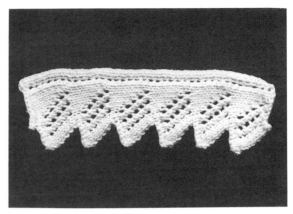

Pattern 44

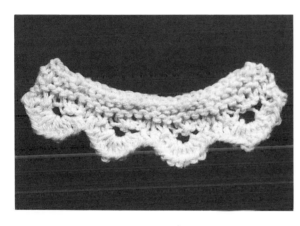

Cast on a multiple of 11 sts, plus 2, for required length of edging.
Row 1: P.
Row 2: K2, *k1, sl this st back onto L.H. needle and lift the next 8 sts on L.H. needle over this st and off the needle, m2, then k first st again, k2*, repeat *—* to end.
Row 3: K1, *p2 tog, drop extra loop of 2 sts made on previous row and into this long loop (k1, k1 tbl) twice, p1*, repeat *—* to last st, k1.
Work 5 rows of garter st. Cast off.

Cast on 13 sts.
Row 1: K3, yfwd, k2 tog, k1, (yfwd, k2 tog) twice, yfwd, k3.
Row 2: P.
Row 3: K3, yfwd, k2 tog, k2, (yfwd, k2 tog) twice, yfwd, k3.
Row 4: P.
Row 5: K3, yfwd, k2 tog, k3, (yfwd, k2 tog) twice, yfwd, k3.
Row 6: P.
Row 7: K3, yfwd, k2 tog, k4, (yfwd, k2 tog) twice, yfwd, k3.
Row 8: P.
Row 9: K3, yfwd, k2 tog, k5, (yfwd, k2 tog) twice, yfwd, k3.
Row 10: P.
Row 11: K3, yfwd, k2 tog, k13.
Row 12: Cast off 5 sts, p to end.
Repeat rows 1–12 until desired length. Cast off.

Pattern 46

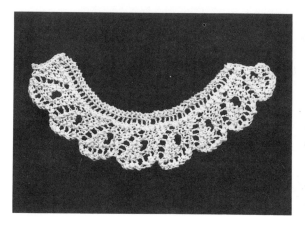

Cast on 10 sts.

Row 1: K.

Row 2: Sl 1, k1, (m1, k2 tog) twice, m4, k2 tog, m1, p2 tog.

Row 3: M1, p2 tog, k1, (k1, p1, k1, p1) into loop made by m4 of previous row, (k1, p1) twice, k2.

Row 4: Sl 1, (k1, m1, k2 tog) twice, k4, m1, p2 tog.

Row 5: M1, p2 tog, k5, (p1, k2) twice.

Row 6: Sl 1, k1, m1, k2 tog, k2, m1, k2 tog, k3, m1, p2 tog.

Row 7: M1, p2 tog, k4, p1, k3, p1, k2.

Row 8: Sl 1, k1, m1, k2 tog, k3, m1, k2 tog, k2, m1, p2 tog.

Row 9: M1, p2 tog, k3, p1, k4, p1, k2.

Row 10: Sl 1, k1, m1, k2 tog, k4, m1, k2 tog, k1, m1, p2 tog.

Row 11: M1, p2 tog, k2, p1, k5, p1, k2.

Row 12: Sl 1, k1, m1, k2 tog, k5, m1, k2 tog, m1, p2 tog.

Row 13: Cast off 3 sts, slip the st from R.H. needle back to L.H. needle, m1, p2 tog, k5, p1, k2.

Repeat rows 2–13 until desired length. Cast off.

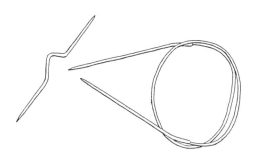

Pattern 47

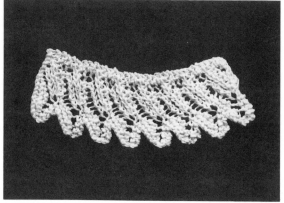

Cast on 10 sts.

Row 1: K.

Row 2: K3, yon, k5, yon, k2.

Row 3: K2, (yon) twice, p1, yon, p2 tog, k4, yon, k2 tog, k1.

Row 4: K3, yon, k2 tog, k1, (k2 tog, yon) twice, k1, p1, k2.

Row 5: K2, (yon) twice, k3, (yon, p2 tog) twice, k2, yon, k2 tog, k1.

Row 6: K4, (k2 tog, yon) twice, k5, p1, k2.

Row 7: K2, (yon) twice, k7, (yon, p2 tog) twice, k3.

Row 8: K2, (k2 tog, yon) twice, k9, p1, k2.

Row 9: Cast off 8 sts, k4, (yon, p2 tog) twice, k1.

Repeat rows 2–9 until desired length. Cast off.

Pattern 48

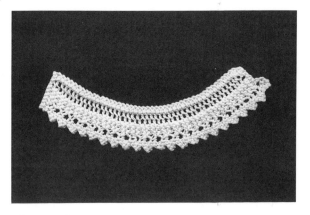

Cast on 9 sts.

Row 1: Sl 1, k2, m1, k2 tog, k2, m2, k2.
Row 2: Sl 1, k2, p1, k4, m1, k2 tog, k1.
Row 3: Sl 1, k2, m1, k2 tog, k6.
Row 4: Cast off 2 sts, k5, m1, k2 tog, k1.
Repeat rows 1–4 until desired length. Cast off.

Pattern 50

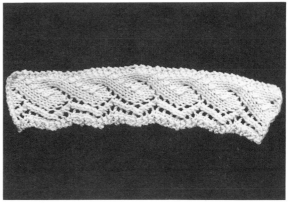

Pattern 49

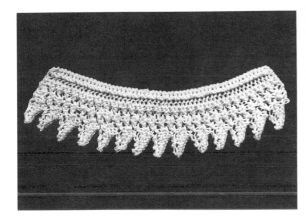

Cast of 12 sts.
Row 1: Sl 1, k2, yfwd, k2 tog, k1, k2 tog, yfwd, k1, yfwd, k2 tog, yfwd, k1.
Row 2: K1, yfwd, k2 tog, yfwd, k3, yfwd, k2 tog, k1, yfwd, k2 tog, k2.
Row 3: Sl 1, k2, yfwd, k2 tog, k1, yfwd, k2 tog, k1, k2 tog, yfwd, k2, yfwd, k1.
Row 4: K1, yfwd, k4, yfwd, sl 1, k2 tog, psso, yfwd, k3, yfwd, k2 tog, k2.
Row 5: Sl 1, k2, yfwd, k2 tog, k1, k2 tog, yfwd, k1, yfwd, k2 tog, k4, yfwd, k1.
Row 6: K1, yfwd, k4, k2 tog, yfwd, k3, yfwd, k2 tog, k1, yfwd, k2 tog, k2.
Row 7: Sl 1, k2, yfwd, k2 tog, k1, yfwd, k2 tog, k1, k2 tog, yfwd, k6, yfwd, k1.
Row 8: Cast off 7 sts, k1, yfwd, sl 1, k2 tog, psso, yfwd, k3, yfwd, k2 tog, k2.
Repeat rows,1–8 until desired length. Cast off.

Cast on 13 sts.
Row 1 and all other alternate rows: K2, p to last 2 sts, k2. [Number of p sts will vary on different rows.]
Row 2: Sl 1, k3, yon, k5, yon, k2 tog, yon, k2.
Row 4: Sl 1, k4, sl 1, k2 tog, psso, k2, (yon, k2 tog) twice, k1.
Row 6: Sl 1, k3, sl 1, k1, psso, k2 (yon, k2 tog) twice, k1.
Row 8: Sl 1, k2, sl 1, k1, psso, k2, (yon, k2 tog) twice, k1.
Row 10: Sl 1, k1, sl 1, k1, psso, k2, (yon, k2 tog) twice, k1.
Row 12: K1, sl 1, k1, psso, k2, yon, k1, yon, k2 tog, yon, k2.
Row 14: Sl 1, (k3, yon) twice, k2 tog, yon, k2.
Repeat rows 1–14 until desired length. Cast off.

Pattern 51

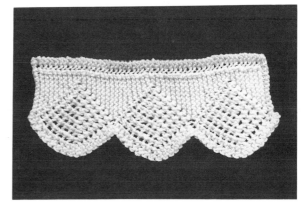

Cast on 16 sts.

Row 1: K.

Row 2: Yon, k2 tog, k1, yon, k10, yon, k2 tog, k1.

Row 3: K2, yon, k2 tog, k12, p1.

Row 4: Yon, k2 tog, k1, yon, k2 tog, yon, k9, yon, k2 tog, k1.

Row 5: K2, yon, k2 tog, k13, p1.

Row 6: Yon, k2 tog, k1, (yon, k2 tog) twice, yon, k8, yon, k2 tog, k1.

Row 7: K2, yon, k2 tog, k14, p1.

Row 8: Yon, k2 tog, k1, (yon, k2 tog) 3 times, yon, k7, yon, k2 tog, k1.

Row 9: K2, yon, k2 tog, k15, p1.

Row 10: Yon, k2 tog, k1, (yon, k2 tog) 4 times, yon, k6, yon, k2 tog, k1.

Row 11: K2, yon, k2 tog, k16, p1.

Row 12: Yon, k2 tog, k1, (yon, k2 tog) 5 times, yon, k5, yon, k2 tog, k1.

Row 13: K2, yon, k2 tog, k17, p1.

Row 14: Yon, k2 tog, k1, (yon, k2 tog) 6 times, yon, k4, yon, k2 tog, k1.

Row 15: K2, yon, k2 tog, k18, p1.

Row 16: Yon, k2 tog, k1, (yon, k2 tog) 7 times, yon, k3, yon, k2 tog, k1.

Row 17: K2, yon, k2 tog, k19, p1.

Row 18: Yon, (k2 tog) twice, (yon, k2 tog) 7 times, k3, yon, k2 tog, k1.

Rows 19, 21, 23, 25, 27, 29 & 31: Repeat rows 15, 13, 11, 9, 7, 5 & 3 respectively.

Row 20: Yon, (k2 tog) twice, (yon, k2 tog) 6 times, k4, yon, k2 tog, k1.

Row 22: Yon, (k2 tog) twice, (yon, k2 tog) 5 times, k5, yon, k2 tog, k1.

Row 24: Yon, (k2 tog) twice, (yon, k2 tog) 4 times, k6, yon, k2 tog, k1.

Row 26: Yon, (k2 tog) twice, (yon, k2 tog) 3 times, k7, yon, k2 tog, k1.

Row 28: Yon, (k2 tog) twice, (yon, k2 tog) twice, k8, yon, k2 tog, k1.

Row 30: Yon, (k2 tog) twice, yon, k2 tog, k9, yon, k2 tog, k1.

Row 32: Yon, (k2 tog) twice, k10, yon, k2 tog, k1.

Row 33: K2, yon, k2 tog, k11, p1.

Repeat rows 2–33 until desired length. Cast off.

Pattern 52

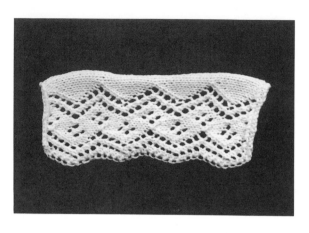

Cast on 18 sts.

Row 1: P.

Row 2: K5, (m1, k2 tog) twice, k1, m1, k2 tog, k2, m1, k2 tog, m1, k2.

Row 3: M1, k2 tog, p to end.

Row 4: K6, (m1, k2 tog) twice, k5, m1, k2 tog, m1, k2.

Row 5: M1, k2 tog, p to end.

Row 6: K7, (m1, k2 tog) twice, k2, m1, k2 tog, k1, m1, k2 tog, m1, k2.

Row 7: M1, k2 tog, p to end.

Row 8: K8, (m1, k2 tog) 4 times, k1, m1, k2 tog, m1, k2.

Row 9: M1, k2 tog, p to end.

Row 10: K6, k2 tog, m1, k2 tog, m1, k3, m1, (K2 tog) twice, (m1, k2 tog) twice, k1.

Row 11: M1, k2 tog, p to end.

Row 12: K5, k2 tog, m1, k2 tog, m1, k5, k2 tog, (m1, k2 tog) twice, k1.

Row 13: M1, k2 tog, p to end.

Row 14: K4, k2 tog, m1, k2 tog, m1, k2, m1, k2 tog, k1, k2 tog, (m1, k2 tog) twice, k1.

Row 15: M1, k2 tog, p to end.

Row 16: K3, k2 tog, m1, k2 tog, m1, k2, m1, k2 tog, m1, sl 1, k2 tog, psso, (m1, k2 tog) twice, k1.

Row 17: M1, k2 tog, p to end.

Repeat rows 2–17 until desired length. Cast off.

Pattern 53

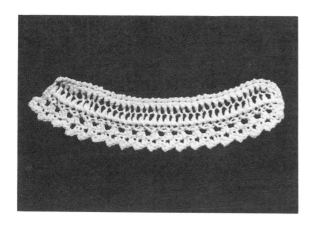

Cast on 11 sts.
Row 1: K9, m1, k2.
Row 2: K2, (k1, p1, k1) in m1 of previous row, m1, k4 tog, k1, m2, k2 tog, m2, k2.
Row 3: Sl 1, (k2, p1) twice, k2, (k1, p1, k1) in m1 of previous row, m1, p4 tog, k1.
Row 4: K2, (k1, p1, k1) in m1 of previous row, m1, p4 tog, k8.
Row 5: Cast off 3 sts, k5, (k1, p1, k1) in m1 of previous row, m1, p4 tog, k1.
Repeat rows 2–5 until desired length. Cast off.

Pattern 54

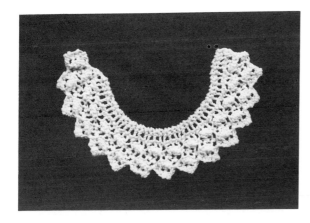

Cast on 9 sts.
Row 1: Sl 1, k1, m1, k2 tog, (m1, k1) 3 times, m1, k2.
Row 2: P11, k2.

Row 3: Sl 1, k1, m1, k2 tog, m1, k3, m1, k1, m1, k3, m1, k2.
Row 4: P15, k2.
Row 5: Sl 1, k1, m1, k2 tog, m1, sl 2, k3 tog, psso, m1, k1, m1, sl 2, k3 tog, psso, m1, k2.
Row 6: Cast off 4 sts, p6, k2.
Repeat rows 1–6 until desired length. Cast off.

Pattern 55

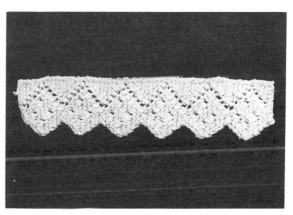

Cast on 11 sts.
Row 1: K6, yon, k2 tog, k1, k2 tog.
Row 2: K.
Row 3: K5, k2 tog, yon, k2, pick up thread between these 2 sts and k tbl [= inc 1 for this pattern only], k1.
Row 4: K.
Row 5: K4, k2 tog, yon, k4, inc 1, k1.
Row 6: K.
Row 7: K3, k2 tog, yon, k3, yon, k2 tog, k1, inc 1, k1.
Row 8: K.
Row 9: K2, k2 tog, yon, k8, inc 1, k1.
Row 10: K.
Row 11: K1, k2 tog, yon, k2, yon, k2 tog, k3, yon, k2 tog, k1, inc 1, k1.
Row 12: K.
Row 13: K2, yon, k2 tog, k9, k2 tog.
Row 14: K.
Row 15: K3, yon, k2 tog, k3, yon, k2 tog, k2, k2 tog.
Row 16: K.
Row 17: K4, yon, k2 tog, k5, k2 tog.
Row 18: K.
Row 19: K5, yon, k2 tog, k3, k2 tog.

Row 20: K.
Row 21: Repeat 1st row.
Repeat rows 1–21 until desired length. Cast off.

Pattern 56

Cast on 20 sts.
Row 1: Sl 1, k1, (m1, k2 tog) 4 times, p3, k2 tog, m1, k3, m1, k2.
Row 2: M1, k2 tog, k19.
Row 3: Sl 1, k2, (m1, k2 tog) 3 times, p3, k2 tog, m1, k5, m1, k2.
Row 4: M1, k2 tog, k20.
Row 5: Sl 1, k1, (m1, k2 tog) 3 times, p3, k2 tog, m1, (k2 tog) twice, m3, k2 tog, k1, m1, k2.
Row 6: M1, k2 tog, k4, p1, k16.
Row 7: Sl 1, k2, (m1, k2 tog) 3 times, p3, k1, m1, k2 tog, k3, k2 tog, m1, k2 tog, k1.
Row 8: M1, k2 tog, k20.
Row 9: Sl 1, k1, (m1, k2 tog) 4 times, p3, k1, m1, k2 tog, k1, k2 tog, m1, k2 tog, k1.
Row 10: M1, k2 tog, k19.
Row 11: Sl 1, k2, (m1, k2 tog) 4 times, p3, k1, m1, sl 1, k2 tog, psso, m1, k2 tog, k1.
Row 12: M1, k2 tog, k18.
Repeat rows 1–12 until desired length. Cast off.

Pattern 57

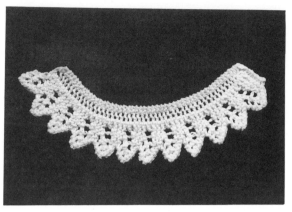

Cast on 10 sts.
Row 1: Sl 1, k2, m1, k2 tog, k1, m2, k2 tog, m2, k2 tog.
Row 2: Sl 1, k1, p1, k2, p1, k3, m1, k2 tog, k1.
Row 3: Sl 1, k2, m1, k2 tog, k3, m2, k2 tog, m2, k2 tog.
Row 4: Sl 1, k1, p1, k2, p1, k5, m1, k2 tog, k1.
Row 5: Sl 1, k2, m1, k2 tog, k5, m2, k2 tog, m2, k2 tog.
Row 6: Sl 1, k1, p1, k2, p1, k7, m1, k2 tog, k1.
Row 7: Sl 1, k2, m1, k2 tog, k11.
Row 8: Cast off 6 sts, k6, m1, k2 tog, k1.
Repeat rows 1–8 until desired length. Cast off.

Pattern 58

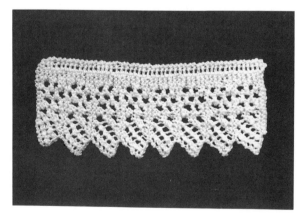

Cast on 19 sts.
Row 1: K.

Row 2: Sl 1, k1, m1, k2 tog, k3, k2 tog, m2, k2 tog, k1, k2 tog, m2, k2 tog, m1, k2 tog, m1, k1.
Row 3: K6, p1, k4, p1, k8.
Row 4: Sl 1, k1, m1, k2 tog, k1, k2 tog, m2, (k2 tog) twice, m2, k2 tog, k2, m1, k2 tog, m1, k2 tog, m1, k1.
Row 5: K10, p1, k3, p1, k6.
Row 6: Sl 1, k1, m1, k2 tog, k3, k2 tog, m2, k2 tog, k5, m1, k2 tog, m1, k2 tog, m1, k1.
Row 7: K13, p1, k8.
Row 8: Sl 1, k1, m1, k2 tog, k1, k2 tog, m2, (k2 tog) twice, m2, sl 1, k2 tog, psso, m2, k2 tog, k1, m1, k2 tog, m1, k2 tog, m1, k1.
Row 9: K9, p1, k2, p1, k3, p1, k6.
Row 10: Sl 1, k1, m1, k2 tog, k3, k2 tog, m2, k2 tog, k7, m1, k2 tog, m1, k2 tog, m1, k1.
Row 11: Cast off 5 sts, k9, p1, k8.
Row 12: Sl 1, k1, m1, k2 tog, k15.
Repeat rows 1–12 until desired length. Cast off.

tog, psso, m2, k2 tog, k1, m1, k2 tog, m1, k2 tog, m1, k1.
Row 9: K9, p1, k2, p1, k3, p1, k2 tog, m2, k2 tog, k1, m1, k2 tog, m1, k2 tog, m1, k1.
Row 10: K9, p1, k2, k2 tog, m2, k2 tog, k7, m1, k2 tog, m1, k2 tog, m1, k1.
Row 11: Cast off 5 sts, k9, p1, k8, m1, k2 tog, m1, k2 tog, m1, k1.
Row 12: Cast off 5 sts, k19.
Repeat rows 1–12 until desired length. Cast off.

Pattern 60

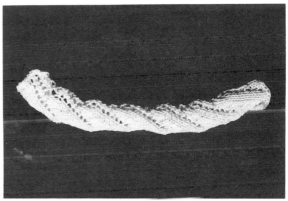

Cast on 16 sts.
Row 1: K2, p to last 4 sts, k4.
Row 2: Sl 1, k1, m1, k2 tog, k3, m1, k5, m1, k2 tog, m1, k2.
Row 3: K2, p to last 4 sts, k4.
Row 4: Sl 1, k1, m1, k2 tog, k4, sl 1, k2 tog, psso, k2, (m1, k2 tog) twice, k1.
Row 5: K2, p to last 4 sts, k4.
Row 6: Sl 1, k1, m1, k2 tog, k3, k2 tog tbl, k2, (m1, k2 tog) twice, k1.
Row 7: K2, p to last 4 sts, k4.
Row 8: Sl 1, k1, m1, k2 tog, k2, k2 tog tbl, k2, (m1, k2 tog) twice, k1.
Row 9: K2, p to last 4 sts, k4.
Row 10: Sl 1, k1, m1, k2 tog, k1, k2 tog tbl, k2, (m1, k2 tog) twice, k1.
Row 11: K2, p to last 4 sts, k4.
Row 12: Sl 1, k1, m1, k2 tog, k2 tog tbl, k2, m1, k1, k2 tog, m1, k2.
Row 13: K2, p to last 4 sts, k4.
Row 14: Sl 1, k1, m1, k2 tog, (k3, m1) twice, k1, m1, k2.
Repeat rows 1–14 until desired length. Cast off.

Pattern 59

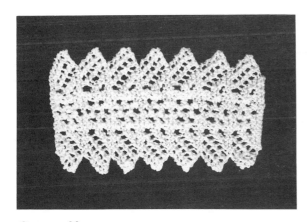

Cast on 20 sts.
Row 1: K.
Row 2: K8, k2 tog, m2, k2 tog, k1, k2 tog, m2, k2 tog, m1, k2 tog, m1, k1.
Row 3: K6, p1, k4, p1, k2, k2 tog, m2, k2 tog, m1, k2 tog, m1, k1.
Row 4: K6, p1, k2 tog, m2, (k2 tog) twice, m2, k2 tog, k2, m1, k2 tog, m1, k2 tog, m1, k1.
Row 5: K10, p1, k3, p1, k3, m1, k2 tog, m1, k2 tog, m1, k1.
Row 6: K10, k2 tog, m2, k2 tog, k5, m1, k2 tog, m1, k2 tog, m1, k1.
Row 7: K13, p1, k6, m1, k2 tog, m1, k2 tog, m1, k1.
Row 8: K9, k2 tog, m2, (k2 tog) twice, m2, sl 1, k2

Pattern 61

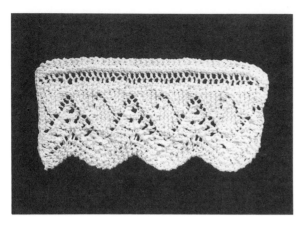

Cast on 17 sts.
Row 1: K.
Row 2: K4, m1, p2 tog, k2, m1, k2, p1, k3, m1, k3.
Row 3: K3, m1, k1, p2 tog, m2, (p2 tog) twice, m1, p5, m1, p2 tog, k2.
Row 4: K4, m1, p2 tog, k4, m1, p2 tog, k1, p1, k3, m1, k3.
Row 5: K3, m1, k1, p2 tog, m2, (p2 tog) twice, m1, k7, m1, p2 tog, k2.
Row 6: K4, m1, p2 tog, k6, m1, p2 tog, k1, p1, k3, m1, k3.
Row 7: K3, m1, k1, p2 tog, m2, (p2 tog) twice, m1, k9, m1, p2 tog, k2.
Row 8: K4, m1, p2 tog, k5, k2 tog, m1, k1, m1, p2 tog, k1, p1, k3, m1, k3.
Row 9: K3, m1, k1, p2 tog, m2, (p2 tog) twice, m1, k3, m1, p2 tog, k6, m1, p2 tog, k2.
Row 10: K4, m1, p2 tog, k3, k2 tog, m1, k5, m1, p2 tog, k1, p1, k3, m1, k3.
Row 11: K3, m1, k1, p2 tog, m2, (p2 tog) twice, m1, k7, m1, p2 tog, k4, m1, p2 tog, k2.
Row 12: K4, m1, p2 tog, k1, k2 tog, m1, k9, m1, k3, p1, k3, m1, k3.
Row 13: K3, m1, k1, p2 tog, m2, p2 tog, p3 tog, m1, k11, m1, p2 tog, k2, m1, p2 tog, k2.
Row 14: K4, m1, p2 tog, k2, m1, sl 1, k1, psso, k7, k2 tog, m1, k4, p1, p2 tog, m1, p2 tog, k2.
Row 15: K2, p2 tog, m1, (p2 tog) twice, m2, p2 tog, k1, m1, p2 tog, k5, p2 tog, m1, k5, m1, p2 tog, k2.
Row 16: K4, m1, p2 tog, k4, m1, sl 1, k1, psso, k3, k2 tog, m1, k1, p2 tog, k1, p1, p2 tog, m1, p2 tog, k2.
Row 17: K2, p2 tog, m1, (p2 tog) twice, m2, p2 tog, m1, p2 tog, k1, p2 tog, m1, k7, m1, p2 tog, k2.
Row 18: K4, m1, p2 tog, k6, m1, p3 tog, m1, k3, p1, p2 tog, m1, p2 tog, k2.
Row 19: K2, p2 tog, m1, (p2 tog) twice, m2, p2 tog, m1, p2 tog, k8, m1, p2 tog, k2.
Row 20: K4, m1, p2 tog, k5, k2 tog, m1, k3, p1, p2 tog, m1, p2 tog, k2.
Row 21: K2, p2 tog, m1, (p2 tog) twice, m2, p2 tog, m1, p2 tog, k6, m1, p2 tog, k2.
Row 22: K4, m1, p2 tog, k3, k2 tog, m1, k3, p1, p2 tog, m1, p2 tog, k2.
Row 23: K2, p2 tog, m1, (p2 tog) twice, m2, p2 tog, m1, p2 tog, k4, m1, p2 tog, k2.
Row 24: K4, m1, p2 tog, k1, k2 tog, m1, k3, p1, p2 tog, m1, p2 tog, k2.
Row 25: K2, p2 tog, m1, (p2 tog) twice, m2, p2 tog, m1, p2 tog, k2, m1, p2 tog, k2.
Repeat rows 2–25 until desired length. Cast off.

Pattern 62

This pattern is worked lengthwise across the edging.
Cast on a multiple of 11 sts, the required number for desired length, allowing 33 sts for each 10 cm of edging.
Row 1: K.
Row 2: P.
Row 3: *(K2 tog) twice, (m1, k1) 3 times, m1, (k2 tog) twice*, repeat *—* to end.
Row 4: P.
Row 5: Repeat row 3.
Row 6: Repeat row 4. Cast off.

Pattern 63

Cast on 20 sts.

Row 1: K.
Row 2: Sl 1, k3, (yon, k2 tog) 7 times, yon, k2.
Row 3: K.
Row 4: Sl 1, k6, (yon, k2 tog) 6 times, yon, k2.
Row 5: K.
Row 6: Sl 1, k9, (yon, k2 tog) 5 times, yon, k2.
Row 7: K.
Row 8: Sl 1, k12, (yon, k2 tog) 4 times, yon, k2.
Row 9: K.
Row 10: Sl 1, k23.
Row 11: Cast off 4 sts, k19
Repeat rows 1-10 until desired length. Cast off.

*Pattern 64

Cast on 6 sts.
Row 1: K.

Row 2: K.
Row 3: K.
Row 4: Cast on 3 sts, k.
Row 5: K.
Row 6: K.
Row 7: K.
Row 8: Cast on 3 sts, k.
Row 9: K.
Row 10: P.
Row 11: K.
Row 12: P.
Row 13: K.
Row 14: K.
Row 15: K.
Row 16: Cast off 3 sts, k.
Row 17: K.
Row 18: K.
Row 19: K.
Row 20: Cast off 3 sts, k.
Repeat rows 1-20 until desired length. Cast off.

Pattern 65

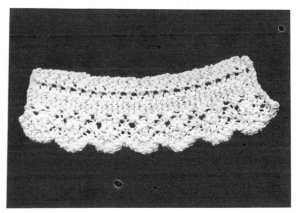

Cast on 9 sts.
Row 1: K4, yfwd, k2 tog, yfwd, k3.
Row 2: Yfwd, k2 tog, k1, yfwd, k2 tog, yfwd, k5.
Row 3: K6, yfwd, k2 tog, yfwd, k3.
Row 4: Yfwd, k2 tog, k1, yfwd, k2 tog, yfwd, k1, yfwd, k2 tog, k4.
Row 5: K3, k2 tog, yfwd, k3, yfwd, k2 tog, yfwd, k3.
Row 6: Yfwd, k2 tog, k1, yfwd, k2 tog, yfwd, k5, yfwd, k2 tog, k2.
Row 7: K4, yfwd, k2 tog, k1, k2 tog, (yfwd, k2 tog) twice, k2.

47

Row 8: Yfwd, k2 tog, k2 tog, yfwd, k2 tog, yfwd, sl 1, k2 tog, psso, yfwd, k5.
Row 9: K5, (k2 tog, yfwd) twice, k2 tog, k2.
Row 10: Yfwd, k2 tog, k2 tog, (yfwd, k2 tog) twice, k4.
Row 11: K3, (k2 tog, yfwd) twice, k2 tog, k2.
Row 12: Yfwd, k2 tog, k2 tog, (yfwd, k2 tog) twice, k2.
Repeat rows 1-12 until desired length. Cast off.

Pattern 67

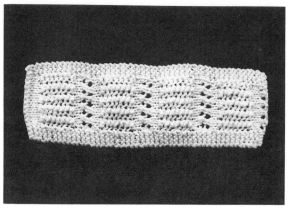

Pattern 66

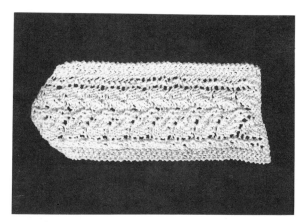

Cast on 25 sts.
Row 1: Sl 1, k3, m1, k2 tog, m1, k1, m1, k2 tog, p1, k2 tog, p1, sl 1, k1, psso, p1, sl 1, k1, psso, m1, k1, m1, sl 1, k1, psso, m1, k4.
Row 2: Sl 1, k2, p7, k1, p1, k1, p1, k1, p7, k3.
Row 3: Sl 1, k3, m1, k2 tog, m1, k3, m1, k3 tog, p1, sl 1, k2 tog, psso, m1, k3, m1, sl 1, k1, psso, m1, k4.
Row 4: Sl 1, k2, p9, k1, p9, k3.
Row 5: Sl 1, k3, m1, k2 tog, m1, k5, m1, sl 1, k2 tog, psso, m1, k5, m1, sl 1, k1, psso, m1, k4.
Row 6: Sl 1, k2, p21, k3.
Row 7: Sl 1, k3, m1, k2 tog, m1, k1, k2 tog, p1, k2 tog, k3, k2 tog, p1, sl 1, k1, psso, k1, m1, sl 1, k1, psso, m1, k4.
Row 8: Sl 1, k2, p6, k1, p5, k1, p6, k3.
Repeat rows 1-8 until desired length. Cast off.

Cast on 17 sts.
Row 1: Sl 1, k3, (m1, k2 tog) 5 times, k3.
Row 2: Sl 1, k3, p10, k3.
Row 3: Sl 1, k16.
Row 4: Sl 1, k3, p10, k3.
Row 5: Sl 1, k16.
Rows 6-18: Sl 1, k3, (m1, k2 tog) 5 times, k3.
Row 19: Sl 1, k16.
Row 20: Sl 1, k3, p10, k3.
Row 21: Sl 1, k16.
Row 22: Sl 1, k3, p10, k3.
Row 23: Sl 1, k3, (m1, k2 tog) 5 times, k3.
Row 24: Sl 1, k3, p10, k3.
Repeat rows 1-24 until desired length. Cast off.

Pattern 68

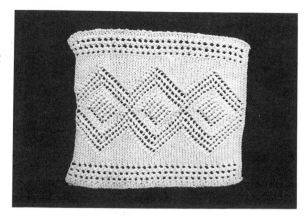

Cast on 55 sts.

Row 1: K2, (k2 tog, m1) 3 times, k13, (k2 tog, m1) 3 times, k1, (m1, k2 tog) 3 times, k13, (m1, k2 tog) 3 times, k2.

Row 2: K.

Row 3: K20, (k2 tog, m1) 3 times, k3, (m1, k2 tog) 3 times, k20.

Row 4: K.

Row 5: K2, (k2 tog, m1) 3 times, k11, (k2 tog, m1) 3 times, k5, (m1, k2 tog) 3 times, k11, (m1, k2 tog) 3 times, k2.

Row 6: K.

Row 7: K18, (k2 tog, m1) 3 times, k7, (m1, k2 tog) 3 times, k18.

Row 8: K.

Row 9: K2, (k2 tog, m1) 3 times, k9, (k2 tog, m1) 3 times, k3, k2 tog, m1, k4, (m1, k2 tog) 3 times, k9, (m1, k2 tog) 3 times, k2.

Row 10: K.

Row 11: K16, (k2 tog, m1) 3 times, k3, k2 tog, m1, k1, m1, k2 tog, k3, (m1, k2 tog) 3 times, k16.

Row 12: K.

Row 13: K2, (k2 tog, m1) 3 times, k7, (k2 tog, m1) 3 times, k3, (k2 tog, m1) twice, k1, m1, k2 tog, k3, (m1, k2 tog) 3 times, k7, (m1, k2 tog) 3 times, k2.

Row 14: K.

Row 15: K14, (k2 tog, m1) 3 times, k3, (k2 tog, m1) 3 times, k1, m1, k2 tog, k3, (m1, k2 tog) 3 times, k14.

Row 16: K.

Row 17: K2, (k2 tog, m1) 3 times, k5, (k2 tog, m1) 3 times, k3, (k2 tog, m1) 4 times, k1, m1, k2 tog, k3, (m1, k2 tog) 3 times, k5, (m1, k2 tog) 3 times, k2.

Row 18: K.

Row 19: K12, (k2 tog, m1) 3 times, k3, (k2 tog, m1) 5 times, k1, m1, k2 tog, k3, (m1, k2 tog) 3 times, k12.

Row 20: K.

Row 21: K2, (k2 tog, m1) 3 times, k6, (m1, k2 tog) 3 times, k2, (k2 tog, m1) 5 times, k3, (k2 tog, m1) 3 times, k6, (m1, k2 tog) 3 times, k2.

Row 22: K.

Row 23: K15, (m1, k2 tog) 3 times, k2, (k2 tog, m1) 4 times, k3, (k2 tog, m1) 3 times, k15.

Row 24: K.

Row 25: K2, (k2 tog, m1) 3 times, k8, (m1, k2 tog) 3 times, k2, (k2 tog, m1) 3 times, k3, (k2 tog, m1) 3 times, k8, (m1, k2 tog) 3 times, k2.

Row 26: K.

Row 27: K17, (m1, k2 tog) 3 times, k2, (k2 tog, m1) twice, k3, (k2 tog, m1) 3 times, k17.

Row 28: K.

Row 29: K2, (k2 tog, m1) 3 times, k10, (m1, k2 tog) 3 times, k2, k2 tog, m1, k3, (k2 tog, m1) 3 times, k10, (m1, k2 tog) 3 times, k2.

Row 30: K.

Row 31: K19, (m1, k2 tog) 3 times, k5, (k2 tog, m1) 3 times, k19.

Row 32: K.

Row 33: K2, (k2 tog, m1) 3 times, k12, (m1, k2 tog) 3 times, k3, (k2 tog, m1) 3 times, k12, (m1, k2 tog) 3 times, k2.

Row 34: K.

Row 35: K21, (m1, k2 tog) 3 times, k1, (k2 tog, m1) 3 times, k21.

Row 36: K.

Row 37: K2, (k2 tog, m1) 3 times, k14, (m1, k2 tog) twice, m1, sl 1, k2 tog, psso, m1, (k2 tog, m1) twice, k14, (m1, k2 tog) 3 times, k2.

Row 38: K.

Row 39: K23, m1, k2 tog, m1, sl 1, k2 tog, psso, (m1, k2 tog) twice, m1, k23.

Row 40: K.

Repeat rows 1–40 until desired length. Cast off.

Pattern 69

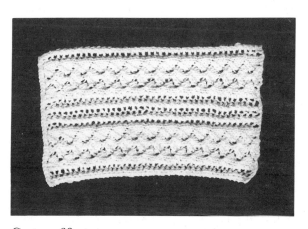

Cast on 38 sts.

Row 1: Sl 1, k2, m1, k2 tog, k1, m1, sl 1, k1, psso, k3, k2 tog, m1, k3, m1, k2 tog, k1, m1, k2 tog, k1, m1, k2 tog, k1, m1, sl 1, k1, psso, k3, k2 tog, m1, k3, m1, k2 tog, k1.

Row 2: Sl 1, p2, m1, p2 tog, p2, m1, p2 tog, p1, p2 tog, m1, p4, m1, p2 tog, p1, m1, p2 tog, p1, m1, p2 tog, p2, m1, p2 tog, p1, p2 tog, m1, p4, m1, p2 tog, p1.

Row 3: Sl 1, k2, m1, k2 tog, k3, m1, sl 1, k2 tog, psso, m1, k5, m1, k2 tog, k1, m1, k2 tog, k1, m1, k2 tog, k3, m1, sl 1, k2 tog, psso, m1, k5, m1, k2 tog, k1.
Row 4: Sl 1, p2, m1, p2 tog, p2, p2 tog, m1, p1, m1, p2 tog, p4, m1, p2 tog, (p1, m1, p2 tog) twice, p2, p2 tog, m1, p1, m1, p2 tog, p4, m1, p2 tog, p1.
Row 5: Sl 1, k2, m1, k2 tog, k1, k2 tog, m1, k3, m1, sl 1, k1, psso, k3, m1, k2 tog, k1, m1, k2 tog, k1, m1, k2 tog, k1, k2 tog, m1, k3, m1, sl 1, k1, psso, k3, m1, k2 tog, k1.
Row 6: Sl 1, p2, m1, p2 tog, p2 tog, m1, p5, m1, p2 tog, p2, m1, p2 tog, p1, m1, p2 tog, p1, m1, p2 tog, p2 tog, m1, p5, m1, p2 tog, p2, m1, p2 tog, p1.
Repeat rows 1–6 until desired length. Cast off.

Pattern 71

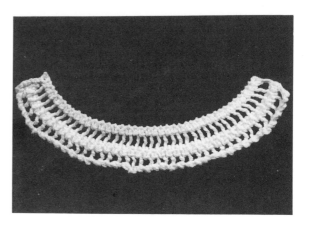

Cast on 8 sts.
Row 1: K2 tog, m2, k2 tog, k1, m2, k2 tog, k1.
Row 2: Sl 1, k2, p1, k2 tog, k1, p1, k1.
Repeat these two rows until desired length. Cast off.

Pattern 70

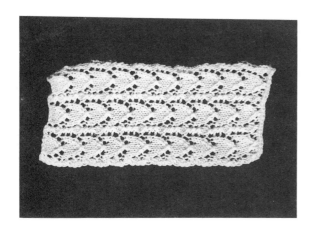

Cast on 27 sts.
Row 1: Sl 1, k2 tog, *m1, k5, m1, sl 1, k2 tog, psso* repeat *—*, m1, k5, m1, sl 1, k1, psso, k1.
Row 2: P.
Row 3: Repeat row 1.
Row 4: P.
Row 5: Sl 1, k2, *m1, sl 1, k1, psso, k1, k2 tog, m1, k3* repeat *—* twice.
Row 6: P.
Row 7: Sl 2, k1, psso, *m1, k1, m1, sl 1, k2 tog, psso, m1, k1, m1, sl 1, k2 tog, psso* repeat *—*, m1, k1, m1, sl 1, k2 tog, psso, m1, k1, m1, sl 1, k1, psso, k1.
Row 8: P.
Repeat rows 1–8 until desired length. Cast off.

Pattern 72

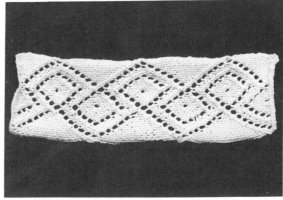

Cast on 21 sts.
Row 1: P.
Row 2: K2, m1, sl 1, k1, psso, k1, m1, sl 1, k1, psso, k3, k2 tog, m1, k1, m1, sl 1, k1, psso, k6.
Row 3: P.
Row 4: K3, (m1, sl 1, k1, psso, k1) twice, k2 tog, m1, k3, m1, sl 1, k1, psso, k5.
Row 5: P.
Row 6: K4, m1, sl 1, k1, psso, k1, m1, k3 tog, m1, k2, m1, sl 1, k1, psso, k1, m1, sl 1, k1, psso, k4.

Row 7: P.
Row 8: K5, m1, sl 1, k1, psso, (k2, m1, k1) twice, m1, sl 1, k1, psso, k1, m1, sl 1, k1, psso, k3.
Row 9: P.
Row 10: K6, m1, sl 1, k1, psso, k1, k2 tog, m1, k3, m1, sl 1, k1, psso, k1, m1, sl 1, k1, psso, k2.
Row 11: P.
Row 12: K7, m1, k3 tog, m1, k5, (m1, sl 1, k1, psso, k1) twice.
Row 13: P.
Row 14: K7, k2 tog, m1, k3, m1, sl 1, k1, psso, k2, m1, sl 1, k1, psso, k1, m1, sl 1, k1, psso.
Row 15: P.
Row 16: K6, k2 tog, m1, k1, m1, sl 1, k1, psso, k3, k2 tog, m1, k1, k2 tog, m1, k2.
Row 17: P.
Row 18: K5, k2 tog, m1, k3, m1, sl 1, k1, psso, (k1, k2 tog, m1) twice, k3.
Row 19: P.
Row 20: K4, k2 tog, m1, k1, k2 tog, m1, k2, m1, sl 1, k2 tog, psso, m1, k1, k2 tog, m1, k4.
Row 21: P.
Row 22: K3, (k2 tog, m1, k1) twice, m1, sl 1, k1, psso, k1, m1, sl 1, k1, psso, k2 tog, m1, k5.
Row 23: P.
Row 24: K2, k2 tog, m1, k1, k2 tog, m1, k3, m1, sl 1, k1, psso, k1, k2 tog, m1, k6.
Row 25: P.
Row 26: (K1, k2 tog, m1) twice, k5, m1, sl 1, k2 tog, psso, m1, k7.
Row 27: P.
Row 28: K2 tog, m1, k1, k2 tog, m1, k2, k2 tog, m1, k3, m1, sl 1, k1, psso, k7.
Repeat rows 1-28 until desired length. Cast off.

Pattern 73

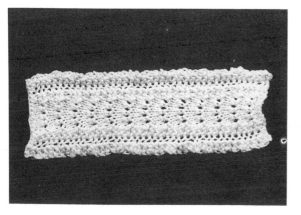

Cast on 19 sts.
Row 1: M1, k2 tog, k4, p7, k6.
Row 2: M1, k2 tog, k1, m1, (k2 tog) twice, k5, sl 1, k1, psso, k1, m1, k2 tog, k2.
Row 3: M1, k2 tog, k1, m1, k2 tog, k8, m1, k2 tog, k2.
Row 4: M1, k2 tog, k1, m1, k2 tog, k2, (m1, k1) 3 times, m1, k3, m1, k2 tog, k2.
Row 5: M1, k2 tog, k1, m1, k2 tog, k1, p9, k2, m1, k2 tog, k2.
Row 6: M1, k2 tog, k1, m1, (k2 tog) twice, k7, sl 1, k1, psso, k1, m1, k2 tog, k2.
Row 7: M1, k2 tog, k1, m1, k2 tog, k1, p7, k2, m1, k2 tog, k2.
Repeat rows 2-7 until desired length. Cast off.

*Pattern 74

Cast on 7 sts.
Row 1: K.
Row 2: K5, k in f & b of next st, k1.
Row 3: K1, k in f & b of next st, k6.
Row 4: K7, k in f & b of next st, k1.
Row 5: K1, k in f & b of next st, k8.
Row 6: K9, k in f & b of next st, k1.
Row 7: K1, k in f & b of next st, k10.
Row 8: K11, k in f & b of next st, k1.
Row 9: K1, k in f & b of next st, k12.
Row 10: K12, k2 tog, k1.
Row 11: K1, k2 tog, k11.
Row 12: K10, k2 tog, k1.
Row 13: K1, k2 tog, k9.
Row 14: K8, k2 tog, k1.
Row 15: K1, k2 tog, k7.
Row 16: K6, k2 tog, k1.

Row 17: K1, k2 tog, k5.
Repeat rows 2–16 until desired length. Cast off.

Cast on 13 sts.
Row 1: K3, yfwd, k2 tog, k1, (yrn twice, k2 tog) 3 times, k1.
Row 2: K3, yfwd, k2 tog, (k1, yfwd, k2 tog) twice, k5.
Row 3: K3, yfwd, k2 tog, k11.
Row 4: Cast off 3 sts, k12.
Repeat rows 1–4 until desired length. Cast off.

Pattern 75

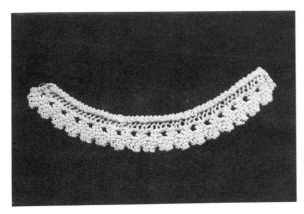

Cast on 7 sts.
Row 1: K.
Row 2: Sl 1, k1, m1, k2 tog, m2, k3.
Row 3: K4, p1, k1, m1, k2 tog, k1.
Row 4: Sl 1, k1, m1, k2 tog, k5.
Row 5: K6, m1, k2 tog, k1.
Row 6: Sl 1, k1, m1, k2 tog, k5.
Row 7: Cast off 2 sts, k3, m1, k2 tog, k1.
Repeat rows 2–7 until desired length. Cast off.

Pattern 77

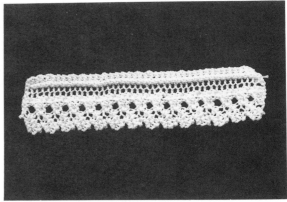

Cast on 11 sts.
Row 1: K4, yrn, p2 tog, k4, yfwd, (k1, p1) in last st.
Row 2: K3, yrn, p2 tog, k4, yrn, p2 tog, k2.
Row 3: K4, yrn, p2 tog, k1, p2 tog, yon, k4.
Row 4: K5, yrn, p2 tog, k2, yrn, p2 tog, k2.
Row 5: K4, yrn, p2 tog, k2, yrn, p2 tog, k3.
Row 6: Cast off 3 sts, yfwd, k5, yrn, p2 tog, k2.
Repeat rows 1–6 until desired length. Cast off.

Pattern 76

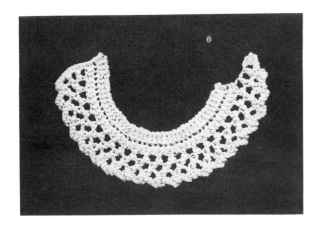

Pattern 78

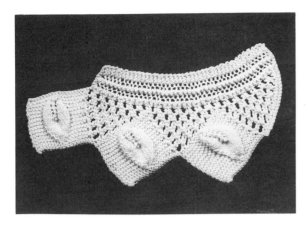

Cast on 30 sts.
Row 1: K.
Row 2: K4, (yfwd, k2 tog, k1) twice, yrn twice, k2 tog, k18.
Row 3: K9, (k1, p1, k1) in next st, k9, (k1, p1) in yrn twice of previous row, k3, (yfwd, k2 tog, k1) twice, k1.
Row 4: K4, (yfwd, k2 tog, k1) twice, k11, p3, k9.
Row 5: K10, yfwd, k1, yfwd, k15, (yfwd, k2 tog, k1) twice, k1.
Row 6: K4, (yfwd, k2 tog, k1) twice, yrn twice, k2 tog, yrn twice, k2 tog, k7, p5, k9.
Row 7: K11, yfwd, k1, yfwd, k11, p1, k2, p1, k3, (yfwd, k2 tog, k1) twice, k1.
Row 8: K4, (yfwd, k2 tog, k1) twice, k13, p7, k9.
Row 9: K12, yfwd, k1, yfwd, k19 (yfwd, k2 tog, k1) twice, k1.
Row 10: K4, (yfwd, k2 tog, k1) twice, (yrn twice, k2 tog) 3 times, k7, p9, k9.
Row 11: K13, yfwd, k1, yfwd, k13 (p1, k2) twice, p1, k3, (yfwd, k2 tog, k1) twice, k1.
Row 12: K4, (yfwd, k2 tog, k1) twice, k16, p11, k9.
Row 13: K14, yfwd, k1, yfwd, k24, (yfwd, k2 tog, k1) twice, k1.
Row 14: K4, (yfwd, k2 tog, k1) twice, (yrn twice, k2 tog) 3 times, yrn twice, sl 1, k2 tog, psso, k7, p13, k9.
Row 15: K9, sl 1, k1, psso, k9, k2 tog, k9, (p1, k2) 3 times, p1, k3, (yfwd, k2 tog, k1) twice, k1.
Row 16: K4, (yfwd, k2 tog, k1) twice, k19, p11, k9.
Row 17: K9, sl 1, k1, psso, k7, k2 tog, k22, (yfwd, k2 tog, k1) twice, k1.
Row 18: K4, (yfwd, k2 tog, k1) twice, (yrn twice, k2 tog) 3 times, (yrn twice, sl 1, k2 tog, psso) twice, k7, p9, k9.
Row 19: K9, sl 1, k1, psso, k5, k2 tog, k9, (p1, k2) 4 times, p1, k3, (yfwd, k2 tog, k1) twice, k1.
Row 20: K4, (yfwd, k2 tog, k1) twice, k22, p7, k9.
Row 21: K9, sl 1, k1, psso, k3, k2 tog, k25, (yfwd, k2 tog, k1) twice, k1.
Row 22: K4, (yfwd, k2 tog, k1) twice, (yrn twice, k2 tog) 3 times, (yrn twice, sl 1, k2 tog, psso) 3 times, k7, p5, k9.
Row 23: K9, sl 1, k1, psso, k1, k2 tog, k9, (p1, k2) 5 times, p1, k3, (yfwd, k2 tog, k1) twice, k1.
Row 24: K4, (yfwd, k2 tog, k1) twice, k25, p3, k9.
Row 25: K9, sl 1, k2 tog, psso, k28, (yfwd, k2 tog, k1) twice, k1.
Row 26: K4, (yfwd, k2 tog, k1) twice, (yrn twice, k2 tog) 3 times, (yrn twice, sl 1, k2 tog, psso) 4 times, k17.
Row 27: K19, (p1, k2) 6 times, p1, k3, (yfwd, k2 tog, k1) twice, k1.
Row 28: K4, (yfwd, k2 tog, k1) twice, k38.
Row 29: Cast off 18 sts, k to last 7 sts, (yfwd, k2 tog, k1) twice, k1.
Repeat rows 2-29 until desired length. Cast off.

Pattern 79

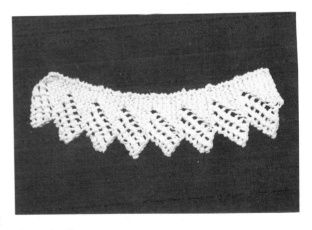

Cast on 9 sts.
Row 1: K4, (yfwd, k2 tog) twice, yfwd, k1.
Row 2 and every alternate row: K.
Row 3: Sl 1, k4, *(yfwd, k2 tog) twice, yfwd, k1.*
Row 5: Sl 1, k5, repeat *—* row 3.
Row 7: Sl 1, k6, repeat *—* row 3.
Row 9: Sl 1, k7, repeat *—* row 3.
Row 11: Sl 1, k8, repeat *—* row 3.
Row 12: Cast off 6 sts, k to end. [9 sts on needle.]
Repeat rows 1-12 until desired length. Cast off.

Pattern 80

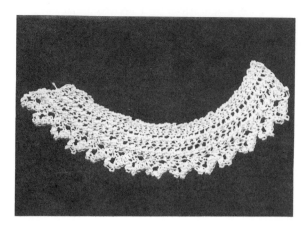

Cast on 11 sts.
Row 1: K.
Row 2: K3, k2 tog, yfwd, k1, k2 tog, yfwd, k3.
Row 3: K9, (yfwd, yrn, k1) twice. [15 sts on needle.]
Row 4: (K2, k1 tbl) twice, (k1, k2 tog, yfwd) twice, k3.
Row 5: K15.
Row 6: Cast off 4 sts, k2, k2 tog, yfwd, k1, k2 tog, yfwd, k3. [11 sts on needle.]
Repeat rows 1–6 until desired length. Cast off.

Pattern 81

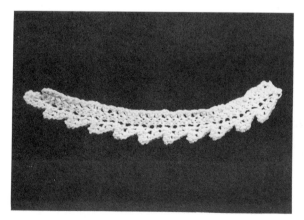

Cast on 6 sts.
Row 1: Yfwd, k2 tog, k2, yfwd, k2. [7 sts on needle.]
Row 2: K5, yfwd, k2 tog.
Row 3: Yfwd, k2 tog, k2, yfwd, k1, yfwd, k2.

Row 4: K7, yfwd, k2 tog.
Row 5: Yfwd, k2 tog, k2, (yfwd, k1) 3 times, yfwd, k2. (13 sts on needle.)
Row 6: Cast off 7 sts, k4, yfwd, k2 tog. [6 sts on needle.]
Repeat rows 1–6 until desired length. Cast off.

Pattern 82

Cast on 7 sts.
Row 1: K3, yfwd, k2 tog, yfwd twice, k2.
Row 2: K3, p1, k2, yfwd, k2 tog, k1.
Row 3: K3, yfwd, k2 tog, k4.
Row 4: Cast off 2 sts, k3, yfwd, k2 tog, k1.
Repeat rows 1–4 until desired length. Cast off.

Pattern 83

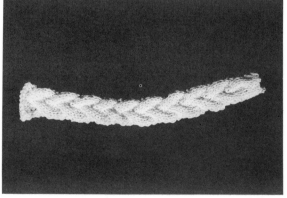

Cast on 11 sts.
Row 1: P1, sl next 3 sts onto dpn, leave at f of work, k3, k3 from dpn, k3, p1.
Row 2 and every alternate row: K1, p to last st, k1.
Row 3: P1, k to last st, p1.
Row 5: P1, k3, sl next 3 sts onto dpn, leave at b of work, k3, k3 from dpn, p1.
Row 7: Repeat row 3.
Row 8: Repeat row 2.
Repeat rows 1–8 until desired length. Cast off.

*Pattern 85

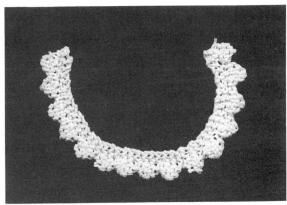

*Pattern 84

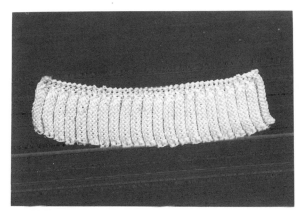

Cast on 6 sts.
Rows 1–3: K.
Row 4: Sl 1, k3, pass 1st, 2nd & 3rd of these sts over the 4th st, k2.
Row 5: K.
Row 6: Cast on 3 sts, k to end.
Repeat rows 1–6 until desired length. Cast off.

Pattern 86

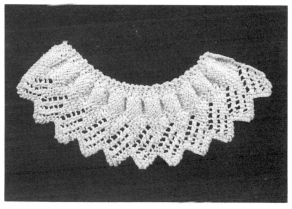

Cast on 15 sts
Row 1: K.
Row 2: P12, turn, k12.
Row 3: P12, k3.
Row 4: K3, p12.
Row 5: K12, turn, p12.
Row 6: K.
Repeat rows 1–6 until desired length. Cast off.
To prevent holes when turning, sl 1, yarn under, pass sl st back. Sl 1st st of each row.

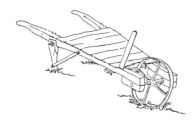

Cast on 16 sts.
Row 1: K10, (yfwd, k2 tog) twice, yfwd, k2.
Row 2: K9, p5, turn.
Row 3: K8, (yfwd, k2 tog) twice, yfwd, k2.
Row 4: K10, p5, k3.
Row 5: K12, (yfwd, k2 tog) twice, yfwd, k2.
Row 6: K11, p5, turn.
Row 7: P5, k5, (yfwd, k2 tog) twice, yfwd, k2.
Row 8: K20.

Row 9: K3, p5, k6, (yfwd, k2 tog) twice, yfwd, k2.
Row 10: K18, turn.
Row 11: P5, k13.
Row 12: Cast off 5 sts, k to end.
Repeat rows 1–12 until desired length. Cast off.

Pattern 87

Cast on 15 sts.
Row 1: Sl 1, k4, (yfwd, k2 tog) 4 times, yfwd, k2.
Row 2: K.
Row 3: Sl 1, k5, (yfwd, k2 tog) 4 times, yfwd, k2.
Row 4: K.
Row 5: Sl 1, k6, (yfwd, k2 tog) 4 times, yfwd, k2.
Row 6: K.
Row 7: Sl 1, k7, (yfwd, k2 tog) 4 times, yfwd, k2.
Row 8: K.
Row 9: Sl 1, k5, k2 tog, (yfwd, k2 tog) 5 times, k1.
Row 10: K.
Row 11: Sl 1, k4, k2 tog, (yfwd, k2 tog) 5 times, k1.
Row 12: K.
Row 13: Sl 1, k3, k2 tog, (yfwd, k2 tog) 5 times, k1.
Row 14: K.
Row 15: Sl 1, k2, k2 tog, (yfwd, k2 tog) 5 times, k1.
Row 16: K.
Repeat rows 1–16 until desired length. Cast off.

Pattern 88

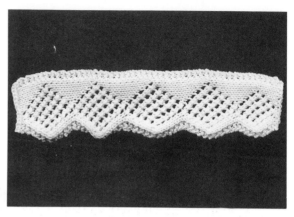

Cast on 13 sts.
Row 1 & all alternate rows: K2, p to last 2 sts, k2.
Row 2: K7, yon, sl 1, k1, psso, yon, k4.
Row 4: K6, (yon, sl 1, k1, psso) twice, yon, k4.
Row 6: K5, (yon, sl 1, k1, psso) 3 times, yon, k4.
Row 8: K4, (yon, sl 1, k1, psso) 4 times, yon, k4.
Row 10: K3, (yon, sl 1, k1, psso) 5 times, yon, k4.
Row 12: K4, (yon, sl 1, k1, psso) 5 times, k2 tog, k2.
Row 14: K5, (yon, sl 1, k1, psso) 4 times, k2 tog, k2.
Row 16: K6, (yon, sl 1, k1, psso) 3 times, k2 tog, k2.
Row 18: K7, (yon, sl 1, k1, psso) twice, k2 tog, k2.
Row 20: K8, yon, sl 1, k1, psso, k2 tog, k2.
Repeat rows 1–20 until desired length. Cast off.

Pattern 89

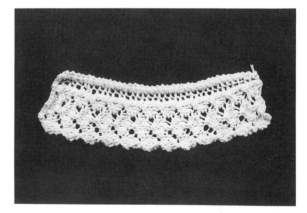

Cast on 13 sts.
Row 1: P.

Row 2: Sl 1, k2, (yon, sl 1, k1, psso, k1) twice, k2 tog, yon, k2.

Row 3: Sl 1 k-wise, p2, yon, sl 1 p-wise, p2 tog, psso, yon, p4, yon, p2 tog, k1.

Row 4: Sl 1 k-wise, k2, yon, sl 1, k1, psso, k3, yon, k1, yon, k4.

Row 5: Sl 1 k-wise, (p3, yon) twice, p2 tog, p3, yon, p2 tog, k1.

Row 6: Sl 1 k-wise, k2, yon, sl 1, k1, psso, k2 tog, yon, k5, yon, k4.

Row 7: (P2 tog) twice, then pass 1st st on R.H. needle over 2nd, yon, p2 tog, p3, p2 tog tbl, yon, p2 tog, p1, yon, p2 tog, k1. [13 sts on needle.]
Repeat rows 2–7 until desired length. Cast off.

Row 15: Yfwd, (k2 tog) twice, (yfwd, k2 tog) twice, k4, (yfwd, k2 tog) 3 times, k1.

Row 17: Yfwd, (k2 tog) twice, yfwd, k2 tog, k5, (yfwd, k2 tog) 3 times, k1.

Row 19: Yfwd, (k2 tog) twice, k6, (yfwd, k2 tog) 3 times, k1.
Repeat rows 1–20 until desired length. Cast off.

Pattern 91

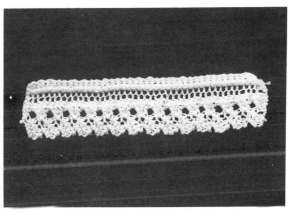

Cast on 11 sts.

Row 1: K4, yrn, p2 tog, k4, yfwd, (k1, p1) into last st.

Row 2: K3, yrn, p2 tog, k4, yrn, p2 tog, k1, sl 1.

Row 3: K4, yrn, p2 tog, k1, p2 tog, yon, k4.

Row 4: K5, yrn, p2 tog, k2, yrn, p2 tog, k1, sl 1.

Row 5: K4, yrn, p2 tog, k2, yrn, p2 tog, k3.

Row 6: Cast off 3 sts, yfwd, k5, yrn, p2 tog, k1, sl 1.
Repeat rows 1–6 until desired length. Cast off.

Pattern 90

Cast on 16 sts.

Row 1: Yfwd, k2 tog, k1, yfwd, k6, (yfwd, k2 tog) 3 times, k1.

Row 2 & alternate rows: Sl 1, k1, (yfwd, k2 tog) 3 times, k to end.

Row 3: Yfwd, k2 tog, k1, yfwd, k2 tog, yfwd, k5, (yfwd, k2 tog) 3 times, k1.

Row 5: Yfwd, k2 tog, k1, (yfwd, k2 tog) twice, yfwd, k4, (yfwd, k2 tog) 3 times, k1.

Row 7: Yfwd, k2 tog, k1, (yfwd, k2 tog) 3 times, yfwd, k3, (yfwd, k2 tog) 3 times, k1.

Row 9: Yfwd, k2 tog, k1, (yfwd, k2 tog) 4 times, yfwd, k2, (yfwd, k2 tog) 3 times, k1.

Row 11: Yfwd, (k2 tog) twice, (yfwd, k2 tog) 4 times, k2, (yfwd, k2 tog) 3 times, k1.

Row 13: Yfwd, (k2 tog) twice, (yfwd, k2 tog) 3 times, k3, (yfwd, k2 tog) 3 times, k1.

Pattern 92

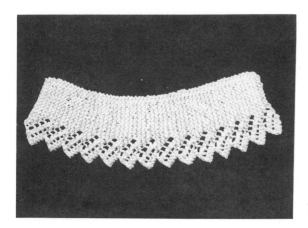

Cast on 15 sts.
Row 1: K11, yfwd, k2 tog, yfwd, k2.
Row 2 & all alternate rows: K.
Row 3: K12, yfwd, k2 tog, yfwd, k2.
Row 5: K13, yfwd, k2 tog, yfwd, k2.
Row 7: K14, yfwd, k2 tog, yfwd, k2.
Row 8: Cast off 4 sts, k to end.
Repeat rows 1–8 until desired length. Cast off.

*Pattern 93

Cast on 5 sts.
Row 1: K.
Row 2: K2, yfwd, k3.
Row 3: K4, yfwd, k2.
Row 4: K3, yfwd, k4.
Row 5: K5, yfwd, k3.

Row 6: Cast off 4 sts, k5.
Repeat rows 1–6 until desired length. Cast off.

Pattern 94

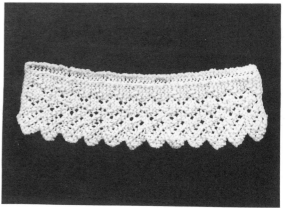

Cast on 17 sts.
Row 1: K.
Row 2: Sl 1, k1, yfwd, k2 tog, k3, k2 tog, yfwd, k1, yfwd, k2 tog, k1, yfwd, k2 tog, yfwd, k2.
Row 3: K15, yfwd, k2 tog, k1.
Row 4: Sl 1, k1, yfwd, k2 tog, k2, k2 tog, yfwd, k3, yfwd, k2 tog, k1, yfwd, k2 tog, yfwd, k2.
Row 5: K16, yfwd, k2 tog, k1.
Row 6: Sl 1, k1, yfwd, k2 tog, k1, k2 tog, yfwd, k5, yfwd, k2 tog, k1, yfwd, k2 tog, yfwd, k2.
Row 7: K17, yfwd, k2 tog, k1.
Row 8: Sl 1, k1, yfwd, k2 tog, k3, yfwd, k2 tog, k1, k2 tog, yfwd, k4, yfwd, k2 tog, yfwd, k2.
Row 9: K18, yfwd, k2 tog, k1.
Row 10: Sl 1, k1, yfwd, k2 tog, k4, yfwd, sl 1, k2 tog, psso, yfwd, k6, yfwd.
Row 11: Cast off 5 sts, k14, yfwd, k2 tog, k1, k2 tog, yfwd, k2.
Repeat rows 2–11 until desired length. Cast off.

Pattern 95

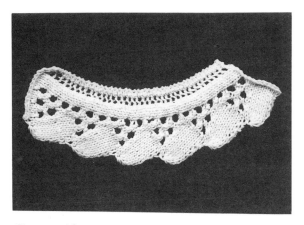

Cast on 16 sts.

Row 1: P.

Row 2: Sl 1, k2, yon, k2 tog, k2, (yon) twice, k2 tog, k7.

Row 3: Sl 1, p8, k1, p3, k1, yon, k2 tog, k1.

Row 4: Sl 1, k2, yon, k2 tog, k12.

Row 5: Sl 1, p12, k1, yon, k2 tog, k1.

Row 6: Sl 1, k2, yon, k2 tog, k2 ([yon] twice, k2 tog) twice, k6.

Row 7: Sl 1, p7, k1, p2, k1, p3, k1, yon, k2 tog, k1.

Row 8: Sl 1, k2, yon, k2 tog, k14.

Row 9: Sl 1, p14, k1, yon, k2 tog, k1.

Row 10: Sl 1, k2, yon, k2 tog, k2 ([yon] twice, k2 tog) 3 times, k6.

Row 11: Sl 1, p7, (k1, p2) twice, k1, p3, k1, yon, k2 tog, k1.

Row 12: Sl 1, k2, yon, k2 tog, k17.

Row 13: P6 tog, p1, pass the p6 tog st over the last st made, p11, k1, yon, k2 tog, k1.

Repeat rows 2–13 until desired length. Cast off.

Pattern 96

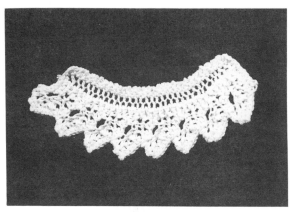

Cast on 11 sts.

Row 1: K.

Row 2: K3, yon, k2 tog, k1, sl 1, k1, psso, cast on 4 sts, k2 tog, k1.

Row 3: K10, yon, k2 tog, k1.

Row 4: K3, yon, k2 tog, sl 1, k1, psso, (yon, k1) 4 times, yon, k2 tog.

Row 5: K13, yon, k2 tog, k1.

Row 6: K3, yon, k2 tog, sl 1, k1, psso, (yon, k1) twice, yon, sl 1, k2 tog, psso, (yon, k1) twice, yon, k2 tog.

Row 7: K15, yon, k2 tog, k1.

Row 8: K3, yon, k2 tog, k11, k2 tog.

Row 9: Cast off 6 sts, k7, yon, k2 tog, k1.

Repeat rows 2–9 until desired length. Cast off.

Pattern 97

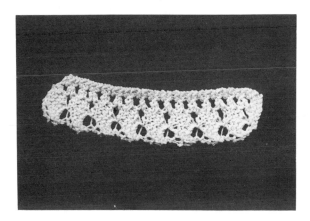

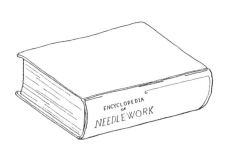

Cast on 8 sts.
Row 1: K.
Row 2: K2, (yon) twice, k2 tog, k3, yon, k1.
Row 3: K7, p1, k2.
Row 4: K9, yon, k1.
Row 5: K.
Row 6: K2, ([yon] twice, k2 tog) twice, k4, yon, k1.
Row 7: K8, (p1, k2) twice.
Row 8: K9, pass 8th st over 9th st, then cast off remaining 5 sts. [8 sts on needle, i.e. 7 sts separated from the last cast off st by a space. On the following row 1 this last st is drawn up to the others.]
Repeat rows 1–8 until desired length. Cast off.

Pattern 99

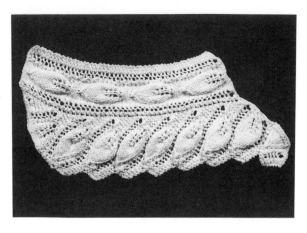

Pattern 98

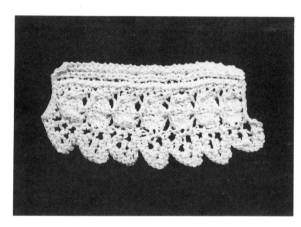

Cast on 14 sts.
Row 1: P.
Row 2: *Sl 1, k2 tog, yon, k1, yon, sl 1, k1, psso, k1*, yon, k1, yon, (k1, yon, k1) in the next st, (yon, k1) twice, (yon) twice, k2 tog, k1.
Row 3: K3, p1, k1, p9, k1, k5, k1.
Row 4: Repeat *—* row 2, (yon, k3) 3 times, yon, (k1, m2) twice, k2 tog, k1.
Row 5: K3, p1, k2, p1, k1, p5, p3 tog, (p5, k1) twice.
Row 6: Repeat *—* row 2, (yon, sl 1, k1, psso, k1, k2 tog, yon, k1) twice, ([yon] twice, k2 tog) 3 times, k1.
Row 7: K3, p1, (k2, p1) twice, k1, p2 tog, p1, p2 tog tbl, p1, p2 tog, p1, p2 tog tbl, k1, p5, k1.
Row 8: Repeat *—* row 2, yon, k3 tog tbl, k1, k3 tog, yon, k11.
Row 9: Cast off 7 sts, k4, p3 tog, k2, p5, k1.
Repeat rows 2–9 until desired length. Cast off.

Cast on 45 sts.
Row 1: K.
Row 2: Sl 1, k3, yon, k2 tog, p8, k1, yon, k2 tog, yon, k3, yon, k2 tog, p1, yon, p1, k2, yon, k2 tog, p1, k1, sl 1, psso, k5, k2 tog, p1, k2, yon, k2 tog, k2.
Row 3: Sl 1, k3, yon, k2 tog, k1, p7, k3, yon, k2 tog, k1, p1, k3, yon, k2 tog, k4, yon, k2 tog, k9, yon, k2 tog, k2.
Row 4: Sl 1, k3, yon, k2 tog, p3, yon, k1, yon, p4, k1, yon, k2 tog, yon, k4, yon, k2 tog, p1, yon, k1, yon, p1, k2, yon, k2 tog, p1, k7, p1, k2, yon, k2 tog, k2.
Row 5: Sl 1, k3, yon, k2 tog, k1, p7, k3, yon, k2 tog, k1, p3, k3, yon, k2 tog, k5, yon, k2 tog, k3, p3, k5, yon, k2 tog, k2.
Row 6: Sl 1, k3, yon, k2 tog, p3, (k1, yon) twice, k1, p4, k1, yon, k2 tog, yon, k5, yon, k2 tog, p1, (k1, yon) twice, k1, p1, k2, yon, k2 tog, p1, k1, sl 1, psso, k3, k2 tog, p1, k2, yon, k2 tog, k2.
Row 7: Sl 1, k3, yon, k2 tog, (k1, p5, k3, yon, k2 tog) twice, k6, yon, k2 tog, k3, p5, k5, yon, k2 tog, k2.
Row 8: Sl 1, k3, yon, k2 tog, p3, k2, yon, k1, yon, k2, p4, k1, yon, k2 tog, yon, k6, yon, k2 tog, p1, k2, yon, k1, yon, k2, p1, k2, yon, k2 tog, p1, sl 1, k1, psso, k1, k2 tog, p1, k2, yon, k2 tog, k2.
Row 9: Sl 1, k3, yon, k2 tog, k1, p3, k3, yon, k2 tog, k1, p7, k3, yon, k2 tog, k7, yon, k2 tog, k3, p7, k5, yon, k2 tog, k2.
Row 10: Sl 1, k3, yon, k2 tog, p3, k3, yon, k1, yon, k3, p4, k1, yon, k2 tog, yon, k7, yon, k2 tog, p1, k3, yon, k1, yon, k3, p1, k2, yon, k2 tog, p1, sl 1, k2 tog, psso, p1, k2, yon, k2 tog, k2.
Row 11: Sl 1, k3, yon, k2 tog, k1, p1, k3, yon, k2 tog, k1, p9, k3, yon, k2 tog, k8, yon, k2 tog, k3, p9, k5, yon, k2 tog, k2.

Row 12: Sl 1, k3, yon, k2 tog, p3, k9, p4, k1, yon, k2 tog, yon, k2, yon, k2 tog, p2, k2, yon, k2 tog, p1, k9, p1, k2, yon, k2 tog, p1, k8.

Row 13: Sl 1, cast off 3 sts, k4, pass 4 sts over the last st worked, k3, yon, k2 tog, k1, p9, k3, yon, k2 tog, k4 (yon, k2 tog, k3) twice, p9, k5, yon, k2 tog, k2.

Row 14: Sl 1, k3, yon, k2 tog, p3, sl 1, k1, psso, k5, k2 tog, p4, k1, yon, k2 tog, yon, k3, yon, k2 tog, p1, yon, p1, k2, yon, k2 tog, p1, sl 1, k1, psso, k5, k2 tog, p1, k2, yon, k2 tog, k2.

Row 15: Sl 1, k3, yon, k2 tog, k1, p7, k3, yon, k2 tog, k1, p1, k3, yon, k2 tog, k4, yon, k2 tog, k3, p7, k5, yon, k2 tog, k2.

Row 16: Sl 1, k3, yon, k2 tog, p3, k7, p4, k1, yon, k2 tog, yon, k4, yon, k2 tog, p1, yon, k1, yon, p1, k2, yon, k2 tog, p1, k7, p1, k2, yon, k2 tog, k2.

Row 17: Sl 1, k3, yon, k2 tog, k1, p7, k3, yon, k2 tog, k1, p3, k3, yon, k2 tog, k5, yon, k2 tog, k3, p7, k5, yon, k2 tog, k2.

Row 18: Sl 1, k3, yon, k2 tog, p3, sl 1, k1, psso, k3, k2 tog, p4, k1, yon, k2 tog, yon, k5, yon, k2 tog, p1, (k1, yon) twice, k1, p1, k2, yon, k2 tog, p1, sl 1, k1, psso, k3, k2 tog, p1, k2, yon, k2 tog, k2.

Row 19: Sl 1, k3, yon, k2 tog, (k1, p5, k3, yon, k2 tog) twice, k6, yon, k2 tog, k3, p5, k5, yon, k2 tog, k2.

Row 20: Sl 1, k3, yon, k2 tog, p3, sl 1, k1, psso, k1, k2 tog, p4, k1, yon, k2 tog, yon, k6, yon, k2 tog, p1, k2, yon, k1, yon, k2, p1, k2, yon, k2 tog, p1, sl 1, k1, psso, k1, k2 tog, p1, k2, yon, k2 tog, k2.

Row 21: Sl 1, k3, yon, k2 tog, k1, p3, k3, yon, k2 tog, k1, p7, k3, yon, k2 tog, k7, yon, k2 tog, k3, p3, k5, yon, k2 tog, k2.

Row 22: Sl 1, k3, yon, k2 tog, p3, sl 1, k2 tog, psso, p4, k1, yon, k2 tog, yon, k7, yon, k2 tog, p1, k3, yon, k1, yon, k3, p1, k2, yon, k2 tog, p1, sl 1, k2 tog, psso, p1, k2, yon, k2 tog, k2.

Row 23: Sl 1, k3, yon, k2 tog, k1, p1, k3, yon, k2 tog, k1, p9, k3, yon, k2 tog, k8, yon, k2 tog, k3, p1, k5, yon, k2 tog, k2.

Row 24: Sl 1, k3, yon, k2 tog, p8, k1, yon, k2 tog, yon, k2, yon, k2 tog, p2, k2, yon, k2 tog, p1, k9, p1, k2, yon, k2 tog, p1, k8.

Row 25: Sl 1, cast off 3 sts, k4, pass 4 sts over last worked st, k3, yon, k2 tog, k1, p9, k3, yon, k2 tog, k4, yon, k2 tog, k3, yon, k2 tog, k9, yon, k2 tog, k2.

Repeat rows 2–25 until desired length. Cast off.

Pattern 100

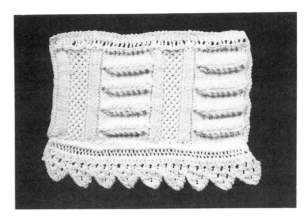

Insertion

Cast on 32 sts.

Row 1: K3, m1, k2 tog, k27.

Row 2: P29, yon, k2 tog, k1.

Row 3: K3, m1, k2 tog, p4, *yon, k1 (yon) twice, p5*, repeat *—* to last 4 sts , p4.

Row 4: K4, *p3, k5*, repeat *—* 3 times, p1, m1, k2 tog, k1.

Row 5: K3, m1, k2 tog, p4, *m1, k3, m1, p5*, repeat *—* 3 times, p4.

Row 6: K4, *p5, k5*, repeat *—* 3 times, p1, m1, k2 tog, k1.

Row 7: K3, m1, k2 tog, p4, *m1, k1, sl 1, k2 tog, psso, k1, m1, p5*, repeat *—* 3 times, p4.

Row 8: K4, *p5, k5*, repeat *—* 3 times, p1, m1, k2 tog, k1.

Rows 9–18: Repeat rows 7–8 five times.

Row 19: K3, m1, k2 tog, p4, *k1, sl 1, k2 tog, psso, k1, p5*, repeat *—* 3 times, p4.

Row 20: K4, *p3, k5*, repeat *—* 3 times, p1, m1, k2 tog, k1.

Row 21: K3, m1, k2 tog, p4, *sl 1, k2 tog, psso, p5*, repeat *—* 3 times, p4.

Row 22: K4, *p1, k5*, repeat *—* 3 times, p1, m1, k2 tog, k1.

Row 23: K3, m1, k2 tog, k27.

Row 24: P29, m1, k2 tog, k1.

Row 25: K3, m1, k2 tog, p27.

Row 26: K28, p1, m1, k2 tog, k1.

Row 27: Repeat row 25.

Row 28: Repeat row 26.

Row 29: Repeat row 23.

Row 30: Repeat row 24.

Row 31: K3, m1, k2 tog, p1, *sl 1 p-wise, p1*, repeat *—* to end.

Row 32: P29, m1, k2 tog, k1.

Row 33: K3, m1, k2 tog, sl 1 p-wise, *p1, sl 1 p-wise*, repeat *—* to end.

Row 34: P29, m1, k2 tog, k1.

Rows 35–42: Repeat rows 31–34 twice.

Row 43: K3, m1, k2 tog, p27.

Row 44: K28, p1, m1, k2 tog, k1.

Row 45: Repeat row 43.

Row 46: Repeat row 44.

Row 47: K3, m1, k2 tog, k27.

Row 48: P29, m1, k2 tog, k1.

Repeat rows 3–48 until desired length. Cast off.

Edging for above insertion

Cast on 9 sts.

Row 1: K.

Row 2: Sl 1, k2, m1, k2 tog, k1, m2, k2 tog, k1.

Row 3: K3, p1, k3, m1, k2 tog, k1.

Row 4: Sl 1, k2, m1, k2 tog, k5.

Row 5: K7, m1, k2 tog, k1.

Row 6: Sl 1, k2, m1, k2 tog, k1, m2, k2 tog, m2, k2.

Row 7: K3, p1, k2, p1, k3, m1, k2 tog, k1.

Row 8: Sl 1, k2, m1, k2 tog, k8.

Row 9: K10, m1, k2 tog, k1.

Row 10: Sl 1, k2, m1, k2 tog, k1, m2, k2 tog, m2, k2 tog, m2, k2 tog, k1.

Row 11: K3, p1, k2, p1, k2, p1, k3, m1, k2 tog, k1.

Row 12: Sl 1, k2, m1, k2 tog, k11.

Row 13: Cast off 7 sts, k5, m1, k2 tog, k1.

Repeat rows 2–13 until desired length. Cast off.

Pattern 101

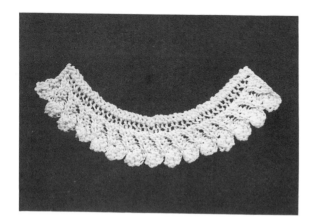

Cast on 13 sts.

Row 1: K.

Row 2: K2, m1, p1, m1, p2 tog, k5, m1, k2 tog, k1.

Row 3: K3, m1, k2 tog, k2, k2 tog, m1, k3, m1, k2.

Row 4: K2, m1, p1, k3, p1, m1, p2 tog, k3, m1, k2 tog, k1.

Row 5: K3, m1, (k2 tog) twice, m1, k7, m1, k2.

Row 6: K2, m1, p1, k7, p1, m1, p2 tog, k1, m1, k2 tog, k1.

Row 7: K3, m1, k2 tog, k4, (with R.H. needle lift the 2nd st on L.H. needle over the first st and off the needle) 8 times, k1, turn, cast on 3 sts.

Repeat rows 2–7 until desired length. Cast off.

Pattern 102

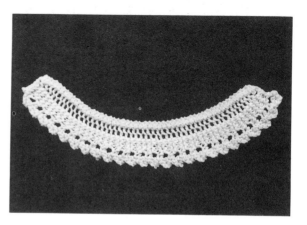

Cast on 9 sts.

Row 1: Sl 1, k2, m1, k2 tog, k2, m2, k2.

Row 2: Sl 1, k2, p1, k4, m1, k2 tog, k1.

Row 3: Sl 1, k2, m1, k2 tog, k6.

Row 4: Cast off 2 sts, k5, m1, k2 tog, k1.

Repeat rows 1–4 until desired length. Cast off.

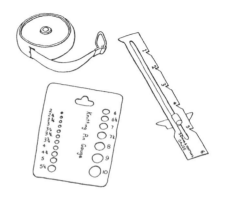

Pattern 103

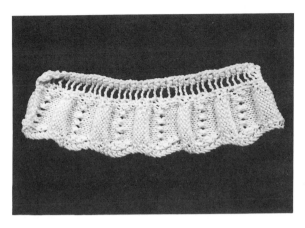

Pattern 104

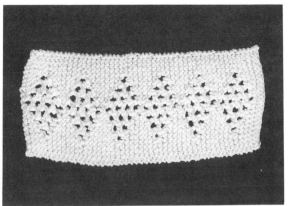

Cast on 16 sts.

Row 1: P.

Row 2: K1, sl 1, k1, psso, m2, k2 tog, p8, inc 1 in next st, k2.

Row 3: K14, p1, k2.

Row 4: K1, sl 1, k1, psso, m2, k2 tog, p9, inc 1 in next st, k2.

Row 5: K12, turn, p9, inc 1 in next st, k2.

Row 6: K16, p1, k2.

Row 7: K1, sl 1, k1, psso, m2, k2 tog, p1, (m1, p2 tog) 5 times, p1, k2.

Row 8: K13, turn, p9, p2 tog, k2.

Row 9: K15, p1, k2.

Row 10: K1, sl 1, k1, psso, m2, k2 tog, p9, p2 tog, k2.

Row 11: K14, p1, k2.

Row 12: K1, sl 1, k1, psso, m2, k2 tog, p8, p2 tog, k2.

Row 13: K13, p1, k2.

Row 14: K1, sl 1, k1, psso, m2, k2 tog, k11.

Row 15: K2, p8, turn, k10.

Row 16: K2, p8, turn, k10.

Row 17: K2, p9, k2, p1, k2.

Repeat rows 2–17 until desired length. Cast off.

Cast on 24 sts.

Row 1: K.

Row 2: Sl 1, k9, k2 tog, m2, k2 tog, k10.

Row 3: Sl 1, k11, p1, k11.

Row 4: Sl 1, k7, k2 tog, m2, (k2 tog) twice, m2, k2 tog, k8.

Row 5: Sl 1, k9, p1, k3, p1, k9.

Row 6: Sl 1, k5, k2 tog, m2, (k2 tog) twice, m2, (k2 tog) twice, m2, k2 tog, k6.

Row 7: Sl 1, k7, p1, k3, p1, k3, p1, k7.

Row 8: Sl 1, k3, k2 tog, m2, (k2 tog) twice, m2, (k2 tog) twice, m2, (k2 tog) twice, m2, k2 tog, k4.

Row 9: Sl 1, k5, p1, k3, p1, k3, p1, k3, p1, k5.

Row 10: Sl 1, k5, k2 tog, m2, (k2 tog) twice, m2, (k2 tog) twice, m2, k2 tog, k6.

Row 11: Sl 1, k7, p1, k3, p1, k3, p1, k7.

Row 12: Sl 1, k7, k2 tog, m2, (k2 tog) twice, m2, k2 tog, k8.

Row 13: Sl 1, k9, p1, k3, p1, k9.

Row 14: Sl 1, k9, k2 tog, m2, k2 tog, k10.

Row 15: Sl 1, k11, p1, k11.

Row 16: Sl 1, k to end.

Row 17: Sl 1, k to end.

Repeat rows 2–17 until desired length. Cast off.

Pattern 105

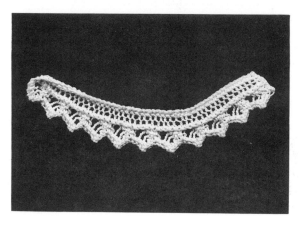

Cast on 8 sts.
Row 1: Sl 1, k2, m1, p2 tog, m2, p2 tog, k1 tbl.
Row 2: Sl 1, k2, p1, k2, m1, p2 tog, k1 tbl.
Row 3: Sl 1, k2, m1, p2 tog, k1, m2, p2 tog, k1 tbl.
Row 4: Sl 1, k2, p1, k3, m1, p2 tog, k1 tbl.
Row 5: Sl 1, k2, m1, p2 tog, k2, m2, p2 tog, k1 tbl.
Row 6: Sl 1, k2, p1, k4, m1, p2 tog, k1 tbl.
Row 7: Sl 1, k2, m1, p2 tog, k5, k1 tbl.
Row 8: Cast off 3 sts, k4, m1, p2 tog, k1 tbl.
Repeat rows 1–8 until desired length. Cast off.

Pattern 106

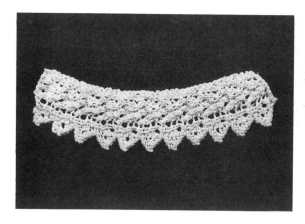

Cast on 12 sts.
Row 1: K2, p2, k1, p5, m1, k2.
Row 2: K3, p1, k1, m1, k3 tog, m1, k2 tog, m1, k
to end.

Row 3: K2, p8, k4.
Row 4: K5, m1, k6, m1, k2 tog, k to end.
Row 5: K2, p9, m1, k2 tog, m1, k2.
Row 6: K3, p1, k1, (k1, p1) into next st, k1, m1, k1,
k2 tog, p1, k2 tog, k1, m1, k2 tog, k to end.
Row 7: K2, p3, k1, p4, k7.
Row 8: Cast off 5 sts, k2, m1, k1, m1, k2 tog, p1, k2
tog, m1, k2 tog, k to end.
Repeat rows 1–8 until desired length. Cast off.

Pattern 107

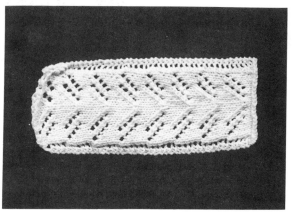

Cast on 22 sts.
Row 1: Sl 1, k1, m1, k2 tog, m1, sl 1, k1, psso, m1,
sl 1, k1, psso, k6, k2 tog, m1, k2 tog, m1, k2 tog,
m1, k2.
Row 2: Sl 1, k1, p18, k2.
Row 3: Sl 1, k1, m1, k2 tog, k1, m1, sl 1, k1, psso,
m1, sl 1, k1, psso, k4, k2 tog, m1, k2 tog, m1, k1,
k2 tog, m1, k2.
Row 4: Repeat row 2.
Row 5: Sl 1, k1, m1, k2 tog, k2, m1, sl 1, k1, psso,
m1, sl 1, k1, psso, k2, k2 tog, m1, k2 tog, m1, k2,
k2 tog, m1, k2.
Row 6: Repeat row 2.
Row 7: Sl 1, k1, m1, k2 tog, k3, m1, sl 1, k1, psso,
m1, sl 1, k1, psso, k2 tog, m1, k2 tog, m1, k3, k2 tog,
m1, k2.
Row 8: Repeat row 2.
Row 9: Sl 1, k1, m1, k2 tog, k14, k2 tog, m1, k2.
Row 10: Repeat row 2.
Repeat rows 1–10 until desired length. Cast off.

Victorian lace-trimmed garments.

Traycloth and napkin—knitted edgings.

Runner—antique knitted lace.

Antique lace.

Chest of drawers cover.

Pattern 108

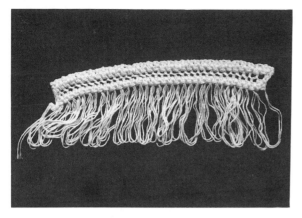

For a fairly thick fringe suitable for trimming lamp shades, curtains etc., use 4 thicknesses of cotton from 4 separate balls.

Cast on 9 sts.

(M1 by passing all 4 strands of cotton round the needle, k2 tog, k1) 3 times. Repeat until required length. Cast off 6 sts and fasten these off. Slip remaining 2 sts off needle and unravel back to beg of work.

Pattern 109

Cast on 9 sts.

Row 1: Sl 2, k2, m1, k2 tog tbl, m3, k2 tog tbl, k1.
Row 2: M1, k2 tog tbl, k1, p1, k3, m1, k2 tog tbl, p2.
Row 3: Sl 2, k2, m1, k2 tog tbl, k5.
Row 4: M1, k2 tog tbl, k5, m1, k2 tog tbl, p2.
Row 5: Sl 2, k2, m1, k2 tog tbl, k5.

Row 6: M1, k2 tog tbl, k5, m1, k2 tog tbl, p2.
Row 7: Sl 2, k2, m1, k2 tog tbl, k2, m3, k2 tog tbl, k1.
Row 8: M1, k2 tog tbl, k1, p1, k5, m1, k2 tog tbl, p2.
Row 9: Sl 2, k2, m1, k2 tog tbl, p2, k5.
Row 10: K9, m1, k2 tog tbl, p2.
Row 11: Sl 2, k2, m1, k2 tog tbl, m3, k2 tog tbl.
The 5 sts remaining are to be cast off as follows: Sl 3, pass 5th st [last st on L.H. needle] over 4th st, pass 3rd st back onto L.H. needle and sl 4th st over it, pass 2nd st back onto L.H. needle and sl 3rd st over it, pass 1st st back onto L.H. needle and sl 2nd st over it. K to end.
Repeat rows 2–11 until desired length. Cast off.

Pattern 110

Cast on 7 sts.
Row 1: K.
Row 2: K1, (m1, k2 tog) twice, m1, k2.
Row 3: M1, k2 tog, k to end.
Row 4: K2, (m1, k2 tog) twice, m1, k2.
Row 5: M1, k2 tog, k to end.
Row 6: K3, (m1, k2 tog) twice, m1, k2.
Row 7: M1, k2 tog, k to end.
Row 8: K4, (m1, k2 tog) twice, m1, k2 tog.
Row 9: M1, k2 tog, k to end.
Row 10: K3, (m1, k2 tog) twice, m1, k3 tog.
Row 11: M1, k2 tog, k to end.
Row 12: K2, (m1, k2 tog) twice, m1, k3 tog.
Row 13: M1, k2 tog, k to end.
Row 14: K1, (m1, k2 tog) twice, m1, k3 tog.
Row 15: M1, k to end.
Repeat rows 3–14 until desired length. Cast off.

Pattern 111

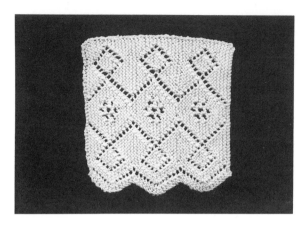

Cast on 41 sts.
Row 1: K.
Row 2: K16, k2 tog, m1, k7, m1, k2 tog, k11, m1, k3.
Row 3: K.
Row 4: K15, k2 tog, m1, k9, m1, k2 tog, k11, m1, k3.
Row 5: K.
Row 6: K7, m1, k2 tog, k5, k2 tog, m1, k11, m1, k2 tog, k5, k2 tog, m1, k4, m1, k3.
Row 7: K.
Row 8: K5, k2 tog, m1, k1, m1, k2 tog, k3, k2 tog, m1, k13, m1, k2 tog, k3, k2 tog, m1, k1, m1, k2 tog, k3, m1, k3.
Row 9: K.
Row 10: K4, k2 tog, m1, k3, m1, k2 tog, k1, k2 tog, m1, k5, k2 tog, m2, k2 tog, k6, m1, k2 tog, k1, k2 tog, m1, k3, m1, k2 tog, k3, m1, k3.
Row 11: K25, p1, k20.
Row 12: K3, k2 tog, m1, k5, m1, k3 tog, m1, k4, k2 tog, m2, (k2 tog) twice, m2, k2 tog, k5, m1, k3 tog, m1, k5, m1, k2 tog, k3, m1, k3.
Row 13: K24, p1, k3, p1, k18.
Row 14: K2, k2 tog, m1, k7, m1, k2 tog, k6, k2 tog, m2, k2 tog, k7, k2 tog, m1, k7, m1, k2 tog, k3, m1, k3.
Row 15: K27, p1, k20.
Row 16: K4, m1, k2 tog, k3, k2 tog, m1, k1, m1, k2 tog, k3, k2 tog, m2, (k2 tog) twice, m2, k2 tog, k4, k2 tog, m1, k1, m1, k2 tog, k3, k2 tog, m1, k3, k2 tog, m1, k2 tog, k2.
Row 17: K24, p1, k3, p1, k18.
Row 18: K5, m1, k2 tog, k1, k2 tog, m1, k3, m1, k2 tog, k4, k2 tog, m2, k2 tog, k5, k2 tog, m1, k3, m1, k2 tog, k1, k2 tog, m1, k3, k2 tog, m1, k2 tog, k2.
Row 19: K25, p1, k20.
Row 20: K6, m1, k3 tog, m1, k5, m1, k2 tog, k11, k2 tog, m1, k5, m1, k3 tog, m1, k3, k2 tog, m1, k2 tog, k2.
Row 21: K.
Row 22: K7, m1, k2 tog, k6, m1, k2 tog, k9, k2 tog, m1, k6, k2 tog, m1, k3, k2 tog, m1, k2 tog, k2.
Row 23: K.
Row 24: K16, m1, k2 tog, k7, k2 tog, m1, k11, k2 tog, m1, k2 tog, k2.
Row 25: K.
Row 26: K17, m1, k2 tog, k5, k2 tog, m1, k11, k2 tog, m1, k2 tog, k2.
Row 27: K.
Row 28: K18, m1, k2 tog, k3, k2 tog, m1, k11, k2 tog, m1, k2 tog, k2.
Row 29: K.
Repeat rows 2–29 until desired length. Cast off.

Pattern 112

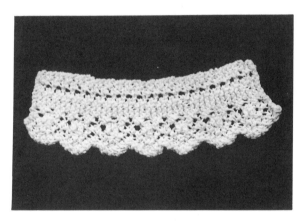

Cast on 14 sts.
Row 1: K.
Row 2: K3, m1, k2 tog, k4, m1, k2 tog, m1, k3.
Row 3: M1, k2 tog, k1, m1, k2 tog, m1, k4, k2 tog, m1, k4.
Row 4: K2, k2 tog, m1, k7, m1, k2 tog, m1, k3.
Row 5: M1, k2 tog, k1, m1, k2 tog, m1, k1, m1, k2 tog, k6, m1, k2 tog, k1.
Row 6: K3, m1, k2 tog, k3, k2 tog, m1, k3, m1, k2 tog, m1, k3.
Row 7: M1, k2 tog, k1, m1, k2 tog, m1, k5, m1, k2 tog, k1, k2 tog, m1, k4.
Row 8: K2, k2 tog, m1, k5, m1, k2 tog, k1, k2 tog, (m1, k2 tog) twice, k2.
Row 9: M1, (k2 tog) twice, m1, k2 tog, m1, sl 1, k2 tog, psso, m1, k7, m1, k2 tog, k1.
Row 10: K3, m1, k2 tog, k5, (k2 tog, m1) twice, k2 tog, k2.

Row 11: M1, (k2 tog) twice, (m1, k2 tog) twice, k3, k2 tog, m1, k4.

Row 12: K2, k2 tog, m1, k4, (k2 tog, m1) twice, k2 tog, k2.

Row 13: M1, (k2 tog) twice, (m1, k2 tog) twice, k4, m1, k2 tog, k1.

Repeat 2-13 until desired length. Cast off.

Pattern 113

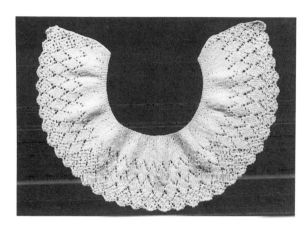

Cast on 40 sts.

Row 1: Sl 1, k6, (m1, k2 tog, k1, m1, k2 tog, k3, k2 tog, m1, k1, k2 tog, m1, k3) twice, m1, k1.

Row 2: K1, (m1, k5, m1, k2 tog, k1, m1, k2 tog, k1, k2 tog, m1, k1, k2 tog) twice, m1, k8.

Row 3: Sl 1, k8, (m1, k2 tog, k1, m1, k3 tog, m1, k1, k2 tog) twice, (m1, k1, m1, k2 tog, k1) twice, m1, k1.

Row 4: K1, (m1, k1, k2 tog, m1, k3, m1, k2 tog, k1, m1, k2 tog, k3, k2 tog) twice, m1, k6, turn leaving 4 sts on L.H. needle.

Row 5: Sl 1, k6, (m1, k2 tog, k1, k2 tog, m1, k1, k2 tog, m1, k5, m1, k2 tog, k1) twice, m1, k1.

Row 6: K1, (m1, k1, k2 tog, m1, k1, k2 tog, k1, m1, k2 tog, k1, m1, k2 tog, k1, m1, k3 tog) twice, m1, k6, turn leaving 6 sts on L.H. needle.

Row 7: Sl 1, k8, m1, k2 tog, k1, m1, k2 tog, k2, k2 tog, m1, k1, k2 tog, m1, k3, m1, k2 tog, k1, m1, k2 tog, k2, k2 tog, m1, k1, k2 tog, m1, k2 tog.

Row 8: K2 tog, m1, k2 tog, k1, m1, k2 tog, k2 tog, m1, k1, k2 tog, m1, k5, m1, k2 tog, k1, m1, k2 tog, m1, k1, k2 tog, m1, k8, turn leaving 8 sts on L.H. needle.

Row 9: Sl 1, k8, m1, k2 tog, k1, m1, k2 tog, (m1, k1, k2 tog) twice, m1, k1, m1, k2 tog, (k1, m1, k2 tog) twice, m1, k1, k2 tog, m1, k2 tog.

Row 10: K2 tog, m1, k2 tog, k3, k2 tog, m1, k1, k2 tog, m1, k3, m1, k2 tog, k1, m1, k2 tog, k3, k2 tog, m1, k8, turn leaving 10 sts on L.H. needle.

Row 11: Sl 1, k8, m1, k2 tog, k1, k2 tog, m1, k1, k2 tog, m1, k5, (m1, k2 tog, k1) twice, k2 tog, m1, k2 tog.

Row 12: K2 tog, m1, k3 tog, m1, k1, k2 tog, m1, k1, (k2 tog, k1, m1) 3 times, k3 tog, m1, k20.

Row 13: Sl 1, k17, k2 tog, m1, k3, m1, k2 tog, k1, m1, k2 tog, k2, k2 tog, m1, k1, k2 tog, m1, k3, m1, k1.

Row 14: K1, m1, k5, m1, k2 tog, k1, m1, (k2 tog) twice, m1, k1, k2 tog, m1, k5, m1, k2 tog, k17.

Row 15: Sl 1, k15, k2 tog, m1, k7, m1, k2 tog, k1, m1, k2 tog, (m1, k1, k2 tog) twice, m1, k1, m1, k2 tog, k1, m1, k1.

Row 16: K1, m1, k1, k2 tog, m1, k3, m1, k2 tog, k1, m1, k2 tog, k3, k2 tog, m1, k9, m1, k2 tog, k11, turn leaving 4 sts on L.H. needle.

Row 17: Sl 1, k9, k2 tog, m1, k11, m1, k2 tog, k1, k2 tog, m1, k1, k2 tog, m1, k5, m1, k2 tog, k1, m1, k1.

Row 18: K1, m1, k1, k2 tog, m1, k1, k2 tog, (k1, m1, k2 tog) twice, k1, m1, k3 tog, m1, k13, m1, k2 tog, k7, turn leaving 6 sts on L.H. needle.

Row 19: Sl 1, k8, m1, k2 tog, k9, k2 tog, m1, k3, m1, k2 tog, k1, m1, k2 tog, k2, k2 tog, m1, k1, k2 tog, m1, k2 tog.

Row 20: K2 tog, m1, k2 tog, k1, m1, (k2 tog) twice, m1, k1, k2 tog, m1, k5, m1, k2 tog, k7, k2 tog, m1, k8, turn leaving 8 sts on L.H. needle.

Row 21: Sl 1, k8, m1, k2 tog, k5, k2 tog, m1, k7, m1, k2 tog, k1, m1, k2 tog, k1, k2 tog, m1, k2 tog.

Row 22: K2 tog, m1, k2 tog, k3, k2 tog, m1, k9, m1, k2 tog, k3, k2 tog, m1, k18.

Row 23: Sl 1, k18, m1, k2 tog, k1, k2 tog, m1, k11, m1, k2 tog, k1, k2 tog, m1, k2 tog.

Row 24: K2 tog, m1, k3 tog, m1, k13, m1, k3 tog, m1, k20.

Row 25: Sl 1, k17, k2 tog, m1, k3, m1, k2 tog, k9, k2 tog, m1, k3, m1, k1.

Row 26: K1, m1, k5, m1, k2 tog, k7, k2 tog, m1, k5, m1, k2 tog, k17.

Row 27: Sl 1, k15, k2 tog, m1, k7, m1, k2 tog, k5, (k2 tog, m1, k1) twice, m1, k2 tog, k1, m1, k1.

Row 28: K1, m1, k1, k2 tog, m1, k3, m1, k2 tog, k1, m1, k2 tog, k3, k2 tog, m1, k9, m1, k2 tog, k11, turn leaving 4 sts on L.H. needle.

Row 29: Sl 1, k9, k2 tog, m1, k11, m1, k2 tog, k1, k2 tog, m1, k1, k2 tog, m1, k5, m1, k2 tog, k1, m1, k1.

Row 30: K1, m1, k1, k2 tog, m1, k1, k2 tog, k1, m1,

(k2 tog, k1, m1) twice, k3 tog, m1, k13, m1, k2 tog, k7, turn leaving 6 sts on L.H. needle.

Row 31: Sl 1, k8, m1, k2 tog, k9, k2 tog, m1, k3, m1, k2 tog, k1, m1, k2 tog, k2 k2 tog, m1, k1, k2 tog, m1, k2 tog.

Row 32: K2 tog, m1, k2 tog, k1, m1, (k2 tog) twice, m1, k1, k2 tog, m1, k5, m1, k2 tog, k7, k2 tog, m1, k8, turn leaving 8 sts on L.H. needle.

Row 33: Sl 1, k8, m1, k2 tog, k5, k2 tog, m1, k7, m1, k2 tog, k1, m1, k2 tog, m1, k1, k2 tog, m1, k2 tog.

Row 34: K2 tog, m1, k2 tog, k3, k2 tog, m1, k9, m1, k2 tog, k3, k2 tog, m1, k18.

Row 35: Sl 1, k18, m1, k2 tog, k1, k2 tog, m1, k11, m1, k2 tog, k1, k2 tog, m1, k2 tog.

Row 36: K2 tog, m1, k3 tog, m1, k13, m1, k3 tog, m1, k20.

Repeat rows 25–36 ten times, then repeat rows 25–32 then:

Row 37: Sl 1, k8, m1, k2 tog, k5, (k2 tog, m1, k1) twice, (m1, k2 tog, k1) twice, m1, k2 tog, m1, k1, k2 tog, m1, k2 tog.

Row 38: K2 tog, m1, k2 tog, k3, k2 tog, m1, k1, k2 tog, m1, k3, m1, k2 tog, k1, m1, k2 tog, k3, k2 tog, m1, k18.

Row 39: Sl 1, k18, m1, k2 tog, (k2, k2 tog, m1) twice, k5, (m1, k2 tog, k1) twice, k2 tog, m1, k2 tog.

Row 40: K2 tog, m1, k3 tog, (m1, k1, k2 tog) twice, (k1, m1, k2 tog) twice, k1, m1, k3 tog, m1, k20.

Row 41: Sl 1, k17, k2 tog, m1, k3, m1, k2 tog, k1, m1, k2 tog, k2, k2 tog, m1, k1, k2 tog, m1, k3, m1, k1.

Row 42: K1, m1, k5, m1, k2 tog, k1, m1, (k2 tog) twice, m1, k1, k2 tog, m1, k5, m1, k2 tog, k17.

Row 43: Sl 1, k15, k2 tog, m1, k1, k2 tog, m1, (k1, m1, k2 tog) 3 times, (m1, k1, k2 tog) twice, m1, k1, m1, k2 tog, k1, m1, k1.

Row 44: K1, m1, k1, k2 tog, m1, k3, m1, k2 tog, k1, m1, k2 tog, k3, k2 tog, m1, k1, k2 tog, m1, k3, m1, k2 tog, k1, m1, k2 tog, k11, turn leaving 4 sts on L.H. needle.

Row 45: Sl 1, k9, k2 tog, m1, k1, k2 tog, m1, k5 (m1, k2 tog, k1) twice, k2 tog, m1, k1, k2 tog, m1, k5, m1, k2 tog, k1, m1, k1.

Row 46: K1, (m1, k1, k2 tog) twice, k1, (m1, k2 tog, k1) twice, m1, k3 tog, (m1, k1, k2 tog) twice, k1 (m1, k2 tog, k1) twice, m1, k2 tog, k7, turn leaving 6 sts on L.H. needle.

This makes one quarter of collar. Repeat rows 7–46 three times for other three quarters. The last time on completion of row 46, put yon before k7, and turn leaving 6 sts on L.H. needle. Then finish with following rows:

Row 47: Sl 1, k4, k2 tog, m1, k3, m1, k2 tog, k1, m1, k2 tog, k2, k2 tog, m1, k1, k2 tog, m1, k3, m1, k2 tog, k1, m1, k2 tog, k2, k2 tog, m1, k1, k2 tog, m1, k2 tog.

Row 48: K2 tog, m1, k2 tog, (k1, m1, k2 tog, k2 tog, m1, k1, k2 tog, m1, k5, m1, k2 tog) twice, k10.

Row 49: Sl 1, k8, (k2 tog, m1, k1) twice, (m1, k2 tog, k1) twice, m1, k2 tog, (m1, k1, k2 tog) twice, m1, k1, (m1, k2 tog, k1) twice, m1, k2 tog, m1, k1, k2 tog, m1, k2 tog.

Row 50: K2 tog, (m1, k2 tog, k3, k2 tog, m1, k1, k2 tog, m1, k3, m1, k2 tog, k1) twice, m1, k2 tog, k8.

Row 51: Sl 1, k6, k2 tog, (m1, k1, k2 tog, m1, k5, m1, k2 tog, k1, m1, k2 tog, k1, k2 tog) twice, m1, k2 tog.

Row 52: K2 tog, (m1, k3 tog, m1, k1, k2 tog, m1, k1, k2 tog, k1, m1, k2 tog, k1, m1, k2 tog, k1) twice, m1, k2 tog, k6. Cast off.

Repeat rows 1–52. Cast off.

Pattern 114

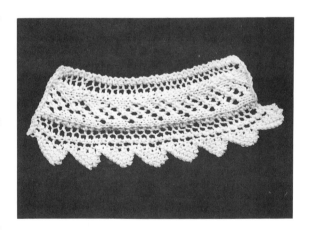

Cast on 18 sts.

Row 1: K6, p7, k5.

Row 2: Sl 1, k2, yon, k2 tog, k2, k2 tog, yon, k5, yon, k2 tog, (yon, k1) twice.

Row 3: K6, yon, k2 tog, p7, k2, yon, k2 tog, k1.

Row 4: Sl 1, k2, yon, k2 tog, k1, (k2 tog, yon) twice, k4, yon, k2 tog, (yon, k1) twice, k2.

Row 5: K8, yon, k2 tog, p7, k2, yon, k2 tog, k1.

Row 6: Sl 1, k2, yon, k2 tog, (k2 tog, yon) 3 times, k3, yon, k2 tog, (yon, k1) twice, k4.

Row 7: K10, yon, k2 tog, p7, k2, yon, k2 tog, k1.

Row 8: Sl 1, k2, yon, k2 tog, k1, (k2 tog, yon) twice, k4, yon, k2 tog, (yon, k1) twice, k6.

Row 9: Cast off 8 sts, k3, yon, k2 tog, p7, k2, yo k2 tog, k1.
Repeat rows 2–9 until desired length. Cast off.

Cast on 36 sts.
Row 1: K to end, join in 2nd ball of cotton.
Row 2: K6, *change yarn and k6 carrying yarn not in use tightly across b of work*, repeat *—* to end.
Row 3: K6, change yarn and k6 carrying yarn not in use tightly across f of work.
Repeat rows 2–3 until desired length. Cast off.

Pattern 115

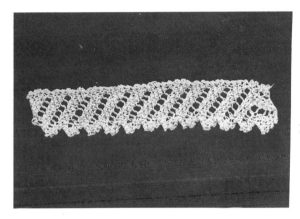

Cast on 8 sts.
Row 1: K2, m1, k2 tog, k2, m1, k2.
Row 2: K.
Row 3: K3, m1, k2 tog, k2, m1, k2.
Row 4: K.
Row 5: K4, m1, k2 tog, k2, m1, k2.
Row 6: K.
Row 7: K5, m1, k2 tog, k4.
Row 8: Cast off first 3 sts, k8.
Repeat rows 1–8 until desired length. Cast off.

Pattern 117

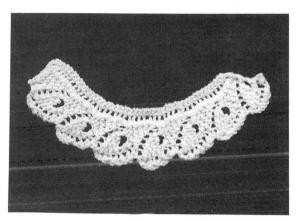

Cast on 10 sts.
Row 1: K.
Row 2: Sl 1, k1, (m1, k2 tog) twice, (m1) 4 times, k2 tog, m1, p2 tog.
Row 3: M1 p-wise, p2 tog, k1, (k1, p1) 4 times, k2.
Row 4: Sl 1, (k1, m1, k2 tog) twice, k4, m1, p2 tog.
Row 5: M1 p-wise, p2 tog, k5, (p1, k2) twice.
Row 6: Sl 1, k1, m1, k2 tog, k2, m1, k2 tog, k3, m1, p2 tog.
Row 7: M1 p-wise, p2 tog, k4, p1, k3, p1, k2.
Row 8: Sl 1, k1, m1, k2 tog, k3, m1, k2 tog, k2, m1, p2 tog.
Row 9: M1 p-wise, p2 tog, k3, p1, k4, p1, k2.
Row 10: Sl 1, k1, m1, k2 tog, k4, m1, k2 tog, k1, m1, p2 tog.
Row 11: M1 p-wise, p2 tog, k2, p1, k5, p1, k2.
Row 12: Sl 1, k1, m1, k2 tog, k5, m1, k2 tog, m1, p2 tog. Cast off 3 sts, then slip the st from R.H. needle back to L.H. needle, m1, p2 tog, k5, p1, k2.
Repeat rows 2–12 until desired length. Cast off.

*Pattern 116

Pattern 118

Cast on 12 sts.
Row 1: Sl 1, k3, (m2, k2 tog) 4 times.
Row 2: (K2, p1) 4 times, k4.
Row 3: Sl 1, k15 sts.
Row 4: Cast off 4 sts, k11.
Repeat rows 1–4 until desired length. Cast off.

Pattern 119

Cast on 24 sts.
Row 1: K.
Row 2: K.
Row 3: K2 tog, m2, k2 tog, (m1, k2 tog) 8 times, m1, k4.
Row 4: Sl 1, k3, p18, k1, p1, k1.
Row 5: K2 tog, m2, k2 tog, (m1, k2 tog) 8 times, m1, k5.
Row 6: Sl 1, k4, p18, k1, p1, k1.

Row 7: K2 tog, m2, k2 tog, (m1, k2 tog) 8 times, m1, k6.
Row 8: Sl 1, k5, p18, k1, p1, k1.
Row 9: Cast off 3 sts, p18, k5.
Row 10: Sl 1, k4, p19.
Repeat rows 3–10 until desired length. Cast off.

Pattern 120

Cast on 24 sts.
Row 1: (K3, yon, k2 tog) twice, k5, (yon, k2 tog) twice, k1, p1, k2 tog, k1.
Row 2 and all even rows: Yon, k2 tog, k2 to last 8 sts, yon, k2 tog, k3, yon, k2 tog, k1.
Row 3: (K3, yon, k2 tog) twice, k3, k2 tog, (yon, k2 tog) twice, (k1, yon) twice, k2.
Row 5: (K3, yon, k2 tog) twice, k2, k2 tog, (yon, k2 tog) twice, k1, yon, k3, yon, k2.
Row 7: (K3, yon, k2 tog) twice, k1, k2 tog (yon, k2 tog) twice, k1, yon, k5, yon, k2.
Row 9: (k3, yon, k2 tog) twice, k2 tog, (yon, k2 tog) twice, k1, yon, k7, yon, k2.
Row 11: (K3, yon, k2 tog) twice, k2 (yon, k2 tog) twice, k1, yon, k2 tog, k3, k2 tog, yon, k2 tog, k1.
Row 13: (K3, yon, k2 tog) twice, k3, (yon, k2 tog) twice, k1, yon, k2 tog, k1, k2 tog, yon, k2 tog, k1.
Row 15: (K3, yon, k2 tog) twice, k4, (yon, k2 tog) twice, k1, yon, sl 1, k2 tog, psso, yon, k2 tog, k1.
Row 16: Repeat row 2.
Repeat rows 1–16 until desired length. Cast off.

Pattern 121

Cast on 5 sts.
Row 1: K.
Row 2: Sl 1, m1, k2 tog, m1, k2.
Row 3: K.
Row 4: Sl 1, m1, k2 tog, m1, k2 tog, m1, k1.
Row 5: K.
Row 6: Sl 1, m1, k2 tog, m1, k2 tog, m1, k2.
Row 7: K.
Row 8: Sl 1, m1, k2 tog, m1, k2 tog, m1, k2 tog, m1, k1.
Row 9: K.
Row 10: Sl 1, m1, k2 tog, m1, k2 tog, m1, k2 tog, m1, k2.
Row 11: K.
Row 12: Sl 1, m1, k2 tog, m1, k2 tog, m1, k2 tog, m1, k2 tog, m1, k1.
Row 13: K.
Row 14: Sl 1, m1, k2 tog, m1, k2 tog, m1, k2 tog, m1, k2 tog, m1, k2.
Row 15: K.
Row 16: Cast off 8 sts, m1, k2 tog, m1, k1.
Row 17: K.
Repeat rows 2–17 until desired length. Cast off.

Pattern 122

Cast on 7 sts.
Row 1: K.
Row 2: K3, m1, k2 tog, m2, k2.
Row 3: K3, p1, k2, m1, k2 tog, k1.
Row 4: K3, m1, k2 tog, k to end.
Row 5: K to last 3 sts, m1, k2 tog, k1.
Row 6: K3, m1, k2 tog, m2, k2 tog, m2, k2.
Row 7: K3, p1, k2, p1, k2, m1, k2 tog, k1.
Row 8: K3, m1, k2 tog, k to end.
Row 9: K to last 3 sts, m1, k2 tog, k1.
Row 10: K3, m1, k2 tog, m2, k2 tog, m2, k2 tog, m2, k2 tog, k1.
Row 11: K3, p1, k2, p1, k2, p1, k2, m1, k2 tog, k1.
Row 12: K3, m1, k2 tog, k to end.
Row 13: Cast off 8 sts, k to last 3 sts, m1, k2 tog, k1.
Repeat rows 2–13 until desired length. Cast off.

Pattern 123

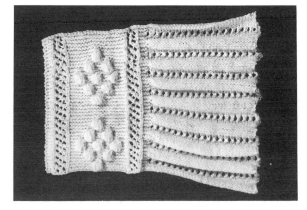

Cast on 70 sts.

Row 1: Sl 1, k2, p5, k19, p5, k38.

Row 2: P35, turn.

Row 3: Sl 1, k34.

Row 4: P35, k4, m1, k2 tog, m1, k2 tog, k20, m1, k2 tog, m1, k2 tog, k3.

Row 5: Sl 1, k2, p5, k19, p5, k38.

Row 6: P35, turn.

Row 7: Sl 1, k34.

Row 8: K40, m1, k2 tog, k22, m1, k2 tog, k4.

Row 9: Sl 1, k2, p5, k19, p5, k3, p34, (p1, k1) in last st.

Row 10: K36, turn.

Row 11: Sl 1, p34, (p1, k1) in last st.

Row 12: K41, m1, k2 tog, m1, k2 tog, k9, mb [*see below*], k10, m1, k2 tog, m1, k2 tog, k3.

Row 13: (Sl 1, k2, p5, k19, p5, k3, m1, p2 tog) 18 times, p1.

Row 14: K42, m1, k2 tog, k22, m1, k2 tog, k4.

Row 15: Sl 1, k2, p5, k19, p5, k3, p35, p2 tog.

Row 16: K36, turn.

Row 17: Sl 1, p33, p2 tog.

Row 18: K39, m1, k2 tog, m1, k2 tog, k20, m1, k2 tog, m1, k2 tog, k3.

Row 19: Sl 1, k2, p5, k19, p5, k38.

Row 20: P35, turn.

Row 21: Sl 1, k34.

Row 22: P35, k5, m1, k2 tog, k7, mb, k5, mb, k8, m1, k2 tog, k4.

Row 23: Sl 1, k2, p5, k19, p5, k38.

Row 24: P35, turn.

Row 25: Sl 1, k34.

Row 26: K39, m1, k2 tog, m1, k2 tog, k20, m1, k2 tog, m1, k2 tog, k3.

Row 27: Sl 1, k2, p5, k19, p5, k3, p34, (p1, k1) in last st.

Row 28: K36, turn.

Row 29: Sl 1, p34, (p1, k1) in last st.

Row 30: K42, m1, k2 tog, k22, m1, k2 tog, k4.

Row 31: Sl 1, k2, p5, k19, p5, k3, (m1, p2 tog) 18 times, p1.

Row 32: K41, m1, k2 tog, m1, k2 tog, k3, mb, k5, mb, k5, mb, k4, m1, k2 tog, m1, k2 tog, k3.

Row 33: Sl 1, k2, p5, k19, p5, k3, p35, p2 tog.

Row 34: K36, turn.

Row 35: Sl 1, p33, p2 tog.

Row 36: K40, m1, k2 tog, k22, m1, k2 tog, k4.

Row 37: Sl 1, k2, p5, k19, p5, k38.

Row 38: P35, turn.

Row 39: Sl 1, k34.

Row 40: P35, k4, m1, k2 tog, m1, k2 tog, k20, m1, k2 tog, m1, k2 tog, k3.

Row 41: Sl 1, k2, p5, k19, p5, k38.

Row 42: P35, turn.

Row 43: Sl 1, k34.

Row 44: K40, m1, k2 tog, k7, mb, k5, mb, k8, m1, k2 tog, k4.

Row 45: Sl 1, k2, p5, k19, p5, k3, p34, (p1, k1) in last st.

Row 46: K36, turn.

Row 47: Sl 1, p34, (p1, k1) in last st.

Row 48: K41, m1, k2 tog, m1, k2 tog, k20, m1, k2 tog, m1, k2 tog, k3.

Row 49: Sl 1, k2, p5, k19, p5, k3, (m1, p2 tog) 18 times, p1.

Row 50: K42, m1, k2 tog, k22, m1, k2 tog, k4.

Row 51: Sl 1, k2, p5, k19, p5, k3, p35, p2 tog.

Row 52: K36, turn.

Row 53: Sl 1, p33, p2 tog.

Row 54: K39, m1, k2 tog, m1, k2 tog, k9, mb, k10, m1, k2 tog, m1, k2 tog, k3.

Row 55: Sl 1, k2, p5, k19, p5, k38.

Row 56: P35, turn.

Row 57: Sl 1, k34.

Row 58: P35, k5, m1, k2 tog, k22, m1, k2 tog, k4.

Row 59: Sl 1, k2, p5, k19, p5, k38.

Row 60: P35, turn.

Row 61: Sl 1, k34.

Row 62: K39, m1, k2 tog, m1, k2 tog, k20, m1, k2 tog, m1, k2 tog, k3.

Row 63: Sl 1, k2, p5, k19, p5, k3, p34, (p1, k1) in last st.

Row 64: K36, turn.

Row 65: Sl 1, p34, (p1, k1) in last st.

Row 66: K42, m1, k2 tog, k22, m1, k2 tog, k4.

Row 67: Sl 1, k2, p5, k19, p5, k3, (m1, p2 tog) 18 times, p1.

Row 68: K41, m1, k2 tog, m1, k2 tog, k20, m1, k2 tog, m1, k2 tog, k3.

Row 69: Sl 1, k2, p5, k19, p5, k3, p35, p2 tog.

Row 70: K36, turn.

Row 71: Sl 1, p33, p2 tog.

Row 72: K40, m1, k2 tog, k22, m1, k2 tog, k4.

Repeat rows 1–72 until desired length. Cast off.

mb thus: ([m1, k1] 3 times) all in next st, turn, p6, turn, sl 1, k5, turn, sl 1, p5, turn, sl 1, k5, turn, (p2 tog) 3 times, turn, sl 1, k2 tog, psso.

Pattern 124

Cast on 19 sts.

Row 1: K.

Row 2: K5, p1, yon, p2 tog, k8, yon, k2 tog, k1.

Row 3: K3, yon, k2 tog, k5, k2 tog, yon, k1, yon, sl 1, k1, psso, k2, (yon) twice, k2.

Row 4: K3, p1, k1, p2 tog tbl, yon, p3, yon, p2 tog, k6, yon, k2 tog, k1.

Row 5: K3, yon, k2 tog, k3, k2 tog, yon, k2, k2 tog, yon, k1, yon, sl 1, k1, psso, k2, (yon) twice, k2.

Row 6: K3, p1, k1, p2 tog tbl, yon, p3, yon, p2 tog, p2, yon, p2 tog, k4, yon, k2 tog, k1.

Row 7: K3, yon, k2 tog, k1, (k2 tog, yon, k2) twice, yon, sl 1, k1, psso, k1, yon, sl 1, k1, psso, k2, (yon) twice, k2.

Row 8: K3, p1, k1, (p2 tog tbl, yon, p1) twice, yon, p2 tog, p1, yon, p2 tog, p2, yon, p2 tog, k2, yon, k2 tog, k1.

Row 9: K3, yon, k3 tog, yon, k2, k2 tog, yon, k1, k2 tog, yon, k3, yon, sl 1, k1, psso, k1, yon, sl 1, k1, psso, k2 tog, (yon) twice, k2 tog.

Row 10: K2, p1, k1, p2, yon, p2 tog, p1, yon, p3 tog, yon, p1, p2 tog tbl, yon, p2, p2 tog tbl, yon, k3, yon, k2 tog, k1.

Row 11: K3, yon, k2 tog, (k2, yon, sl 1, k1, psso) twice, k3, k2 tog, yon, k2, sl 1, k2, psso, (yon) twice, k2 tog.

Row 12: K2, p5, yon, p2 tog, p1, p2 tog tbl, yon, p2, p2 tog tbl, yon, k5, yon, k2 tog, k1.

Row 13: K3, yon, k2 tog, k4, yon, sl 1, k1, psso, k2, yon, k3 tog, yon, k2, k3 tog, yon, k2 tog, k1.

Row 14: K3, p1, k3, yon, p2 tog, p1, p2 tog tbl, yon, k7, yon, k2 tog, k1.

Row 15: K3, yon, k2 tog, k6, yon, k3 tog, yon, k2, k3 tog, yon, k3 tog.

Repeat rows 2–15 until desired length. Cast off.

Pattern 125

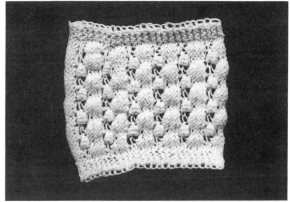

Cast on a multiple of 6 sts, plus 3, for required width of edging.

Row 1: P.

Row 2: K.

Row 3: P.

Row 4: K1, p3 tog, (k1, p1, k1, p1, k1) into next st, *p5 tog, (k1, p1, k1, p1, k1) into next st, repeat *—* to last 4 sts, p3 tog, k1.

Row 5: P.

Row 6: K1, (k1, p1, k1) into next st, p5 tog, *(k1, p1, k1, p1, k1) into next st, p5 tog*, repeat *—* to last 2 sts, (k1, p1, k1) into next st, k1.

Row 7: P.

Row 8: K.

Repeat rows 1–8 until desired length. Cast off.

Pattern 126

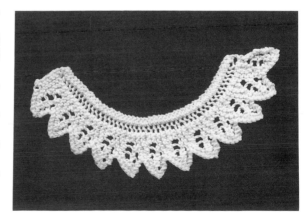

Cast on 10 sts.
Row 1: Sl 1, k2, yfwd, k2 tog, k1, (yfwd) twice, k2 tog, (yfwd) twice, k2 tog.
Row 2: Sl 1, k1, p1, k2, p1, k3, yfwd, k2 tog, k1.
Row 3: Sl 1, k2, yfwd, k2 tog, k3, (yfwd) twice, k2 tog, (yfwd) twice, k2 tog.
Row 4: Sl 1, k1, p1, k2, p1, k5, yfwd, k2 tog, k1.
Row 5: Sl 1, k2, yfwd, k2 tog, k5, (yfwd) twice, k2 tog, m2, k2 tog.
Row 6: Sl 1, k1, p1, k2, p1, k7, yfwd, k2 tog, k1.
Row 7: Sl 1, k2, yfwd, k2 tog, k11.
Row 8: Cast off 6 sts, k6, yfwd, k2 tog, k1.
Repeat rows 1–8 until desired length. Cast off.

Pattern 128

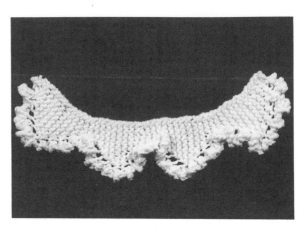

Cast on 5 sts.
Row 1: K.
Row 2: K4, m1, *(k1) 3 times into last st, turn, k3, turn, k3, (sl 2nd to last st over the last st) twice*.
Row 3: K6.
Row 4: K5, m1, repeat *—* row 2.
Row 5: K7.
Row 6: K6, m1, repeat *—* row 2.
Row 7: K8.
Row 8: K7, m1, repeat *—* row 2.
Row 9: K9.
Row 10: K8, m1, repeat *—* row 2.
Row 11: K10.
Row 12: K9, repeat *—* row 2.
Row 13: K10.
Row 14: K7, sl 1, k1, psso, repeat *—* row 2.
Row 15: K9.
Row 16: K6, sl 1, k1, psso, repeat *—* row 2.
Row 17: K8.
Row 18: K5, sl 1, k1, psso, repeat *—* row 2.
Row 19: K7.
Row 20: K4, sl 1, k1, psso, repeat *—* row 2.
Row 21: K6.
Row 22: K3, sl 1, k1, psso, repeat *—* row 2.
Row 23: K5.
Repeat rows 2–23 until desired length. Cast off.

Pattern 127

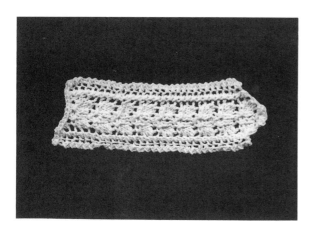

Cast on 17 sts.
Row 1: Sl 1 p-wise, k1, yon, sl 1, k1, psso, yon, k1, yon, sl 1, k2 tog, psso, p1, sl 1, k2 tog, psso, yon, k1, yon, k2, yon, sl 1, k1, psso.
Row 2: Sl 1, p1, yon, p2 tog, p4, k1, p6, yon, p2 tog.
Row 3: Sl 1 p-wise, k1, yon, sl 1, k1, psso, yon, k3, yon, sl 1, k2 tog, psso, yon, k3, yon, k2, yon, sl 1, k1, psso.
Row 4: Sl 1, p1, yon, p2 tog, p5, k1, p7, yon, p2 tog.
Row 5: Sl 1 p-wise, k1, yon, sl 1, k1, psso, yon, sl 1, k1, psso, k1, k2 tog, p1, sl 1, k1, psso, k1, k2 tog, yon, k2, yon, sl 1, k1, psso.
Row 6: Sl 1, p1, yon, p2 tog, p4, k1, p6, yon, p2 tog.
Repeat rows 1–6 until desired length. Cast off.

Pattern 129

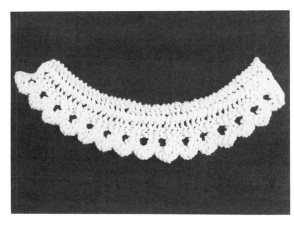

Cast on 8 sts.
Row 1: K.
Row 2: Sl 1, k1, m2, p2 tog, k2, m3, k2.
Row 3: K2, k first loop, p second loop, k third loop, k2, m2, p2 tog, k2.
Row 4: Sl 1, k1, m2, p2 tog, k7.
Row 5: K7, m2, p2 tog, k2.
Row 6: Sl 1, k1, m2, p2 tog, k7.
Row 7: Cast off 3 sts, k3, m2, p2 tog, k2.
Repeat rows 2–7 until desired length. Cast off.

Pattern 130

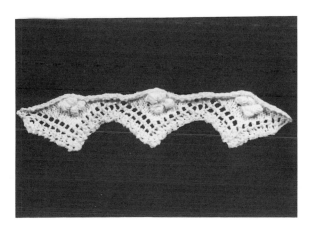

Cast on 8 sts.
Row 1: K3, (yfwd, k2 tog) twice, k1.
Row 2: P5, k3.
Row 3: Inc 1 k-wise, k1, (yfwd, k2 tog) twice, k2.

Row 4: P6, k3.
Row 5: Inc 1 k-wise, k1, (yfwd, k2 tog) twice, k3.
Row 6: P7, k3.
Row 7: Inc 1 k-wise, k1, (yfwd, k2 tog) twice, k4.
Row 8: P8, k3.
Row 9: Inc 1 k-wise, k1, (yfwd, k2 tog) twice, k5.
Row 10: P9, k3.
Row 11: Inc 1 k-wise, k1, (yfwd, k2 tog) twice, k6.
Row 12: P10, k3.
Row 13: Inc 1 k-wise, k1, (yfwd, k2 tog) twice, k3, mb [see below], k3.
Row 14: P11, k3.
Row 15: Inc 1 k-wise, k1, (yfwd, k2 tog) twice, k3, mb, k1, mb, k2.
Row 16: P12, k3.
Row 17: Sl 1, k1, psso, k2, (yfwd, k2 tog) twice, k3, mb, k3.
Row 18: P11, k3.
Row 19: Sl 1, k1, psso, k2, (yfwd, k2 tog) twice, k6.
Row 20: P10, k3.
Row 21: Sl 1, k1, psso, k2, (yfwd, k2 tog) twice, k5.
Row 22: P9, k3.
Row 23: Sl 1, k1, psso, k2, (yfwd, k2 tog) twice, k4.
Row 24: P8, k3.
Row 25: Sl 1, k1, psso, k2, (yfwd, k2 tog) twice, k3.
Row 26: P7, k3.
Row 27: Sl 1, k1, psso, k2, (yfwd, k2 tog) twice, k2.
Row 28: P6, k3.
Row 29: Sl 1, k1, psso, k2, (yfwd, k2 tog) twice, k1.
Row 30: P5, k3.
Row 31: K3, (yfwd, k2 tog) twice, k1.
Row 32: P5, k3.
Repeat rows 1–32 until desired length. Cast off.

mb thus: (K1, p1, k1, p1) all into next st, turn, k4, turn, p4, turn, (k2 tog) twice, turn, sl 1, k1, psso.

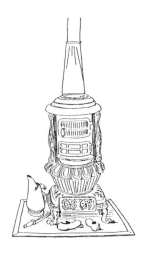

Pattern 131

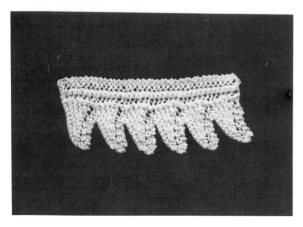

Cast on 8 sts.
Row 1: K.
Row 2: Sl 1, k1, (yon, k2 tog) twice, yon, k2.
Row 3: K2, yon, k2, (yon, k2 tog) twice, k1.
Row 4: Sl 1, k1, (yon, k2 tog) twice, k2, yon, k2.
Row 5: K2, yon, k4, (yon, k2 tog) twice, k1.
Row 6: Sl 1, k1, (yon, k2 tog) twice, k4, yon, k2.
Row 7: K2, yon, k6, (yon, k2 tog) twice, k1.
Row 8: Sl 1, k1, (yon, k2 tog) twice, k6, yon, k2.
Row 9: K2, yon, k8, (yon, k2 tog) twice, k1.
Row 10: Sl 1, k1, (yon, k2 tog) twice, k8, yon, k2.
Row 11: K2, yon, k10, (yon, k2 tog) twice, k1.
Row 12: Sl 1, k1, (yon, k2 tog) twice, k10, yon, k2.
Row 13: Cast off 11 sts, k2, (yon, k2 tog) twice, k1.
Repeat rows 2–13 until desired length. Cast off.

Pattern 132

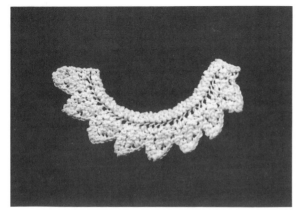

Cast on 6 sts.
Row 1: K.
Row 2: K2, yon, k2 tog, yon, k2.
Row 3: K2, (yon, k1) twice, yon, k2 tog, k1.
Row 4: K2, yon, k2 tog, yon, k3, yon, k2.
Row 5: K2, yon, k5, yon, k1, yon, k2 tog, k1.
Row 6: K2, yon, k2 tog, yon, k1, sl 1, psso, k3, k2 tog, yon, k2.
Row 7: K3, yon, k1, sl 1, psso, k1, k2 tog, yon, k2, yon, k2 tog, k1.
Row 8: K2, yon, k2 tog, k2, yon, sl 1, k2 tog, psso, yon, k4.
Row 9: Cast off 7 sts, k2, yon, k2 tog, k1.
Repeat rows 2–9 until desired length. Cast off.

Pattern 133

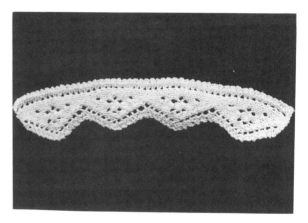

Cast on 8 sts.
Row 1: K1, p1, yon, k3, yon, k2 tog tbl, k1.
Row 2 and even numbered rows: 1 selvedge st [always worked k-wise], p to end.
Row 3: K1, p1, yon, k4, yon, k2 tog tbl, k1.
Row 5: K1, p1, yon, k5, yon, k2 tog tbl, k1.
Row 7: K1, p1, yon, k2, k2 tog, yon, k2, yon, k2 tog tbl, k1.
Row 9: K1, p1, yon, k7, yon, k2 tog tbl, k1.
Row 11: K1, p1, yon, k2, yon, sl 1, k2 tog, psso, yon, k3, yon, k2 tog, k1.
Row 13: K1, p1, yon, k2 tog, yon, k3, yon, k2 tog tbl, k1, yon, k1, k2 tog tbl, k1.
Row 15: K1, p2 tog, yon, k2 tog, k1, yon, sl 1, k2 tog, psso, yon, k3, yon, k2 tog tbl, k1.
Row 17: K1, p2 tog, yon, k2 tog, k6, yon, k2 tog tbl, k1.
Row 19: K1, p2 tog, yon, k2 tog, k1, k2 tog, yon, k2, yon, k2 tog tbl, k1.

Row 21: K1, p2 tog, yon, k2 tog, k4, yon, k2 tog tbl, k1.

Row 23: K1, p2 tog, yon, k2 tog, k3, yon, k2 tog tbl, k1.

Row 25: K1, p2 tog, yon, k2 tog, k2, yon, k2 tog tbl, k1.

Row 26: Repeat row 2.

Repeat rows 3–26 until desired length. Cast off.

Pattern 134

Cast on 20 sts.

Row 1: K2, m1, k2 tog, k3, cast on 6 sts, k5, cast on 6 sts, k2, m1, k2 tog, k1, m2, k2 tog, k1.

Row 2: P3, k1, p1, k4, p2 tog [the first 2 of the cast on sts], p2, p2 tog [the last 2 of the cast on sts], k5, p2 tog, p2, p2 tog, k7.

Row 3: K2, m1, k2 tog, k18, m1, k2 tog, k5.

Row 4: P5, k4, (p2 tog) twice, k5, (p2 tog) twice, k7.

Row 5: K2, m1, k2 tog, k2, k1, cast on 6 sts, k2, (k2 tog) twice, k1, m1, k2 tog, k1, m2, k2 tog, m2, k2 tog.

Row 6: P2, k1, p2, k1, p1, k7, p2 tog, p2, p2 tog, k9.

Row 7: K2, m1, k2 tog, k14, m1, k2 tog, k7.

Row 8: P7, k7, (p2 tog) twice, k9.

Row 9: K2, m1, k2 tog, k3, cast on 6 sts, k1, (k2 tog) twice, k2, cast on 6 sts, k2, m1, k2 tog, k1, (m2, k2 tog) 3 times.

Row 10: (P2, k1) 3 times, p1, k4, p2 tog, p2, p2 tog, k5, p2 tog, p2, p2 tog, k7.

Row 11: K2, m1, k2 tog, k18, m1, k2 tog, k10.

Row 12: Cast off 6 sts, p3, k4, (p2 tog) twice, k5, (p2 tog) twice, k7.

Row 13: K2, m1, k2 tog, k2, (k2 tog) twice, k1, cast on 6 sts, k2, (k2 tog) twice, k1, m1, k2 tog, k1, m2, k2 tog, k1.

Row 14: P3, k1, p1, k7, p2 tog, p2, p2 tog, k9.

Row 15: K2, m1, k2 tog, k14, m1, k2 tog, k5.

Row 16: P5, k7, (p2 tog) twice, k9.

Row 17: K2, m1, k2 tog, k3, cast on 6 sts, k1, (k2 tog) twice, k2, cast on 6 sts, k2, m1, k2 tog, k1, m2, k2 tog, m2, k2 tog.

Row 18: P2, k1, p2, k1, p1, k4, p2 tog, p2, p2 tog, k5, p2 tog, p2, p2 tog, k7.

Row 19: K2, m1, k2 tog, k18, m1, k2 tog, k7.

Row 20: P7, k4, (p2 tog) twice, k5, (p2 tog) twice, k7.

Row 21: K2, m1, k2 tog, k2 (k2 tog) twice, k1, cast on 6 sts, k2, (k2 tog) twice, k1, m1, k2 tog, k1, (m2, k2 tog) 3 times.

Row 22: (P2, k1) 3 times, p1, k7, p2 tog, p2, p2 tog, k9.

Row 23: K2, m1, k2 tog, k14, m1, k2 tog, k10.

Row 24: Cast off 6 sts, p3, k7, (p2 tog) twice, k9.

Row 25: K2, m1, k2 tog, k3, cast on 6 sts, k1, (k2 tog) twice, k2, cast on 6 sts, k2, m1, k2 tog, k1, m2, k2 tog, k1.

Repeat rows 2–25 until desired length. Cast off.

Pattern 135

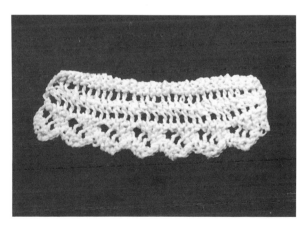

Cast on 10 sts.

Row 1: K3, (yfwd, k2 tog) twice, y2rn, k2 tog, k1.

Row 2: K3, p1, k2, (yfwd, k2 tog) twice, k1.

Row 3: K3, (yfwd, k2 tog) twice, k1, y2rn, k2 tog, k1.

Row 4: K3, p1, k3, (yfwd, k2 tog) twice, k1.

Row 5: K3, (yfwd, k2 tog) twice, k2, y2rn, k2 tog, k1.

Row 6: K3, p1, k4, (yfwd, k2 tog) twice, k1.
Row 7: K3, (yfwd, k2 tog) twice, k6.
Row 8: Cast off 3 sts, k4, (yfwd, k2 tog) twice, k1.
Repeat rows 1–8 until desired length. Cast off.

*Pattern 136

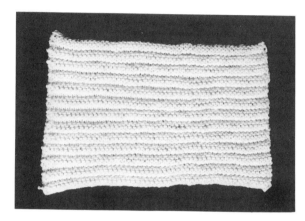

Cast on 52 sts.
Row 1: K.
Row 2: P.
Row 3: K.
Repeat rows 1–3 until desired length, allowing extra fullness at corners.

Pattern 137

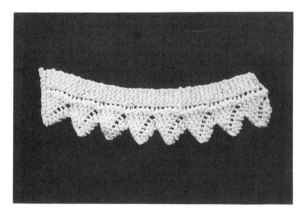

Cast on 8 sts.
Row 1: K4, yfwd, k2 tog, yfwd, k2.

Row 2: K.
Row 3: K4, yfwd, k2 tog, k1, yfwd, k2.
Row 4: K.
Row 5: K4, yfwd, k2 tog, k2, yfwd, k2.
Row 6: K.
Row 7: K4, yfwd, k2 tog, k3, yfwd, k2.
Row 8: K.
Row 9: K4, yfwd, k2 tog, k4, yfwd, k2.
Row 10: K.
Row 11: K4, yfwd, k2 tog, k5, yfwd, k2.
Row 12: Cast off 6 sts, k to end.
Repeat rows 1–12 until desired length. Cast off.

Pattern 138

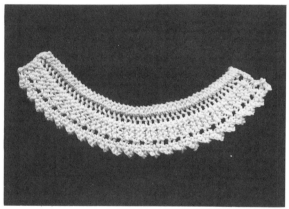

Cast on 9 sts.
Row 1: Sl 1, k2, yfwd, k2 tog, k2, m2, k2.
Row 2: Sl 1, k2, p1, k4, yfwd, k2 tog, k1.
Row 3: Sl 1, k2, yfwd, k2 tog, k6.
Row 4: Cast off 2 sts, k5, yfwd, k2 tog, k1.
Repeat rows 1–4 until desired length. Cast off.

Pattern 139

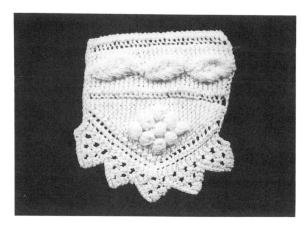

Cast on 25 sts.

Row 1: Sl 1, k2, m1, k2 tog, k3, m1, k1, m1, k5, m1, k2 tog, k2, m1, k2 tog, m1, k2, m2, k2 tog, k1.

Row 2: K3, p1, k9, m1, k2 tog, k3, p3, k5, m1, k2 tog, k1.

Row 3: Sl 1, k2, m1, k2 tog, k3, m1, k3, m1, k5, m1, k2 tog, k3, m1, k2 tog, m1, k6.

Row 4: K14, m1, k2 tog, k3, p5, k5, m1, k2 tog, k1.

Row 5: Sl 1, k2, m1, k2 tog, k3, m1, k5, m1, k5, m1, k2 tog, k4, m1, k2 tog, m1, k2, m2, k2 tog, m2, k2.

Row 6: K3, p1, k2, p1, k11, m1, k2 tog, k3, p7, k5, m1, k2 tog, k1.

Row 7: Sl 1, k2, m1, k2 tog, k3, m1, k7, m1, k5, m1, k2 tog, k5, m1, k2 tog, m1, k9.

Row 8: K19, m1, k2 tog, k3, p9, k5, m1, k2 tog, k1.

Row 9: Sl 1, k2, m1, k2 tog, k3, m1, k9, m1, k5, m1, k2 tog, k6, m1, k2 tog, m1, k2, m2, k2 tog, m2, k2 tog, m2, k2 tog, k1.

Row 10: K3, p1, k2, p1, k2, p1, k13, m1, k2 tog, k3, p11, k5, m1, k2 tog, k1.

Row 11: Sl 1, k2, m1, k2 tog, k7, sl 1, k2 tog, psso, k9, m1, k2 tog, k7, m1, k2 tog, m1, k12.

Row 12: Cast off 7 sts, k16, m1, k2 tog, k3, p9, k5, m1, k2 tog, k1.

Row 13: Sl 1, k2, m1, k2 tog, k6, sl 1, k2 tog, psso, k8, m1, k2 tog, k8, m1, k2 tog, m1, k2, m2, k2 tog, k1.

Row 14: K3, p1, k15, m1, k2 tog, k3, p7, k5, m1, k2 tog, k1.

Row 15: Sl 1, k2, m1, k2 tog, k5, sl 1, k2 tog, psso, k7, m1, k2 tog, k9, m1, k2 tog, m1, k6.

Row 16: K20, m1, k2 tog, k3, p5, k5, m1, k2 tog, k1.

Row 17: Sl 1, k2, m1, k2 tog, k4, sl 1, k2 tog, psso, k6, m1, k2 tog, k10, m1, k2 tog, m1, k2, m2, k2 tog, m2, k2.

Row 18: K3, p1, k2, p1, k17, m1, k2 tog, k3, p3, k5, m1, k2 tog, k1.

Row 19: Sl 1, k2, m1, k2 tog, k3, sl 1, k2 tog, psso, k5, m1, k2 tog, k11, m1, k2 tog, m1, k9.

Row 20: K25, m1, k2 tog, k3, p1, k5, m1, k2 tog, k1.

Row 21: Sl 1, k2, m1, k2 tog, k3, m1, k1, m1, k5, m1, k2 tog, k12, m1, k2 tog, m1, k2, m2, k2 tog, m2, k2 tog, m2, k2 tog, k1.

Row 22: K3, p1, k2, p1, k2, p1, k19, m1, k2 tog, k3, p3, k5, m1, k2 tog, k1.

Row 23: Sl 1, k2, m1, k2 tog, k3, m1, k3, m1, k5, m1, k2 tog, k6, mb [*see below*] k6, m1, k2 tog, m1, k12.

Row 24: Cast off 7 sts, k22, m1, k2 tog, k3, p5, k5, m1, k2 tog, k1.

Row 25: Sl 1, k2, m1, k2 tog, k3, m1, k5, m1, k5, m1, k2 tog, k14, m1, k2 tog, m1, k2, m2, k2 tog, k1.

Row 26: K3, p1, k21, m1, k2 tog, k3, p7, k5, m1, k2 tog, k1.

Row 27: Sl 1, k2, m1, k2 tog, k3, m1, k7, m1, k5, m1, k2 tog, k4, mb, k3, mb, k6, m1, k2 tog, m1, k6.

Row 28: K26, m1, k2 tog, k3, p9, k5, m1, k2 tog, k1.

Row 29: Sl 1, k2, m1, k2 tog, k3, m1, k9, m1, k5, m1, k2 tog, k16, m1, k2 tog, m1, k2, m2, k2 tog, m2, k2.

Row 30: K3, p1, k2, p1, k23, m1, k2 tog, k3, p11, k5, m1, k2 tog, k1.

Row 31: Sl 1, k2, m1, k2 tog, k7, sl 1, k2 tog, psso, k9, m1, k2 tog, k2, mb, k3, mb, k3, mb, k3, k2 tog, m1, k2 tog, m1, k2 tog, k8.

Row 32: K29, m1, k2 tog, k3, p9, k5, m1, k2 tog, k1.

Row 33: Sl 1, k2, m1, k2 tog, k6, sl 1, k2 tog, psso, k8, m1, k2 tog, k13, k2 tog, m1, k2 tog, m1, k2 tog, k1, m2, k2 tog, m2, k2 tog, m2, k2 tog, k1.

Row 34: K3, p1, k2, p1, k2, p1, k21, m1, k2 tog, k3, p7, k5, m1, k2 tog, k1.

Row 35: Sl 1, k2, m1, k2 tog, k5, sl 1, k2 tog, psso, k7, m1, k2 tog, k4, mb, k3, mb, k3, k2 tog, m1, k2 tog, m1, k2 tog, k11.

Row 36: Cast off 7 sts, k22, m1, k2 tog, k3, p5, k5, m1, k2 tog, k1.

Row 37: Sl 1, k2, m1, k2 tog, k4, sl 1, k2 tog, psso, k6, m1, k2 tog, k11, k2 tog, m1, k2 tog, m1, k2 tog, k1, m2, k2 tog, k1.

Row 38: K3, p1, k19, m1, k2 tog, k3, p3, k5, m1, k2 tog, k1.

Row 39: Sl 1, k2, m1, k2 tog, k3, sl 1, k2 tog, psso, k5, m1, k2 tog, k6, mb, k3, k2 tog, m1, k2 tog, m1, k2 tog, k5.

Row 40: K22, m1, k2 tog, k3, p1, k5, m1, k2 tog, k1.

Row 41: Sl 1, k2, m1, k2 tog, k3, m1, k1, m1, k5,

m1, k2 tog, k9, k2 tog, m1, k2 tog, m1, k2 tog, k1, m2, k2 tog, m2, k2.
Row 42: K3, p1, k2, p1, k17, m1, k2 tog, k3, p3, k5, m1, k2 tog, k1.
Row 43: Sl 1, k2, m1, k2 tog, k3, m1, k3, m1, k5, m1, k2 tog, k8, k2 tog, m1, k2 tog, m1, k2 tog, k8.
Row 44: K23, m1, k2 tog, k3, p5, k5, m1, k2 tog, k1.
Row 45: Sl 1, k2, m1, k2 tog, k3, m1, k5, m1, k5, m1, k2 tog, k7, k2 tog, m1, k2 tog, m1, k2 tog, k1, m2, k2 tog, m2, k2 tog, m2, k2 tog, k1.
Row 46: K3, p1, k2, p1, k2, p1, k15, m1, k2 tog, k3, p7, k5, m1, k2 tog, k1.
Row 47: Sl 1, k2, m1, k2 tog, k3, m1, k7, m1, k5, m1, k2 tog, k6, k2 tog, m1, k2 tog, m1, k2 tog, k11.
Row 48: Cast off 7 sts, k16, m1, k2 tog, k3, p9, k5, m1, k2 tog, k1.
Row 49: Sl 1, k2, m1, k2 tog, k3, m1, k9, m1, k5, m1, k2 tog, k5, k2 tog, m1, k2 tog, m1, k2 tog, k1, m2, k2 tog, k1.
Row 50: K3, p1, k13, m1, k2 tog, k3, p11, k5, m1, k2 tog, k1.
Row 51: Sl 1, k2, m1, k2 tog, k7, sl 1, k2 tog, psso, k9, m1, k2 tog, k4, k2 tog, m1, k2 tog, m1, k2 tog, k5.
Row 52: K16, m1, k2 tog, k3, p9, k5, m1, k2 tog, k1.
Row 53: Sl 1, k2, m1, k2 tog, k6, sl 1, k2 tog, psso, k8, m1, k2 tog, k3, k2 tog, m1, k2 tog, m1, k2 tog, k1, m2, k2 tog, m2, k2.
Row 54: K3, p1, k2, p1, k11, m1, k2 tog, k3, p7, k5, m1, k2 tog, k1.
Row 55: Sl 1, k2, m1, k2 tog, k5, sl 1, k2 tog, psso, k7, m1, k2 tog, k2, k2 tog, m1, k2 tog, m1, k2 tog, k8.
Row 56: K17, m1, k2 tog, k3, p5, k5, m1, k2 tog, k1.
Row 57: Sl 1, k2, m1, k2 tog, k4, sl 1, k2 tog, psso, k6, m1, k2 tog, k1, k2 tog, m1, k2 tog, m1, k2 tog, k1, m2, k2 tog, m2, k2 tog, m2, k2 tog, k1.
Row 58: K3, p1, k2, p1, k2, p1, k9, m1, k2 tog, k3, p3, k5, m1, k2 tog, k1.
Row 59: Sl 1, k2, m1, k2 tog, k3, sl 1, k2 tog, psso, k5, m1, k2 tog, k2 tog, m1, k2 tog, m1, k2 tog, k11.
Row 60: Cast off 7 sts, k10, m1, k2 tog, k3, p1, k5, m1, k2 tog, k1.
Repeat rows 1–60 until desired length. Cast off.

mb thus: ([m1, k1] 3 times) all in next st, turn, p6, turn, sl 1, k5, turn, sl 1, p5, turn, sl 1, k5, turn, (p2 tog) 3 times, turn, sl 1, k2 tog, psso.

Pattern 140

Cast on a multiple of 10 sts, plus 2, for required width of edging.
Row 1: P.
Row 2: K.
Row 3: P.
Row 4: K1, *(k5, turn, p5, turn) 3 times, k10*, repeat *—* to last st, k1.
Row 5: P.
Row 6: K.
Row 7: P.
Row 8: K6, repeat *—* row 4 to end, ending k6 instead of k10.
Repeat rows 1–8 until desired length. Cast off.

Pattern 141

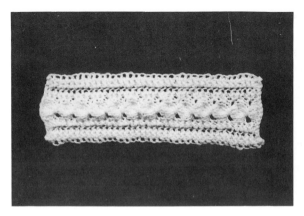

Cast on 18 sts.
Row 1: M1, k2 tog, k4, p6, k6.

Antique knitted strip bedspread—cable edging. Knitted edgings on pillows.

Lace-trimmed napkin—antique.

Preserve covers—knitted.

Victorian tea cloth.

Towels with edgings.

Victorian tea cloth.

Row 2: M1, k2 tog, k1, m1, k2 tog, k9, m1, k2 tog, k2.

Row 3: M1, k2 tog, k1, m1, k2 tog, k1, p6, k2, m1, k2 tog, k2.

Row 4: M1, k2 tog, k1, m1, k2 tog, k9, m1, k2 tog, k2.

Row 5: M1, k2 tog, k1, m1, k2 tog, k1, p6, k2, m1, k2 tog, k2.

Row 6: M1, k2 tog, k1, m1, k2 tog, k1, draw the 4th st on L.H. needle over the 3 sts that are nearer to the point of the needle [the R.H. needle should be inserted in the st from right to left to lift it over], draw 5th and 6th sts over in the same way [this brings 3 sts drawn over 3, all still on L.H. needle], m1, k1 st of the group of three, k1 in f & b of next st, k1 in last st of group, m1, k2, m1, k2 tog, k2.

Row 7: M1, k2 tog, k1, m1, k2 tog, k1, p6, k2, m1, k2 tog, k2.

Repeat rows 2–7 until desired length. Cast off.

twice, k8, (k1, p1) into the double yon of previous row, k3.

Row 8: K1, k2 tog, (yon) twice, k2 tog, (yon) twice, k2 tog, k16, yon, k2 tog, k1.

Row 9: Sl 1, k2, yon, k2 tog, k5 (yon, k2 tog) twice, k6, (k1, p1) into double yon of previous row, k1, (k1, p1) into double yon of previous row, k2.

Row 10: K2 tog, k1, k2 tog, (yon) twice, k2 tog, k3, yon, k1, yon, k2 tog, k11, yon, k2 tog, k1.

Row 11: Sl 1, k2, yon, k2 tog, k3, k2 tog, (yon, k3) twice, yon, k2 tog, k2, (k1, p1) into double yon of previous row, k2 tog, k1.

Row 12: K2 tog, k3, k2 tog, yon, k5, yon, k2 tog, k10, yon, k2 tog, k1.

Row 13: Sl 1, k2, yon, k2 tog, k2, (k2 tog, yon) twice, k3, yon, k7, yon, k2 tog, k1, k2 tog.

Repeat rows 2–13 until desired length. Cast off.

Pattern 143

Pattern 142

Cast on 26 sts.

Row 1: K.

Row 2: K2 tog, k1, yon, k2 tog, k5, k2 tog, yon, k2 tog, k9, yon, k2 tog, k1.

Row 3: Sl 1, k2, yon, k2 tog, k1, k2 tog, (yon, k2 tog) twice, k2, yon, k2 tog, k3, k2 tog, yon, k3.

Row 4: Yon, k4, yon, k2 tog, k1, k2 tog, yon, k11, yon, k2 tog, k1.

Row 5: Sl 1, k2, yon, k2 tog, k3, (yon, k2 tog) twice, k3, yon, sl 1, k2 tog, psso, yon, k6.

Row 6: Yon, k1, k2 tog, (yon) twice, k18, yon, k2 tog, k1.

Row 7: Sl 1, k2, yon, k2 tog, k4, (yon, k2 tog)

Cast on 13 sts.

Row 1: K.

Row 2: Sl 1, k1, m1, k2 tog, k5, m1, k2 tog, m1, k2.

Row 3: M1, k2 tog, k12.

Row 4: Sl 1, k1, m1, k2 tog, k4, m1, k2 tog, m1, k2 tog, m1, k2.

Row 5: M1, k2 tog, k13.

Row 6: Sl 1, k1, m1, k2 tog, k3, (m1, k2 tog) 3 times, m1, k2.

Row 7: M1, k2 tog, k14.

Row 8: Sl 1, k1, m1, k2 tog, k2, (m1, k2 tog) 4 times, m1, k2.

Row 9: M1, k2 tog, k15.

Row 10: Sl 1, k1, m1, k2 tog, k1, (m1, k2 tog) 5 times, m1, k2.

Row 11: M1, k2 tog, k16.

Row 12: Sl 1, k1, m1, k2 tog, k1, k2 tog, (m1, k2 tog) 5 times, k1.
Row 13: M1, k2 tog, k15.
Row 14: Sl 1, k1, m1, k2 tog, k2, k2 tog, (m1, k2 tog) 4 times, k1.
Row 15: M1, k2 tog, k14.
Row 16: Sl 1, k1, m1, k2 tog, k3, k2 tog, (m1, k2 tog) 3 times, k1.
Row 17: M1, k2 tog, k13.
Row 18: Sl 1, k1, m1, k2 tog, k4, k2 tog, m1, k2 tog, m1, k2 tog, k1.
Row 19: M1, k2 tog, k12.
Row 20: Sl 1, k1, m1, k2 tog, k5, k2 tog, m1, k2 tog, k1.
Row 21: M1, k2 tog, k11.
Repeat rows 2-21 until desired length. Cast off.

Row 17: K1, k2 tog, m1, (k2 tog) 14 times, k7.
Row 18: K.
Row 19: K1, k2 tog, m1, (k2 tog) 14 times, k6.
Row 20: K.
Row 21: K1, k2 tog, m1, (k2 tog) 14 times, k5.
Row 22: K.
Row 23: K.
Repeat rows 2-23 until desired length. Cast off.

Pattern 145

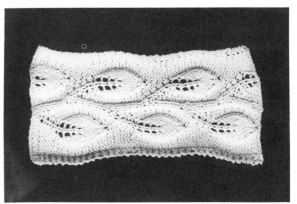

Cast on 26 sts.
Row 1: K5, p5, k4, p3, k9.
Row 2: P7, p2 tog, k into f & b of next st, k2, p4, k2, yon, k1, yon, k2, p5.
Row 3: K5, p7, k4, p2, k1, p1, k8.
Row 4: P6, p2 tog, k1, p into f & b of next st, k2, p4, k3, yon, k1, yon, k3, p5.
Row 5: K5, p9, k4, p2, k2, p1, k7.
Row 6: P5, p2 tog, k1, p into f & b of next st, p1, k2, p4, sl 1, k1, psso, k5, k2 tog, p5.
Row 7: K5, p7, k4, p2, k3, p1, k6.
Row 8: P4, p2 tog, k1, p into f & b of next st, p2, k2, p4, sl 1, k1, psso, k3, k2 tog, p5.
Row 9: K5, p5, k4, p2, k4, p1, k5.
Row 10: P5, yon, k1, yon, p4, k2, p4, sl 1, k1, psso, k1, k2 tog, p5.
Row 11: K5, p3, k4, p2, k4, p3, k5.
Row 12: P5, (k1, yon) twice, k1, p4, k1, pick up thread between st just worked and next st and k into b of this thread [thus making one st], k1, p2 tog, p2, sl 2, k-wise, k1, p2sso, p5.
Row 13: K9, p3, k4, p5, k5.
Row 14: P5, k2, yon, k1, yon, k2, p4, k1, k into f & b of next st, k1, p2 tog, p7.
Row 15: K8, p1, k1, p2, k4, p7, k5.

Pattern 144

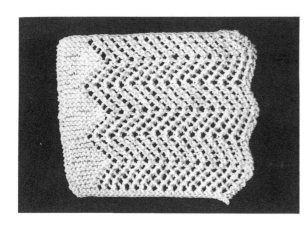

Cast on 35 sts.
Row 1: K.
Row 2: Sl 1, k6, m1, (k2 tog) 13 times, m1, k2.
Row 3: K.
Row 4: Sl 1, k7, m1, (k2 tog) 13 times, m1, k2.
Row 5: K.
Row 6: Sl 1, k8, m1, (k2 tog) 13 times, m1, k2.
Row 7: K.
Row 8: Sl 1, k9, m1, (k2 tog) 13 times, m1, k2.
Row 9: K.
Row 10: Sl 1, k10, m1, (k2 tog) 13 times, m1, k2.
Row 11: K.
Row 12: K.
Row 13: K1, k2 tog, m1, (k2 tog) 14 times, k9.
Row 14: K.
Row 15: K1, k2 tog, m1, (k2 tog) 14 times, k8.
Row 16: K.

Row 16: P5, k3, yon, k1, yon, k3, p4, k2, p into f & b of next st, k1, p2 tog, p6.
Row 17: K7, p1, k2, p2, k4, p9, k5.
Row 18: P5, sl 1, k1, psso, k5, k2 tog, p4, k2, p1, p into f & b of next st, k1, p2 tog, p5.
Row 19: K6, p1, k3, p2, k4, p7, k5.
Row 20: P5, sl 1, k1, psso, k3, k2 tog, p4, k2, p2, p into f & b of next st, k1, p2 tog, p4.
Row 21: K5, p1, k4, p2, k4, p5, k5.
Row 22: P5, sl 1, k1, psso, k1, k2 tog, p4, k2, p4, yon, k1, yon, p5.
Row 23: K5, p3, k4, p2, k4, p3, k5.
Row 24: P5, sl 2 k-wise, k1, p2sso, p2, p2 tog, k1, m1, k1, p4, (k1, yon) twice, k1, p5.
Repeat rows 1–24 until desired length. Cast off.

Pattern 146

Cast on 8 sts.
Row 1: K3, (yfwd, k2 tog) twice, k1.
Row 2: K.
Row 3: Inc 1 k-wise, k1, (yfwd, k2 tog) twice, k2.
Row 4: K.
Row 5: Inc 1 k-wise, k1, (yfwd, k2 tog) twice, k3.
Row 6: K.
Row 7: Inc 1 k-wise, k1, (yfwd, k2 tog) twice, k4.
Row 8: K.
Row 9: Inc 1 k-wise, k1, (yfwd, k2 tog) twice, k5.
Row 10: K.
Row 11: Inc 1 k-wise, k1, (yfwd, k2 tog) twice, k6.
Row 12: K.
Row 13: Inc 1 k-wise, k1, (yfwd, k2 tog) twice, k3, mb[see below], k3.
Row 14: K.
Row 15: Inc 1 k-wise, k1, (yfwd, k2 tog) twice, k3, mb, k1, mb, k2.

Row 16: K.
Row 17: Sl 1, k1, psso, k2, (yfwd, k2 tog) twice, k3, mb, k3.
Row 18: K.
Row 19: Sl 1, k1, psso, k2, (yfwd, k2 tog) twice, k6.
Row 20: K.
Row 21: Sl 1, k1, psso, k2, (yfwd, k2 tog) twice, k5.
Row 22: K.
Row 23: Sl 1, k1, psso, k2, (yfwd, k2 tog) twice, k4.
Row 24: K.
Row 25: Sl 1, k1, psso, k2, (yfwd, k2 tog) twice, k3.
Row 26: K.
Row 27: Sl 1, k1, psso, k2, (yfwd, k2 tog) twice, k2.
Row 28: K.
Row 29: Sl 1, k1, psso, k2, (yfwd, k2 tog) twice, k1.
Row 30: K.
Row 31: K3, (yfwd, k2 tog) twice, k1.
Row 32: K.
Repeat rows 1–32 until desired length. Cast off.

mb thus: (k1, p1, k1) into next st, turn, p4 sts just made, turn, (k2 tog) twice, sl first st over second st.

Pattern 147

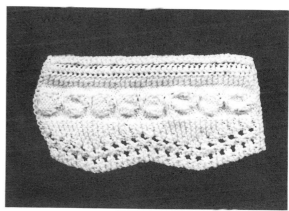

Cast on 23 sts.
Row 1: K.
Row 2: K2, m1, k2 tog, m1, k2 tog, k10, k2 tog, m2, k2 tog, m2, k2 tog, k1.
Row 3: K3, p1, k2, p1, k3, p3, m1, p1, m1, p3, k2, m1, k2 tog, m1, k2 tog, k1.
Row 4: K2, m1, k2 tog, m1, k2 tog, k4, m1, k3, m1, k13.
Row 5: K10, p3, m1, p5, m1, p3, k2, m1, k2 tog, m1, k2 tog, k1.

Row 6: K2, m1, k2 tog, m1, k2 tog, k4, m1, k7, m1, k6, k2 tog, m2, k2 tog, m2, k2 tog, k1.

Row 7: K3, p1, k2, p1, k4, p15, k2, m1, k2 tog, m1, k2 tog, k1.

Row 8: K2, m1, k2 tog, m1, k2 tog, k4, m1, sl 1, k2 tog, psso, k3, sl 1, k2 tog, psso, m1, k14.

Row 9: K11, p3, m1, p3 tog, p1, p3 tog, m1, p3, k2, m1, k2 tog, m1, k2 tog, k1.

Row 10: K2, m1, k2 tog, m1, k2 tog, k4, m1, k2 tog, sl 1, k2 tog, psso, pass the previous '2 tog' st over [thus decreasing again], m1, k7, k2 tog, m2, k2 tog, m2, k2 tog, k1.

Row 11: K3, p1, k2, p1, k5, p3, p3 tog, p3, k2, m1, k2 tog, m1, k2 tog, k1.

Row 12: K2, m1, k2 tog, m1, k2 tog, k20.

Row 13: K12, p3, m1, p1, m1, p3, k2, m1, k2 tog, m1, k2 tog, k1.

Row 14: K2, m1, k2 tog, m1, k2 tog, k4, m1, k3, m1, k8, k2 tog, m2, k2 tog, m2, k2 tog, k1.

Row 15: K3, p1, k2, p1, k6, p3, m1, p5, m1, p3, k2, m1, k2 tog, m1, k2 tog, k1.

Row 16: K2, m1, k2 tog, m1, k2 tog, k4, m1, k7, m1, k16.

Row 17: K13, p15, k2, m1, k2 tog, m1, k2 tog, k1.

Row 18: K2, m1, k2 tog, m1, k2 tog, k4, m1, sl 1, k2 tog, psso, k3, sl 1, k2 tog, psso, m1, k9, k2 tog, m2, k2 tog, m2, k2 tog, k1.

Row 19: K3, p1, k2, p1, k7, p3, m1, p3 tog, p1, p3 tog, m1, p3, k2, m1, k2 tog, m1, k2 tog, k1.

Row 20: K2, m1, k2 tog, m1, k2 tog, k4, m1, k2 tog, sl 1, k2 tog, psso, pass the previous '2 tog' st over, m1, k17.

Row 21: K14, p3, p3 tog, p3, k2, m1, k2 tog, m1, k2 tog, k1.

Row 22: K2, m1, k2 tog, m1, k2 tog, k12, (k2 tog) twice, m2, k2 tog, m2, (k2 tog) twice.

Row 23: K3, p1, k2, p1, k6, p3, m1, p1, m1, p3, k2, m1, k2 tog, m1, k2 tog, k1.

Row 24: K2, m1, k2 tog, m1, k2 tog, k4, m1, k3, m1, k16.

Row 25: K13, p3, m1, p5, m1, p3, k2, m1, k2 tog, m1, k2 tog, k1.

Row 26: K2, m1, k2 tog, m1, k2 tog, k4, m1, k7, m1, k6, (k2 tog) twice, m2, k2 tog, m2, (k2 tog) twice.

Row 27: K3, p1, k2, p1, k5, p15, k2, m1, k2 tog, m1, k2 tog, k1.

Row 28: K2, m1, k2 tog, m1, k2 tog, k4, m1, sl 1, k2 tog, psso, k3, sl 1, k2 tog, psso, m1, k15.

Row 29: K12, p3, m1, p3 tog, p1, p3 tog, m1, p3, k2, m1, k2 tog, m1, k2 tog, k1.

Row 30: K2, m1, k2 tog, m1, k2 tog, k4, m1, k2 tog, sl 1, k2 tog, psso, pass the previous '2 tog' st over, m1, k5, k2 tog, k2 tog, m2, k2 tog, m2, k2 tog, k2 tog.

Row 31: K3, p1, k2, p1, k4, p3, k3 tog, p3, k2, m1, k2 tog, m1, k2 tog, k1.

Row 32: K2, m1, k2 tog, m1, k2 tog, k19.

Row 33: K11, p3, m1, p1, m1, p3, k2, m1, k2 tog, m1, k2 tog, k1.

Row 34: K2, m1, k2 tog, m1, k2 tog, k4, m1, k3, m1, k4, k2 tog, k2 tog, m2, k2 tog, m2, k2 tog, k2 tog.

Row 35: K3, p1, k2, p1, k3, p3, m1, p5, m1, p3, k2, m1, k2 tog, m1, k2 tog, k1.

Row 36: K2, m1, k2 tog, m1, k2 tog, k4, m1, k7, m1, k13.

Row 37: K10, p15, k2, m1, k2 tog, m1, k2 tog, k1.

Row 38: K2, m1, k2 tog, m1, k2 tog, k4, m1, sl 1, k2 tog, psso, k3, sl 1, k2 tog, psso, m1, k3, (k2 tog) twice, m2, k2 tog, m2, (k2 tog) twice.

Row 39: K3, p1, k2, p1, k2, p3, m1, p3 tog, p1, p3 tog, m1, p3, k2, m1, k2 tog, m1, k2 tog, k1.

Row 40: K2, m1, k2 tog, m1, k2 tog, k4, m1, k2 tog, sl 1, k2 tog, psso, pass the previous '2 tog' st over, m1, k12.

Row 41: K9, p3, p3 tog, p3, k2, m1, k2 tog, m1, k2 tog, k1.

Repeat rows 2–41 until desired length. Cast off.

Pattern 148

Cast on 7 sts.

Row 1: Sl 1, p3, m1, p2 tog, p1.

Row 2: P1, m1, p2 tog, p4.

Row 3: Sl 1, p3, m1, p2 tog, m1, (p1, k1) in last st.

Row 4: P1, m1, p2, m1, p2 tog, p4.

Row 5: Sl 1, p3, m1, p2 tog, m1, p3, (p1, k1) in last st.

Row 6: P1, m1, p2, m1, p2 tog, turn, m1, p2 tog, m1, p3, (p1, k1) in last st.
Row 7: Cast off 5 sts, m1, p2 tog, p1, m1, p2 tog, p4.
Row 8: Sl 1, p3, m1, p2 tog, (p1, k1) in next st, m1, p2 tog, m1, (p1, k1) in last st.
Row 9: P3, m1, p2 tog, turn, m1, p2 tog, m1, p2, m1, (p1, k1) in last st.
Row 10: Cast off 5 sts, m1, p2 tog, m1, p2, m1, p2 tog, p4.
Row 11: Sl 1, p3, m1, p2 tog, p2, (p1, k1) in next st, m1, p2 tog, m1, (p1, k1) in last st.
Row 12: P3, m1, p2 tog, turn, m1, p2 tog, m1, p2, m1, (p1, k1) in last st.
Row 13: Cast off 5 sts, m1, p2 tog, m1, p4, m1, p2 tog, p4.
Row 14: Sl 1, p3, m1, p2 tog, p4, (p1, k1) in next st, m1, p2 tog, m1, (p1, k1) in last st.
Row 15: P3, m1, p2 tog, turn, m1, p2 tog, m1, p2, m1, (p1, k1) in last st.
Row 16: Cast off 5 sts, m1, p2 tog, m1, p6, m1, p2 tog, p4.
Row 17: Sl 1, p3, m1, p2 tog, p6, (p1, k1) in next st, m1, p2 tog, m1, (p1, k1) in last st.
Row 18: P3, m1, p2 tog, turn, m1, p2 tog, m1, p2, m1, (p1, k1) in last st.
Row 19: Cast off 5 sts, m1, p2 tog, m1, p8, m1, p2 tog, p4.
Row 20: Sl 1, p3, m1, p2 tog, p8, (p1, k1) in next st, m1, p2 tog, m1, (p1, k1) in last st.
Row 21: P3, m1, p2 tog, turn, m1, p2 tog, m1, p2, m1, (p1, k1) in last st.
Row 22: Cast off 5 sts, m1, p2 tog, m1, sl 1, p2 tog, psso, p7, m1, p2 tog, p4.
Row 23: Sl 1, p3, m1, p2 tog, p6, p2 tog, p1, m1, p2 tog, m1, (p1, k1) in last st.
Row 24: P3, m1, p2 tog, turn, m1, p2 tog, m1, p2, m1, (p1, k1) in last st.
Row 25: Cast off 5 sts, m1, p2 tog, m1, sl 1, p2 tog, psso, p5, m1, p2 tog, p4.
Row 26: Sl 1, p3, m1, p2 tog, p4, p2 tog, p1, m1, p2 tog, m1, (p1, k1) in last st.
Row 27: P3, m1, p2 tog, turn, m1, p2 tog, m1, p2, m1, (p1, k1) in last st.
Row 28: Cast off 5 sts, m1, p2 tog, m1, sl 1, p2 tog, psso, p3, m1, p2 tog, p4.
Row 29: Sl 1, p3, m1, p2 tog, p2, p2 tog, p1, m1, p2 tog, m1, (p1, k1) in last st.
Row 30: P3, m1, p2 tog, turn, m1, p2 tog, m1, p2, m1, (p1, k1) in last st.
Row 31: Cast off 5 sts, m1, p2 tog, m1, sl 1, p2 tog, psso, p1, m1, p2 tog, p4.

Row 32: Sl 1, p3, m1, p2 tog, p2 tog, p1, m1, p2 tog, m1, (p1, k1) in last st.
Row 33: P3, m1, p2 tog, turn, m1, p2 tog, m1, p2, m1, (p1, k1) in last st.
Row 34: Cast off 5 sts, m1, p2 tog, p2 tog, m1, p2 tog, p4.
Row 35: Sl 1, p3, m1, p2 tog, p3 tog, p1.
Row 36: P2 tog, m1, p2 tog, p4.
Rows 37–48: Repeat rows 1 & 2 alternately 4 times.
Repeat rows 3–48 until desired length. Cast off.

Pattern 149

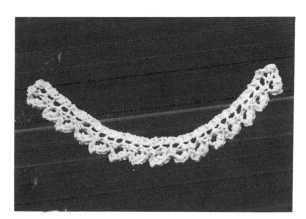

Cast on 4 sts.
Row 1: K1, p3.
Row 2: K1, m1, k1 tbl, m1, sl 1, k1, psso.
Row 3: K1, p2, (k1, p1, k1, p1) into next st, p1.
Row 4: Cast off 4 sts, k1, m1, sl 1, k1, psso.
Repeat rows 1–4 until desired length. Cast off.

Pattern 150

Pattern 151

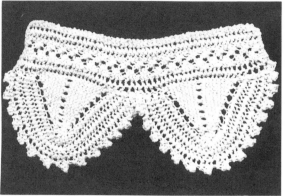

Cast on 31 sts.

Row 1: K.

Row 2: Sl 1, k3, m1, k2 tog, k1, m1, k1, k2 tog, p1, sl 1, k1, psso, k1, m1, p1, m1, k1, k2 tog, p1, sl 1, k1, psso, k1, m1, k3, m1, k2 tog, m2, k2 tog, m2, k2.

Row 3: K3, (p1, k2) twice, m1, k2 tog, p4, k1, (p3, k1) twice, p6, m1, k2 tog, k2.

Row 4: Sl 1, k3, m1, k2 tog, k1, m1, k1, k2 tog, p1, sl 1, k1, psso, k1, p1, k1, k2 tog, p2, sl 1, k1, psso, k1, m1, k3, m1, k2 tog, k7.

Row 5: K9, m1, k2 tog, p4, k1, (p2, k1) twice, p6, m1, k2 tog, k2.

Row 6: Sl 1, k3, m1, k2 tog, (k1, m1) twice, k2 tog, p1, sl 1, k1, psso, p1, k2 tog, p1, sl 1, k1, psso, m1, k1, m1, k3, m1, k2 tog, (m2, k2 tog) twice, m2, k3.

Row 7: K4, (p1, k2) 3 times, m1, k2 tog, p5, (k1, p1) twice, k1, p7, m1, k2 tog, k2.

Row 8: Sl 1, k3, m1, k2 tog, k1, m1, k3, m1, sl 1, k2 tog, psso, p1, sl 1, k2 tog, psso, (m1, k3) twice, m1, k2 tog, k11.

Row 9: Cast off 7 sts, k5, m1, k2 tog, p7, k1, p9, m1, k2 tog, k2.

Row 10: Sl 1, k3, m1, k2 tog, k1, m1, k5, m1, sl 1, k2 tog, psso, m1, k5, m1, k3, m1, k2 tog, k4.

Row 11: K6, m1, k2 tog, p19, m1, k2 tog, k2.

Repeat rows 2–11 until desired length. Cast off.

Cast on 14 sts.

Row 1: K.

Row 2: K2, yon, p2 tog, k1, k2 tog, yon, k3, yon, p2 tog, ([k1, p1] into next st) twice.

Row 3: K4, yon, p2 tog, k4, yon, k2 tog, yon, p2 tog, k2.

Row 4: K2, yon, p2 tog, k2, yon, k2 tog, k2, yon, p2 tog, (k1, p1) into next st, k2, (k1, p1) into next st.

Row 5: K3, yon, p2 tog, yon, k1, yon, p2 tog, k1, k2 tog, yon, k3, yon, p2 tog, k2.

Row 6: K2, yon, p2 tog, k4, yon, k2 tog, yon, p2 tog, (k1, p1) into next st, k1, yon, p2 tog, k2, (k1, p1) into last st.

Row 7: Cast off 3 sts, (yon, p2 tog) twice, yon, k1, yon, p2 tog, k2, yon, k2 tog, k2, yon, p2 tog, k2.

Row 8: K2, yon, p2 tog, k1, k2 tog, yon, k3, yon, p2 tog, (k1, p1) into next st, k1, (yon, p2 tog) twice, (k1, p1) into last st.

Row 9: K2, (yon, p2 tog) 3 times, yon, k1, yon, p2 tog, k4, yon, k2 tog, yon, p2 tog, k2.

Row 10: K2, yon, p2 tog, k2, yon, k2 tog, k2, yon, p2 tog, k1, (k1, p1) into next st, (yon, p2 tog) 3 times, k1, (k1, p1) into last st.

Row 11: *K3, (yon, p2 tog) 3 times, turn, (yon, p2 tog) 3 times, k2, (k1, p1) , turn, cast off 3 sts, (yon, p2 tog) 3 times, yon*, k3, yon, p2 tog, k1, k2 tog, yon, k3, yon, p2 tog, k2.

Row 12: K2, yon, p2 tog, k4, yon, k2 tog, yon, p2 tog, k3, (k1, p1) into next st, (yon, p2 tog) 3 times, (k1, p1) into last st

Row 13: *K2, (yon, p2 tog) 3 times, turn, (yon, p2 tog) 3 times, k1, (k1, p1), turn, k3, (yon, p2 tog) 3 times, yon*, k5, yon, p2 tog, k2, yon, k2 tog, k2, yon, p2 tog, k2.

Row 14: K2, yon, p2 tog, k1, k2 tog, yon, k3, yon,

p2 tog, k5, (k1, p1) into next st, (yon, p2 tog) 3 times, k2, (k1, p1) into last st.

Row 15: Cast off 3 sts, (yon, p2 tog) 3 times, turn, (yon, p2 tog) 3 times, (k1, p1) into next st, turn, k2, (yon, p2 tog) 3 times, *yon, k7, yon, p2 tog, k4, yon, k2 tog, yon, p2 tog, k2.

Row 16: K2, yon, p2 tog, k2, yon, k2 tog, k2, yon, p2 tog, k7, (k1, p1) into next st, (yon, p2 tog) 3 times, k1, (k1, p1) into last st.

Row 17: Repeat *—* row 11, k9, yon, p2 tog, k1, k2 tog, yon, k3, yon, p2 tog, k2.

Row 18: K2, yon, p2 tog, k4, yon, k2 tog, yon, p2 tog, k9, (k1, p1) into next st, (yon, p2 tog) 3 times, (k1, p1) into last st.

Row 19: Repeat *—* row 13, k11, yon, p2 tog, k2, yon, k2 tog, k2, yon, p2 tog, k2.

Row 20: K2, yon, p2 tog, k1, k2 tog, yon, k3, yon, p2 tog, k11, (k1, p1) into next st, (yon, p2 tog) 3 times, k2, (k1, p1) into last st.

Row 21: Repeat *—* row 15, yon, k13, yon, p2 tog, k4, yon, k2 tog, yon, p2 tog, k2.

Row 22: K2, yon, p2 tog, k2, yon, k2 tog, k2, yon, p2 tog, k13, (k1, p1) into next st, (yon, p2 tog) 3 times, k1, (k1, p1) into last st.

Row 23: Repeat *—* row 11, k15, yon, p2 tog, k1, k2 tog, yon, k3, yon, p2 tog, k2.

Row 24: K2, yon, p2 tog, k4, yon, k2 tog, yon, p2 tog, k15, (k1, p1) into next st, (yon, p2 tog) 3 times, (k1, p1) into last st.

Row 25: Repeat *—* row 13, k17, yon, p2 tog, k2, yon, k2 tog, k2, yon, p2 tog, k2.

Row 26: K2, yon, p2 tog, k1, k2 tog, yon, k3, yon, p2 tog, k1, (yon, k2 tog) 8 times, yon, (k1, p1) into next st, (yon, p2 tog) 3 times, k2, (k1, p1) into last st.

Row 27: **Repeat *—* row 15, turn (yon, p2 tog) 3 times, k1, (k1, p1) into next st, turn, k3, (yon, p2 tog) 3 times, yon, sl 1, k2 tog, psso**, k17, yon, p2 tog, k4, yon, k2 tog, yon, p2 tog, k2.

Row 28: K2, yon, p2 tog, k2, yon, k2 tog, k2, yon, p2 tog, k16, k2 tog, k1, (yon, p2 tog) 3 times, k2, (k1, p1) into last st.

Row 29: Repeat **—** row 27, k15, yon, p2 tog, k1, k2 tog, yon, k3, yon, p2 tog, k2.

Row 30: K2, yon, p2 tog, k4, yon, k2 tog, yon, p2 tog, k14, k2 tog, k1, (yon, p2 tog) 3 times, k2, (k1, p1) into last st.

Row 31: Repeat *—* row 15, yon, sl 1, k2 tog, psso, k13, yon, p2 tog, k2, yon, k2 tog, k2, yon, p2 tog, k2.

Row 32: K2, yon, p2 tog, k1, k2 tog, yon, k3, yon, p2 tog, k12, k2 tog, k1, (yon, p2 tog) 3 times, k1, (k1, p1) into last st.

Row 33: Repeat *—* row 11, sl 1, k2 tog, psso, k11, yon, p2 tog, k4, yon, k2 tog, yon, p2 tog, k2.

Row 34: K2, yon, p2 tog, k2, yon, k2 tog, k2, yon, p2 tog, k10, k2 tog, k1, (yon, p2 tog) 3 times, (k1, p1) into last st.

Row 35: Repeat *—* row 13, sl 1, k2 tog, psso, k9, yon, p2 tog, k1, k2 tog, yon, k3, yon, p2 tog, k2.

Row 36: K2, yon, p2 tog, k4, yon, k2 tog, yon, p2 tog, k8, k2 tog, k1, (yon, p2 tog) 3 times, k2, (k1, p1) into last st.

Row 37: Repeat *—* row 15, yon, sl 1, k2 tog, psso, k7, yon, p2 tog, k2, yon, k2 tog, k2, yon, p2 tog, k2.

Row 38: K2, yon, p2 tog, k1, k2 tog, yon, k3, yon, p2 tog, k6, k2 tog, k1, (yon, p2 tog) 3 times, k1, (k1, p1) into last st.

Row 39: Repeat *—* row 11, sl 1, k2 tog, psso, k5, yon, p2 tog, k4, yon, k2 tog, yon, p2 tog, k2.

Row 40: K2, yon, p2 tog, k2, yon, k2 tog, k2, yon, p2 tog, k4, k2 tog, k1, (yon, p2 tog) 3 times, (k1, p1) into last st.

Row 41: Repeat *—* row 13, sl 1, k2 tog, psso, k3, yon, p2 tog, k1, k2 tog, yon, k3, yon, p2 tog, k2.

Row 42: K2, yon, p2 tog, k4, yon, k2 tog, yon, p2 tog, k2, k2 tog, k1, (yon, p2 tog) 3 times, k2, (k1, p1) into last st.

Row 43: Repeat *—* row 15, yon, sl 1, k2 tog, psso, k1, yon, p2 tog, k2, yon, k2 tog, k2, yon, p2 tog, k2.

Row 44: K2, yon, p2 tog, k1, k2 tog, yon, k3, yon, p2 tog, k2 tog, k1, (yon, p2 tog) 3 times, k1, (k1, p1) into last st.

Row 45: K3, (yon, p2 tog) 3 times, yon, k2 tog, yon, p2 tog, k4, yon, k2 tog, yon, p2 tog, k2.

Row 46: K2, yon, p2 tog, k2, yon, k2 tog, k2, yon, p2 tog, k2 tog, (yon, p2 tog) 3 times, k2, (k1, p1) into last st.

Row 47: Cast off 3 sts, (yon, p2 tog) 3 times, k1, yon, p2 tog, k1, k2 tog, yon, k3, yon, p2 tog, k2.

Row 48: K2, yon, p2 tog, k4, yon, k2 tog, yon, p2 tog, sl 1, k2 tog, psso, (yon, p2 tog) twice, (k1, p1) into last st.

Row 49: K2, (yon, p2 tog) twice, k1, yon, p2 tog, k2, yon, k2 tog, k2, yon, p2 tog, k2.

Row 50: K2, yon, p2 tog, k1, k2 tog, yon, k3, yon, p2 tog, sl 1, k2 tog, psso, yon, p2 tog, k1, (k1, p1) into last st.

Row 51: K3, yon, p2 tog, k1, yon, p2 tog, k4, yon, k2 tog, yon, p2 tog, k2.

Row 52: K2, yon, p2 tog, k2, yon, k2 tog, k2, yon, p2 tog, sl 1, k2 tog, psso, k2, (k1, p1) into last st.

Row 53: Cast off 3 sts, k1, yon, p2 tog, k1, k2 tog, yon, k3, yon, p2 tog, k2.

Row 54: K2, yon, p2 tog, k4, yon, k2 tog, yon, p2 tog, k2.
Row 55: K2, yon, p2 tog, k2, yon, k2 tog, k2, yon, p2 tog, k2.
Repeat rows 2–55 until desired length. Cast off.

Pattern 152

Cast on 11 sts.
Row 1: K.
Row 2: K3, (m1, sl 1, k1, psso, k1) twice, m2, k1, m2, k1.
Row 3: (K2, p1) 4 times, k3.
Row 4: K3, m1, sl 1, k1, psso, k1, m1, sl 1, k1, psso, k7.
Row 5: Cast off 4 sts, k3, p1, k2, p1, k3.
Repeat rows 2–5 until desired length. Cast off.

Cast on 21 sts.
Row 1: K.
Row 2: Sl 1, k1, k2 tog, m2, k2 tog, k2 tog, m2, k2 tog, k2, m2, k2 tog, k7.
Row 3: K9, p1, k4, p1, k3, p1, k3.
Row 4: Sl 1, k1, k2 tog, m2, k2 tog, k2 tog, m2, k2 tog, k1, mb [*see below*], k2, m2, k2 tog, k6.
Row 5: K8, p1, k6, p1, k3, p1, k3.
Row 6: Sl 1, k1, k2 tog, m2, k2 tog, k2 tog, m2, k2 tog, k3, mb, k2, m2, k2 tog, k5.
Row 7: K7, p1, k8, p1, k3, p1, k3.
Row 8: Sl 1, k1, k2 tog, m2, k2 tog, k2 tog, m2, k2 tog, k5, mb, k2, m2, k2 tog, k4.
Row 9: K6, p1, k10, p1, k3, p1, k3.
Row 10: Sl 1, k1, k2 tog, m2, k2 tog, k2 tog, m2, k2 tog, k7, mb, k2, m2, k2 tog, k3.
Row 11: K5, p1, k12, p1, k3, p1, k3.
Row 12: Sl 1, k1, k2 tog, m2, k2 tog, k2 tog, m2, k2 tog, k9, mb, k2, m2, k2 tog, k2.
Row 13: K4, p1, k14, p1, k3, p1, k3.
Row 14: Sl 1, k1, k2 tog, m2, k2 tog, k2 tog, m2, k2 tog, k11, mb, k2, m2, k2 tog, k1.
Row 15: K3, p1, k16, p1, k3, p1, k3.
Row 16: Sl 1, k1, k2 tog, m2, k2 tog, k2 tog, m2, k2 tog, k18.
Row 17: Cast off 7 sts, k12, p1, k3, p1, k3.
Repeat rows 2–17 until desired lenght. Cast off.

mb thus: cast on 3 sts, k next st off L.H. needle, turn, sl 1, k3, turn, sl 1, p3, turn, sl 1, k3, turn, sl 1, k3 tog, pass sl st over 'k3 tog' sts.

Pattern 154

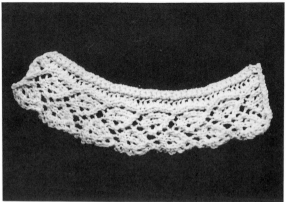

Cast on 15 sts.

Pattern 153

Row 1: K1, m1, k3, m1, sl 1, k1, psso, k1, k2 tog, m1, k2 tog, k1, m1, k2 tog, k1.

Row 2: K2, m1, k2 tog, p to end.

Row 3: K1, m1, k2 tog, m1, k1, m1, sl 1, k1, psso, m1, sl 1, k2 tog, psso, m1, k2 tog, k1, m1, k2 tog, k1.

Row 4: K2, m1, k2 tog, p to end.

Row 5: Sl 1, k1, psso, m1, sl 1, k1, psso, m1, k1, m1, k2 tog, m1, k1, m1, sl 1, k2 tog, psso, k1, m1, k2 tog, k1.

Row 6: K2, m1, k2 tog, p to end.

Row 7: Sl 1, k1, psso, m1, sl 1, k1, psso, k1, k2 tog, m1, k3, m1, k2, m1, k2 tog, k1.

Row 8: K2, m1, k2 tog, p to end.

Row 9: Sl 1, k1, psso, m1, sl 1, k2 tog, psso, m1, k2 tog, m1, k1, m1, sl 1, k1, psso, m1, k2, m1, k2 tog, k1.

Row 10: K2, m1, k2 tog, p to end.

Row 11: Sl 1, k2 tog, psso, m1, k1, m1, sl 1, k1, psso, m1, k1, m1, k2 tog, m1, k2 tog, k1, m1, k2 tog, k1.

Row 12: K2, m1, k2 tog, p to end.

Repeat rows 1–12 until desired length. Cast off.

Row 8: K4, (p1, k3) twice, p1, k5, (m1, p2 tog) twice, k1.

Row 9: K3, (m1, p2 tog) twice, k2 tog, (m2, k2 tog, k2 tog) 3 times, m2, k2 tog.

Row 10: K2, (p1, k3) 4 times, (m1, p2 tog) twice, k1.

Row 11: K3, (m1, p2 tog) twice, k2, k2 tog, (m2, k2 tog, k2 tog) 3 times.

Row 12: K2 tog, k1, (p1, k3) twice, p1, k5, (m1, p2 tog) twice, k1.

Row 13: K3, (m1, p2 tog) twice, k4, k2 tog, (m2, k2 tog, k2 tog) twice.

Row 14: K2 tog, k1, p1, k3, p1, k7 (m1, p2 tog) twice, k1.

Row 15: K3, (m1, p2 tog) twice, k6, k2 tog, m2, (k2 tog) twice.

Row 16: K2 tog, k1, p1, k9, (m1, p2 tog) twice, k1.

Repeat rows 1–16 until desired length. Cast off.

Pattern 156

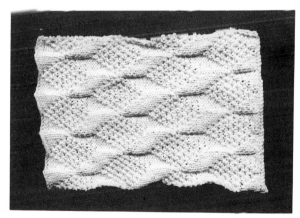

Pattern 155

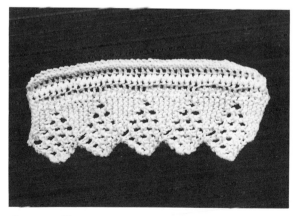

Cast on 17 sts.

Row 1: K3, (m1, p2 tog) twice, k10.

Row 2: K12, (m1, p2 tog) twice, k1.

Row 3: K3, (m1, p2 tog) twice, k6, k2 tog, m2, k1, inc 1 k-wise in last st.

Row 4: K4, p1, k9, (m1, p2 tog) twice, k1.

Row 5: K3, (m1, p2 tog) twice, k4, k2 tog, m2, (k2 tog) twice, m2, k1, inc 1 in last st.

Row 6: K4, p1, k3, p1, k7, (m1, p2 tog) twice, k1.

Row 7: K3, (m1, p2 tog) twice, k2, k2 tog, (m2, k2 tog, k2 tog) twice, m2, k1, inc 1 in last st.

Cast on a multiple of 12 sts.

Rows 1 & 2: *K6, p6*, repeat *—* to end.

Rows 3 & 4: *P1, k5, p5, k1*, repeat *—* to end.

Rows 5 & 6: *K1, p1, k4, p4, k1, p1*, repeat *—* to end.

Rows 7 & 8: *P1, k1, p1, k3, p3, k1, p1, k1*, repeat *—* to end.

Rows 9 & 10: *(K1, p1) twice, k2, p2, (k1, p1) twice*, repeat *—* to end.

Rows 11 & 12: *P1, k1*, repeat *—* to end.

Rows 13 & 14: *K1, p1*, repeat *—* to end.

Rows 15 & 16: *(P1, k1) twice, p2, k2, (p1, k1) twice*, repeat *—* to end.

Rows 17 & 18: *K1, p1, k1, p3, k3, p1, k1, p1*, repeat *—* to end.

Rows 19 & 20: *P1, k1, p4, k4, p1, k1*, repeat *—* to end.

Rows 21 & 22: *K1, p5, k5, p1*, repeat *—* to end.

Rows 23 & 24: *P6, k6*, repeat *—* to end.

Rows 25 & 26: *P5, k1, p1, k5*, repeat *—* to end.

Rows 27 & 28: *P4, (k1, p1) twice, k4*, repeat *—* to end.

Rows 29 & 30: *P3, (k1, p1) 3 times, k3*, repeat *—* to end.

Rows 31 & 32: *P2, (k1, p1) 4 times, k2*, repeat *—* to end.

Rows 33 & 34: *P1, k1*, repeat *—* to end.

Rows 35 & 36: *K1, p1*, repeat *—* to end.

Rows 37 & 38: *K2, (p1, k1) 4 times, p2*, repeat *—* to end.

Rows 39 & 40: *K3, (p1, k1) 3 times, p3*, repeat *—* to end.

Rows 41 & 42: *K4, (p1, k1) twice, p4*, repeat *—* to end.

Rows 43 & 44: *K5, p1, k1, p5*, repeat *—* to end.

Repeat rows 1–44 until desired length. Cast off.

Pattern 157

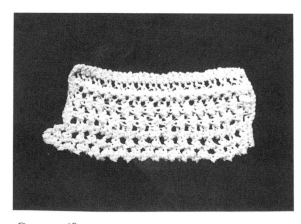

Cast on 19 sts.

Row 1: K.

Row 2: Sl 1, k1, m1, k2 tog, k3, k2 tog, m2, k2 tog, m1, k2 tog, m1, k1.

Row 3: K6, p1 (in second half of 'm2' st of previous row), k4, p1, k8.

Row 4: Sl 1, k1, m1, k2 tog, k1, k2 tog, m2, k2 tog, m2, k2 tog, k2, m1, k2 tog, m1, k1.

Row 5: K10, p1, k3, p1, k6.

Row 6: Sl 1, k1, m1, k2 tog, k3, k2 tog, m2, k2 tog, k5, m1, k2 tog, m1, k2 tog, m1, k1.

Row 7: K13, p1, k8.

Row 8: Sl 1, k1, m1, k2 tog, k1, k2 tog, m2, k2 tog, k2 tog, m2, sl 1, k2 tog, psso, m2, k2 tog, k1, m1, k2 tog, m1, k2 tog, m1, k1.

Row 9: K9, p1, k2, p1, k3, p1, k6.

Row 10: Sl 1, k1, m1, k2 tog, k3, k2 tog, m2, k2 tog, k7, m1, k2 tog, m1, k2 tog, m1, k1.

Row 11: Cast off 5 sts, k9, p1, k8.

Row 12: Sl 1, k1, m1, k2, k15.

Repeat rows 1–12 until desired length. Cast off.

Pattern 158

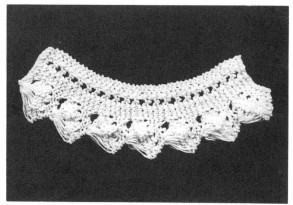

Cast on 13 sts.

Row 1: K.

Row 2: Sl 1, k12.

Row 3: Sl 1, k1, k2 tog, m2, k2 tog, k7.

Row 4: Sl 1, k8, p1, k3.

Row 5: Sl 1, k12.

Row 6: Sl 1, k12.

Row 7: Sl 1, k1, k2 tog, m2, k2 tog, k2, m2, (k1, m2) 3 times, k2.

Row 8: Sl 1, (k2, p1) 4 times, k4, p1, k3.

Row 9: Sl 1, k20.

Row 10: Sl 1, k20.

Row 11: Sl 1, k1, k2 tog, m2, k2 tog, k15.

Row 12: K12 wrapping yrn 3 times for each st, m3, k5, p1, k3.

Row 13: Sl 1, k9, p1, k1, sl the remaining 12 sts to R.H. needle dropping extra wraps to make 12 long loops, sl these 12 long loops back to L.H. needle and k them all together as one st.

Repeat rows 2–13 until desired length. Cast off.

Pattern 159

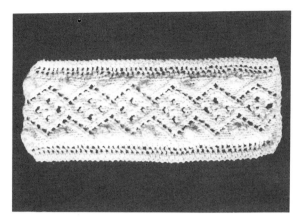

mb thus: (k1, p1, k1, p1) into next st, turn, k4, turn, p4, turn, (k2 tog) twice, turn, sl 1, k1, psso.

Cast on 24 sts.

Row 1: Sl 1, k2, m1, k2 tog, k1, mb [*see below*], k3, m1, sl 1, k1, psso, k2 tog, m1, k3, mb, k3, m1, k2 tog, k1.

Row 2: Sl 1, k2, m1, k2 tog, p14, k2, m1, k2 tog, k1.

Row 3: Sl 1, k2, m1, k2 tog, k3, k2 tog, m1, k4, m1, sl 1, k1, psso, k5, m1, k2 tog, k1.

Row 4: Sl 1, k2, m1, k2 tog, p14, k2, m1, k2 tog, k1.

Row 5: Sl 1, k2, m1, k2 tog, k2, k2 tog, m1, k1, k2 tog, m2, sl 1, k1, psso, k1, m1, sl 1, k1, psso, k4, m1, k2 tog, k1.

Row 6: Sl 1, k2, m1, k2 tog, p6, k1, p7, k2, m1, k2 tog, k1.

Row 7: Sl 1, k2, m1, k2 tog, k1, k2 tog, m1, k8, m1, sl 1, k1, psso, k3, m1, k2 tog, k1.

Row 8: Sl 1, k2, m1, k2 tog, p14, k2, m1, k2 tog, k1.

Row 9: Sl 1, k2, m1, (k2 tog) twice, m1, k1, k2 tog, m2, sl 1, k1, psso, k2 tog, m2, sl 1, k1, psso, k1, m1, sl 1, k1, psso, k2, m1, k2 tog, k1.

Row 10: Sl 1, k2, m1, k2 tog, p4, k1, p3, k1, p5, k2, m1, k2 tog, k1.

Row 11: Sl 1, k2, m1, k2 tog, k2, m1, sl 1, k1, psso, k6, k2 tog, m1, k4, m1, k2 tog, k1.

Row 12: Sl 1, k2, m1, k2 tog, p14, k2, m1, k2 tog, k1.

Row 13: Sl 1, k2, m1, k2 tog, k3, m1, sl 1, k1, psso, k2 tog, m2, sl 1, k1, psso, k2 tog, m1, k5, m1, k2 tog, k1.

Row 14: Sl 1, k2, m1, k2 tog, p6, k1, p7, k2, m1, k2 tog, k1.

Row 15: Sl 1, k2, m1, k2 tog, k4, m1, sl 1, k1, psso, k2, k2 tog, m1, k6, m1, k2 tog, k1.

Row 16: Sl 1, k2, m1, k2 tog, p14, k2, m1, k2 tog, k1.

Repeat rows 1–16 until desired length. Cast off.

Pattern 160

Cast on 17 sts.

Row 1: K.

Row 2: Sl 1, k1, yon, k2 tog, yon, k1, yon, (k2 tog) twice, (yon) twice, (k2 tog) twice, yon, k1, yon, k3.

Row 3: Sl 1, k8, p1, k9.

Row 4: Sl 1, k1, yon, k2 tog, yon, k2, yon, k2 tog, k4, k2 tog, yon, k2, yon, k3.

Row 5: Sl 1, k20.

Row 6: Sl 1, k1, yon, k2 tog, yon, k3, yon, k2 tog, k4, k2 tog, (yon, k3) twice.

Row 7: Sl 1, k22.

Row 8: Sl 1, k7, yon, (k2 tog) twice, (yon) twice, (k2 tog) twice, yon, k1, yon, k2 tog, k1, yon, k3.

Row 9: Sl 1, k11, p1, k11.

Row 10: Cast off 3 sts, k4, yon, k2 tog, k4, k2 tog, yon, k2, yon, k2 tog, k1, yon, k3.

Row 11: Sl 1, k21.

Row 12: Sl 1, k1, yon, k2 tog, yon, k1, yon, k2 tog, k4, k2 tog, yon, k3, yon, k2 tog, k1, yon, k3.

Row 13: Sl 1, k23.

Row 14: Sl 1, k1, yon, k2 tog, yon, k2, yon, (k2 tog) twice, (yon) twice, (k2 tog) twice, yon, k1, (yon, k2 tog, k1) twice, yon, k3.

Row 15: Sl 1, k14, p1, k10.

Row 16: Sl 1, k1, yon, k2 tog, yon, k3, yon, k2 tog, k4, k2 tog, yon, k2, (yon, k2 tog, k1) twice, yon, k3.

Row 17: Sl 1, k27.

Row 18: Sl 1, k7, yon, k2 tog, k4, k2 tog, yon, k3, (yon, k2 tog, k1) twice, yon, k3.

Row 19: Sl 1, k28.

Row 20: Cast off 3 sts, k4, yon, (k2 tog) twice,

(yon) twice, (k2 tog) twice, yon, k1, (yon, k2 tog, k1) 3 times, yon, k3.

Row 21: Sl 1, k17, p1, k8.

Row 22: Sl 1, k1, yon, k2 tog, yon, k1, yon, k2 tog, k4, k2 tog, yon, k2, (yon, k2 tog, k1) 3 times, yon, k3.

Row 23: Sl 1, k28.

Row 24: Sl 1, k1, yon, k2 tog, yon, k2, yon, k2 tog, k4, k2 tog, yon, k3, (yon, k2 tog, k1) 3 times, yon, k3.

Row 25: Sl 1, k30.

Row 26: Sl 1, k1, yon, k2 tog, yon, k3, yon, (k2 tog) twice, (yon) twice, (k2 tog) twice, yon, k1, (yon, k2 tog, k1) 4 times, yon, k3.

Row 27: Sl 1, k20, p1, k11.

Row 28: Sl 1, k7, yon, k2 tog, k4, k2 tog, yon, k2, (yon, k2 tog, k1) 4 times, yon, k3.

Row 29: Sl 1, k33.

Row 30: Cast off 3 sts, k4, yon, k2 tog, k4, k2 tog, yon, k18.

Row 31: Cast off 14 sts loosely, k16.

Repeat rows 2–31 until desired length. Cast off.

Pattern 161

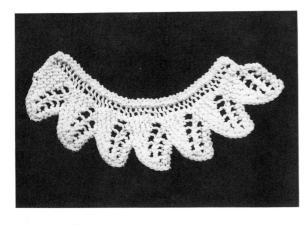

Cast on 10 sts.

Row 1: K.

Row 2: Sl 1, k2, yon, k2 tog, (yon) twice, k2 tog, (yon) twice, k2 tog, k1.

Row 3: Sl 1, (k2, p1) twice, k2, yon, k2 tog, k1.

Row 4: Sl 1, k2, yon, k2 tog, k2, (yon) twice, k2 tog, (yon) twice, k2 tog, k1.

Row 5: Sl 1, (k2, p1) twice, k4, yon, k2 tog, k1.

Row 6: Sl 1, k2, yon, k2 tog, k4, (yon) twice, k2 tog, (yon) twice, k2 tog, k1.

Row 7: Sl 1, (k2, p1) twice, k6, yon, k2 tog, k1.

Row 8: Sl 1, k2, yon, k2 tog, k6, (yon) twice, k2 tog, (yon) twice, k2 tog, k1.

Row 9: Sl 1, (k2, p1) twice, k8, yon, k2 tog, k1.

Row 10: Sl 1, k2, yon, k2 tog, k8, (yon) twice, k2 tog, (yon) twice, k2 tog, k1.

Row 11: Sl 1, (k2, p1) twice, k10, yon, k2 tog, k1.

Row 12: Sl 1, k2, yon, k2 tog, k15.

Row 13: Cast off 10 sts, k6, yon, k2 tog, k1.

Repeat rows 2–13 until desired length. Cast off.

Pattern 162

Cast on 42 sts. K2 sts at each end, these are edge sts and not referred to in pattern.

Row 1: P5, *k2 tog, k3, m1, k1, m1, k3, sl 1, k1, psso*, p9, repeat *—*, p4.

Row 2: K4, p11, k9, p11, k5.

Row 3: P4, *k2 tog, k3, m1, k3, m1, k3, sl 1, k1, psso*, p7, repeat *—*, p3.

Row 4: K3, p13, k7, p13, k4.

Row 5: P3, *k2 tog, k3, m1, k5, m1, k3, sl 1, k1, psso*, p5, repeat *—*, p2.

Row 6: K2, p15, k5, p15, k3.

Row 7: P2, *k2 tog, k3, m1, k7, m1, k3, sl 1, k1, psso*, p3, repeat *—*, p1.

Row 8: K1, p17, k3, p17, k2.

Row 9: P1, *k2 tog, k3, m1, k9, m1, k3, sl 1, k1, psso*, p1, repeat *—*.

Row 10: P19, k to end.

Repeat rows 1–10 until desired length. Cast off.

Pattern 163

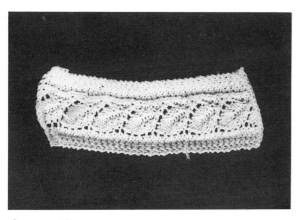

Cast on 18 sts.

Row 1: P.

Row 2: Sl 1, k2, p2, yon, k5, yon, sl 1, k1, psso, k1 tbl, p2, k3.

Row 3 and every even row: Sl 1 k-wise, k4, purl the p sts and k the k sts and p the yons of previous row, k5.

Row 4: Sl 1, k2, p2, yon, k1, sl 1, k1, psso, p1, k2 tog, k1, yon, p1, k1 tbl, p2, k3.

Row 6: Sl 1, k2, p2, yon, k1, sl 1, k1, psso, p1, k2 tog, k1, p1, k1 tbl, p2, k3

Row 8: Sl 1, k2, p2, yon, k1, yon, sl 1, k1, psso, p1, k2 tog, p1, k1 tbl, p2, k3.

Row 10: Sl 1, k2, p2, yon, k3, yon, sl 1, k2 tog, psso, p1, k1 tbl, p2, k3.

Row 11: Repeat row 2.

Repeat rows 2–11 until desired length. Cast off.

Cast on 15 sts.

Row 1: K.

Row 2: K2, yon, p2 tog, k2, (yon) twice, k2 tog, yon, k1, yon, k2 tog tbl, (yon) twice, k2, (yon) twice, k2.

Row 3: K3, p1, k3, p7, k4, yon, p2 tog, k1.

Row 4: K2, yon, p2 tog, k2 (yon) twice, k2 tog, k2, yon, k1, yon, k2, k2 tog tbl, (yon) twice, (yon) twice, k2.

Row 5: K3, p1, k5, p11, k4, yon, p2 tog, k1.

Row 6: K2, yon, p2 tog, k2, (yon) twice, k2 tog, k4, yon, k1, yon, k4, k2 tog tbl, (yon) twice, k6, (yon) twice, k2.

Row 7: K3, p1, k7, p15, k4, yon, p2 tog, k1.

Row 8: K2, yon, p2 tog, k3, (yon) twice, k3 tog tbl, k9, k3 tog, (yon) twice, k11.

Row 9: Cast off 8 sts, k3, p13, k5, yon, p2 tog, k1.

Row 10: K2, yon, p2 tog, k4, (yon) twice, k3 tog tbl, k7, k3 tog, (yon) twice, k2, (yon) twice, k2.

Row 11: K3, p1, k3, p11, k6, yon, p2 tog, k1.

Row 12: K2, yon, p2 tog, k5, (yon) twice, k3 tog tbl, k5, k3 tog, (yon) twice, k5, (yon) twice, k2.

Row 13: K3, p1, k6, p9, k7, yon, p2 tog, k1.

Row 14: K2, yon, p2 tog, k6, (yon) twice, k3 tog tbl, k3, k3 tog, (yon) twice, k8, (yon) twice, k2.

Row 15: K3, p1, k9, p7, k8, yon, p2 tog, k1.

Row 16: K2, yon, p2 tog, k7, k3 tog tbl, k4 tog, pass the 'k3 tog tbl' st over the 'k4 tog' st, k13.

Row 17: Cast off 10 sts, k2, p1, k8, yon, p2 tog, k1.

Repeat rows 2–17 until desired length. Cast off.

Pattern 165

Cast on a multiple of 15 sts, plus 14, for required width of edging.

Pattern 164

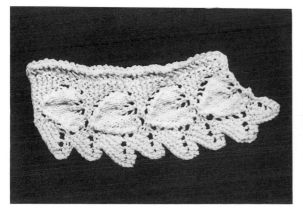

Row 1: (P2, k2) 3 times, p2, *pick up thread betwen st just worked and next st and k into b of this thread thus making one st [= m1 for this pattern only], p1, m1, p2, (k2, p2) 3 times*, repeat *—* to end.

Row 2: (K2, p2) 3 times, k2, *p1, k1, p1, k2 (p2, k2) 3 times*, repeat *—* to end.

Row 3: (P2, k2) 3 times, p2, *m1, p1, k1, p1, m1, p2, (k2, p2) 3 times*, repeat *—* to end.

Row 4: (K2, p2) 3 times, k2, *(p1, k1) twice, p1, k2, (p2, k2) 3 times*, repeat *—* to end.

Row 5: (P2, k2) 3 times, p2, *m1, (p1, k1) twice, p1, m1, p2, (k2, p2) 3 times, repeat *—* to end.

Row 6: (K2, p2) 3 times, k2, *(p1, k1) 3 times, p1, k2, (p2, k2) 3 times*, repeat *—* to end.

Row 7: (P2, k2) 3 times, p2, *m1, (p1, k1) 3 times, p1, m1, p2, (k2, p2) 3 times*, repeat *—* to end.

Row 8: (K2, p2) 3 times, k2, *(p1, k1) 4 times, p1, k2, (p2, k2) 3 times*, repeat *—* to end.

Row 9: (P2, k2) 3 times, p2, *m1, (p1, k1) 4 times, p1, m1, p2, (k2, p2) 3 times, repeat *—*.

Row 10: *K1, inc 1 in next st, sl 10 wyib, pass the first of the 10 sl sts over the other 9 sts, k2, (p1, k1) 5 times*, p1, repeat *—*, k1, inc 1 k-wise in next st, sl 10 wyib, pass 1st sl st over the other 9 sts, k2.

Row 11: (P2, k2) 3 times, p2, *sl 1, k1, psso, (p1, k1) 3 times, p1, k2 tog, p2, (k2, p2) 3 times*, repeat *—* to end.

Row 12: (K2, p2) 3 times, k2, *(p1, k1) 4 times, p1, k2, (p2, k2) 3 times*, repeat *—* to end.

Row 13: (P2, k2) 3 times, p2, sl 1, k1, psso, (p1, k1) twice, p1, k2 tog, p2, (k2, p2) 3 times, repeat *—*.

Row 14: (K2, p2) 3 times, k2, *(p1, k1) 3 times, p1, k2, (p2, k2) 3 times*, repeat *—* to end.

Row 15: (P2, k2) 3 times, p2, sl 1, k1, psso, p1, k1, p1, k2 tog, p2, (k2, p2) 3 times*, repeat *—* to end.

Row 16: (K2, p2) 3 times, k2, *(p1, k1) twice, p1, k2, (p2, k2) 3 times*, repeat *—* to end.

Row 17: (P2, k2) 3 times, p2, *sl 1, k1, psso, p1, k2 tog*, repeat *—* to end.

Row 18: (K2, p2) 3 times, k2, *p1, k1, p1, k2, (p2, k2) 3 times, repeat *—* to end.

Row 19: (P2, k2) 3 times, p2, *sl 1, k2 tog, psso, p2, (k2, p2) 3 times*, repeat *—* to end.

Row 20· (K2, p2) 3 times, k2, *p1, k2, (p2, k2) 3 times*, repeat *—* to end.

Repeat rows 1–20 until desired length. Cast off.

Pattern 166

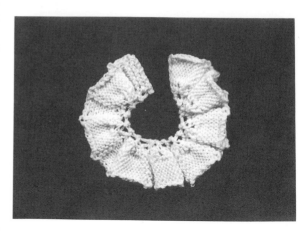

Cast on 9 sts.
Row 1: K.
Row 2: K2, p7.
Row 3: K7, turn, p7.
Row 4: K7, turn, p7.
Row 5: K8, turn, k1, p7.
Row 6: K8, turn, k1, p7.
Row 7: P7, k2.
Row 8: K.
Row 9: P7, turn, k7.
Row 10: P7, turn, k7.
Row 11: P7, k1, turn p8.
Row 12: P7, k1, turn, p8.
Repeat rows 1–12 until desired length. Cast off.

Pattern 167

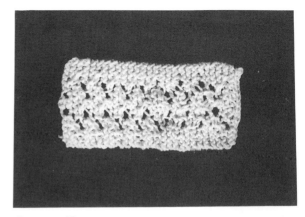

Cast on 15 sts.

Row 1: K6, yon, sl 1, k2 tog, psso, yon, k6.
Row 2: K4, p2 tog tbl, yon, k3, yon, p2 tog, k4.
Row 3: K3, k2 tog, yon, k5, yon, sl 1, k1, psso, k3.
Row 4: K2, p2 tog tbl, yon, k7, yon, p2 tog, k2.
Row 5: K4, yon, sl 1, k1, psso, k3, k2 tog, yon, k4.
Row 6: K5, yon, p2 tog, k1, p2 tog tbl, yon, k5.
Repeat rows 1–6 until desired length. Cast off.

Pattern 168

Cast on 28 sts.
Row 1: P2, k2, m1, k2 tog, p2, k3, m1, k2 tog, k4, m1, k2 tog, k1, p2, k2, m1, k2 tog, p2.
Row 2: K2, p2, m1, p2 tog, k2, p3, m1, p2 tog, p4, m1, p2 tog, p1, k2, p2, m1, p2 tog, k2.
Row 3: P2, k2, m1, k2 tog, p2, k3, m1, k2 tog, k4, m1, k2 tog, k1, p2, k2, m1, k2 tog, p2.
Row 4: K2, p2, m1, p2 tog, k2, p3, m1, p2 tog, p4, m1, p2 tog, p1, k2, p2, m1, p2 tog, k2.
Row 5: P2, *sl 2 onto dpn and leave at f of work to end*, k2, p2, k3, m1, k2 tog, k4, m1, k2 tog, k1, p2, repeat *—*, k2, p2.
Row 6: K2, p2 from dpn, p2, k2, p3, m1, p2 tog, p4, m1, p2 tog, p1, k2, p2 from dpn, p2, k2.
Rows 7–16: Repeat rows 1 & 2 five times.
Row 17: P2, repeat *—* row 5, k2, p2, k3, m1, k2 tog, k4, m1, k2 tog, k1, p2, repeat *—* row 5, k2, p2.
Row 18: K2, p2 from dpn, p2, k2, p3, m1, p2 tog, p4, m1, p2 tog, p1, k2, p2 from dpn, p2, k2.
Row 19: P2, k2, m1, k2 tog, p2, k3, m1, k2 tog, k4, m1, k2 tog, k1, p2, k2, m1, k2 tog, p2.
Row 20: K2, p2, m1, p2 tog, k2, p3, m1, p2 tog, p4, m1, p2 tog, p1, k2, p2, m1, p2 tog, k2.
Row 21: P2, k2, m1, k2 tog, p2, k12, p2, k2, m1, k2 tog, p2.

Row 22: K2, p2, m1, p2 tog, k2, p12, k2, p2, m1, p2 tog, k2.
Row 23: P2, k2, m1, k2 tog, p2, *sl 4 onto dpn and leave at f of work*, k8, p2, k2, m1, k2 tog, p2.
Row 24: K2, p2, m1, p2 tog, k2, p4, p4 from dpn, p4, k2, p2, m1, p2 tog, k2.
Row 25: P2, k2, m1, k2 tog, p2, k12, p2, k2, m1, k2 tog, p2.
Row 26: K2, p2, m1, p2 tog, k2, p12, k2, p2, m1, p2 tog, k2.
Row 27: P2, k2, m1, k2 tog, p2, k12, p2, k2, m1, k2 tog, p2.
Row 28: K2, p2, m1, p2 tog, k2, p12, k2, p2, m1, p2 tog, k2.
Row 29: P2, repeat *—* row 5, k2, p2, k8, repeat *—* row 23, p2, repeat *—* row 5, k2, p2.
Row 30: K2, p2 from dpn, p2, k2, p4, p4 from dpn, p4, k2, p2 from dpn, p2, k2.
Row 31: P2, k2, m1, k2 tog, p2, k12, p2, k2, m1, k2 tog, p2.
Row 32: K2, p2, m1, p2 tog, k2, p12, k2, p2, m1, p2 tog, k2.
Row 33: P2, k2, m1, k2 tog, p2, repeat *—* row 23, k8, p2, k2, m1, k2 tog, p2.
Row 34: K2, p2, m1, p2 tog, k2, p4, p4 from dpn, p4, k2, p2, m1, p2 tog, k2.
Row 35: P2, k2, m1, k2 tog, p2, k12, p2, k2, m1, k2 tog, p2.
Row 36: K2, p2, m1, p2 tog, k2, p12, k2, p2, m1, p2 tog, k2.
Row 37: P2, k2, m1, k2 tog, p2, k8, repeat *—* row 23, p2, k2, m1, k2 tog, p2.
Row 38: K2, p2, m1, p2 tog, k2, p4, p4 from dpn, p4, k2, p2, m1, p2 tog, k2.
Row 39: P2, repeat *—* row 5, k2, p2, k12, p2, repeat *—* row 5, k2, p2.
Row 40: K2, p2 from dpn, p2, k2, p12, k2, p2 from dpn, p2, k2.
Row 41: P2, k2, m1, k2 tog, p2, k12, p2, k2, m1, k2 tog, p2.
Row 42: K2, p2, m1, p2 tog, k2, p12, k2, p2, m1, p2 tog, k2.
Row 43: P2, k2, m1, k2 tog, p2, repeat *—* row 23, k8, p2, k2, m1, k2 tog, p2.
Row 44: K2, p2, m1, p2 tog, k2, p4, p4 from dpn, p4, k2, p2, m1, p2 tog, k2.
Row 45: P2, k2, m1, k2 tog, p2, k12, p2, k2, m1, k2 tog, p2.
Row 46: K2, p2, m1, p2 tog, k2, p12, k2, p2, m1, p2 tog, k2.
Row 47: P2, k2, m1, k2 tog, p2, k12, p2, k2, m1, k2 tog, p2.
Row 48: K2, p2, m1, p2 tog, k2, p12, k2, p2, m1, p2 tog, k2.

Row 49: P2, k2, m1, k2 tog, p2, k8, repeat *—* row 23, p2, k2, m1, k2 tog, p2.

Row 50: K2, p2, m1, p2 tog, k2, p4, p4 from dpn, p4, k2, p2, m1, p2 tog, k2.

Row 51: P2, repeat *—* row 5, k2, p2, k12, p2, repeat *—* row 5, k2, p2.

Row 52: K2, p2 from dpn, p2, k2, p12, k2, p2 from dpn, p2, k2.

Row 53: P2, k2, m1, k2 tog, p2, k12, p2, k2, m1, k2 tog, p2.

Row 54: K2, p2, m1, p2 tog, k2, p12, k2, p2, m1, p2 tog, k2.

Row 55: P2, k2, m1, k2 tog, p2, p12, p2, k2, m1, k2 tog, p2.

Row 56: K2, p2, m1, p2 tog, k2, p12, k2, p2, m1, p2 tog, k2.

Repeat rows 1-56 until desired length. Cast off.

Pattern 169

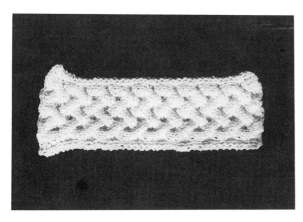

Cast on 29 sts.

Row 1: K1, p1, k3, (p4, k6) twice, p3, k1.

Row 2 and alternate rows: Work all sts as they appear: if they show as purl, p them, as knit, k them.

Row 3: K1, p1, k3, *p4, sl next 3 sts onto dpn, leave at f of work, k3, k3 from dpn*, repeat *—*, p3, k1.

Row 5: K1, p1 *sl the next 3 sts onto dpn, leave at f of work, p2, k3 from dpn [= cross 5 left], sl next 2 sts onto dpn, leave at b of work, k3, then p2 from dpn [= cross 5 right]*, repeat *—*, cross 5 left, p1, k1.

Row 7: K1, p3, *sl next 3 sts onto dpn, leave at b of work, k3, then k3 from dpn, p4*, repeat *—*, k3, p1, k1.

Row 9: K1, p1, *cross 5 right, cross 5 left*, repeat *—*, cross 5 right, p1, k1.

Row 10: Repeat row 2.

Repeat rows 3-10 until desired length. Cast off.

Pattern 170

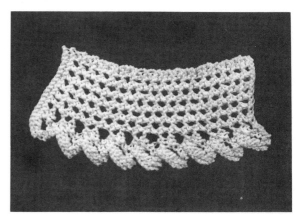

Cast on 15 sts.

Row 1: K.

Row 2: K2, (yon) 4 times, k2 tog, (yon, k2 tog) 5 times, k1.

Row 3: K12, (k1, p1) twice into the 4 yon loop, k2.

Row 4: K.

Row 5: K.

Row 6: K2, (yon) 5 times, k2 tog, k1, (yon, k2 tog) 6 times, k1.

Row 7: K.

Row 8: K.

Row 9: Cast off 7 sts, k1, (yon) 4 times, k2 tog, (yon, k2 tog) 5 times, k1.

Repeat rows 3-9 until desired length. Cast off.

Pattern 171

Cast on 16 sts.

Row 1: K6, m1, k2 tog, m1, k2 tog, (yon) 4 times, k2 tog, k1, m1, k2 tog, k1.

Row 2: K2, p4, k1, p1, k1, p2, k1, p1, k6.

Row 3: K2, m1, k2 tog, k3, m1, k2 tog, m1, k2 tog, k4, k2 tog, m1, k2.

Row 4: K2, p8, k1, p1, k7.

Row 5: K2, k2 tog, (yon) twice, k2 tog, k2, m1, k2 tog, m1, k2 tog, k3, k2 tog, m1, k2.

Row 6: K2, p7, k1, p1, k4, p1, k3.

Row 7: K2, m1, k2 tog, k5, m1, k2 tog, m1, k2 tog, k2, k2 tog, m1, k2.

Row 8: K2, p6, k1, p2, k8.

Row 9: K2, k2 tog, (yon) twice, k2 tog, k4, m1, k2 tog, m1, k2 tog, k1, k2 tog, m1, k2.

Row 10: K2, p5, k1, p3, k4, p1, k3.

Row 11: K2, m1, k2 tog, k7, m1, k2 tog, m1, (k2 tog) twice, m1, k2.

Row 12: K2, p4, k1, p4, k8.

Row 13: K12, m1, k2 tog, m1, k2 tog, k3.

Row 14: Cast off 3 sts, p1, k1, p5, k8.

Repeat rows 1–14 until desired length. Cast off.

Pattern 172

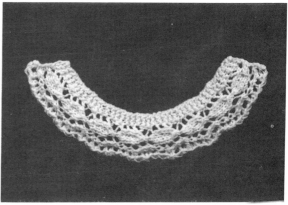

Cast on 9 sts.

Row 1: K3, p4, (p1, k1) into next st, p1.

Row 2: Sl 1, k2 tog, psso, m1, sl 1, k1, psso, m1, k1 tbl, m1, k2 tog, k2.

Row 3: K3, p4, (p1, k1) into next st, p1.

Row 4: Sl 1, k2 tog, psso, m1, k1 tbl, (m1, k3) twice.

Row 5: K3, p6, (p1, k1) into next st, p1.

Row 6: Sl 1, k2 tog, psso, m1, k1 tbl, m1, k2 tog, k1, sl 1, k1, psso, m1, k3.

Row 7: K3, p6, (p1, k1) into next st, p1.

Row 8: Sl 1, k2 tog, psso, m1, k1 tbl, m1, k2 tog, k1, sl 1, k1, psso, m1, k3.

Row 9: K3, p6, (p1, k1) into next st, p1.

Row 10: Sl 1, k2 tog, psso, m1, sl 1, k1, psso, m1, sl 1, k2 tog, psso, m1, k2 tog, k2.

Repeat rows 1–10 until desired length. Cast off.

Pattern 173

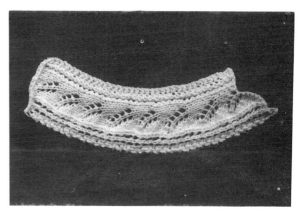

Cast on 18 sts.

Row 1: K3, m1, k2 tog, k1, m1, k1, m1, k5, k2 tog, m1, k2 tog, m1, k1, k into f & b of last st.

Row 2: Cast off 2 sts, p3, p2 tog, p9, yrn, p2 tog, k2.

Row 3: K3, m1, k2 tog, k2, m1, k1, m1, k4, k2 tog, m1, k2 tog, m1, k1, k into f & b of last st.

Row 4: Cast off 2 sts, p3, p2 tog, p9, yrn, p2 tog, k2.

Row 5: K3, m1, k2 tog, k3, m1, k1, m1, k3, k2 tog, m1, k2 tog, m1, k1, k into f & b of last st.

Row 6: Cast off 2 sts, p3, p2 tog, p9, yrn, p2 tog, k2.

Row 7: K3, m1, k2 tog, k4, m1, k1, m1, k2, k2 tog, m1, k2 tog, m1, k1, k into f & b of last st.

Row 8: Cast off 2 sts, p3, p2 tog, p9, yrn, p2 tog, k2.

Repeat rows 1–8 until desired length. Cast off.

Pattern 174

Cast on 14 sts.

Row 1: Sl 1, k2, m1, k2 tog, k4, m1, k1, m1, k4.

Row 2: K4, m1, k3, m1, k2 tog, k3, m1, k2 tog, k2.

Row 3: Sl 1, k2, m1, k2 tog, k1, k2 tog, m1, k5, m1, k4.

Row 4: Cast off 3 sts, m1, k2 tog, k3, k2 tog, m1, k2 tog, k1, m1, k2 tog, k2.

Row 5: Sl 1, k2, m1, k2 tog, k2, m1, k2 tog, k1, k2 tog, m1, k2.

Row 6: K3, m1, sl 1, k2 tog, psso, m1, k4, m1, k2 tog, k2.

Repeat rows 1–6 until desired length. Cast off.

Pattern 175

Cast on 47 sts.

Row 1 and alternate rows: K.

Row 2: Yfwd, (k2 tog) twice, (yfwd, k2 tog) 3 times, k10, (yfwd, k2 tog) 3 times, k1, yfwd, k2 tog, k16, yfwd, k2 tog.

Row 4: Yfwd, (k2 tog) twice, (yfwd, k2 tog) 18 times, k4, yfwd, k2 tog.

Row 6: Yfwd, k1, (k2 tog, yfwd) 3 times, k10, (k2 tog, yfwd) 3 times, k2, yfwd, k2 tog, k1, (yfwd, k2 tog) 6 times, k3, yfwd, k2 tog.

Row 8: Yfwd, k1, (k2 tog, yfwd) 3 times, k10, (k2 tog, yfwd) 3 times, k3, yfwd, k2 tog, k2, (yfwd, k2 tog) 6 times, k2, yfwd, k2 tog.

Row 10: Yfwd, k1, (k2 tog, yfwd) 3 times, k10, (k2 tog, yfwd) 3 times, k4, yfwd, k2 tog, k16, yfwd, k2 tog.

Row 12: Yfwd, k1, (k2 tog, yfwd) 3 times, k10, (k2 tog, yfwd) 3 times, k5, yfwd, k2 tog, k2, yfwd, k2 tog, k3, yfwd, k2 tog, k3, yfwd, k2 tog, k2, yfwd, k2 tog.

Row 14: Yfwd, (k2 tog) twice, (yfwd, k2 tog) 3 times, k10, (yfwd, k2 tog) 3 times, k3, yfwd, (k2 tog) twice, yfwd, k1, yfwd, (k2 tog) twice, yfwd, k1, yfwd, (k2 tog) twice, yfwd, k1, yfwd, k2 tog, k1, yfwd, k2 tog.

Row 16: Yfwd, (k2 tog) twice, (yfwd, k2 tog) 3 times, k10, (yfwd, k2 tog) 3 times, k2, yfwd, (k2 tog) twice, yfwd, k1, yfwd, (k2 tog) twice, yfwd, k1, yfwd, (k2 tog) twice, yfwd, k1, yfwd, k2 tog, k1, yfwd, k2 tog.

Repeat rows 1–16 until desired length. Cast off.

Pattern 176

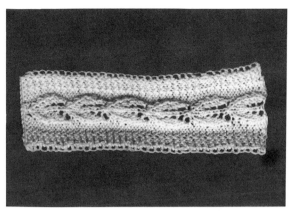

Cast on 17 sts.

Row 1: M1, k2 tog, k2, p3, (k1, yon) twice, k1, p3, k2, k2 tog, m1.

Row 2: M1, k2 tog, k2, k3, p5, k3, k2, k2 tog, m1.

Row 3: M1, k2 tog, k2, p3, k2, yon, k1, yon, k2, k3, k2, k2 tog, m1.

Row 4: M1, k2 tog, k2, k3, p7, k3, k2, k2 tog, m1.

Row 5: M1, k2 tog, k2, p3, k1, sl 1, psso, k1, (yon, k1) twice, k2 tog, p3, k2, k2 tog, m1.

Row 6: M1, k2 tog, k2, k3, p7, k3, k2, k2 tog, m1.

Row 7: M1, k2 tog, k2, p3, k1, sl 1, psso, k3, k2 tog, p3, k2, k2 tog, m1.

Row 8: M1, k2 tog, k2, k3, p5, k3, k2, k2 tog, m1.

Row 9: M1, k2 tog, k2, p3, k1, sl 1, psso, k1, k2 tog, p3, k2, k2 tog, m1.

Row 10: M1, k2 tog, k2, k3, p3, k3, k2, k2 tog, m1.

Row 11: M1, k2 tog, k2, p3, yon, sl 2 k-wise, k1, p2sso, yon, p3, k2, k2 tog, m1.

Row 12: M1, k2 tog, k2, k3, p3, k3, k2, k2 tog, m1.

Repeat rows 1–12 until desired length. Cast off.

Pattern 177

Cast on 25 sts.

Row 1: Sl 1, k19, yrn, p2 tog, k1, yfwd, k2.

Row 2: K4, yrn, p2 tog, k18, turn.

Row 3: Sl 1, k17, yrn, p2 tog, k2, yfwd, k2.

Row 4: K5, yrn, p2 tog, k16, turn.

Row 5: Sl 1, k15, yrn, p2 tog, k3, yfwd, k2.

Row 6: K6, yrn, p2 tog, k14, turn.

Row 7: Sl 1, k13, yrn, p2 tog, k2 tog, y2rn, k2, yfwd, k2.

Row 8: K6, p1, k1, yrn, p2 tog, k12, turn.

Row 9: Sl 1, k11, yrn, p2 tog, k8.

Row 10: Cast off 5 sts, k2, p2 tog, k10, turn.

Row 11: Sl 1, k9, yrn, p2 tog, k1, yfwd, k2.

Row 12: K4, yrn, p2 tog, k8, turn.

Row 13: Sl 1, k7, yrn, p2 tog, k2, yfwd, k2.

Row 14: K5, yrn, p2 tog, k6, turn.

Row 15: Sl 1, k5, yrn, p2 tog, k3, yfwd, k2.

Row 16: K6, yrn, p2 tog, k4, turn.

Row 17: Sl 1, k3, yrn, p2 tog, k2 tog, y2rn, k2, yfwd, k2.

Row 18: K6, p1, k1, yrn, p2 tog, k2, turn.

Row 19: Sl 1, k1, yrn, p2 tog, k8.

Row 20: Cast off 5 sts, k2, yrn, p2 tog, k2, (yfwd, k2 tog) 8 times, k2.

Repeat these 20 rows 7 times. Cast off on the 20th row.

Pattern 178

Cast on 32 sts.

Row 1: K3, m1, k2 tog, k3, turn, cast on 6 sts, turn, k5, m1, k2 tog, k3, m1, p2 tog, m1, p2 tog, m1, p3 tog, m1, p5, m2, p2 tog.

Row 2: M1, k2, p1, k3, k2 tog, m1, k12, m1, k2 tog, k3, (m1, k1) 6 times, k5, m1, k2 tog, k1.

Row 3: K3, m1, k2 tog, k2 tog, k14, k2 tog, k2, m1, k2 tog, k3, m1, p2 tog, m1, p2 tog, m1, p2 tog, p2, m1, p2 tog, p2, m2, p2 tog, m2, p2 tog.

Row 4: K2, p1, k2, p1, k1, k2 tog, m1, k14, m1, k2 tog, k2 tog, k12, k2 tog, k2, m1, k2 tog, k1.

Row 5: K3, m1, k2 tog, p2 tog, p10, p2 tog, k2, m1, k2 tog, k3, m1, p2 tog, m1, p2 tog, m1, p2 tog, p4, m1, p2 tog, p4, m1, p2 tog.

Row 6: Cast off 4 sts, k3, m1, k2 tog, k13, m1, (k2 tog) twice, k8, k2 tog, k2, m1, k2 tog, k1.

Row 7: K3, m1, k2 tog, p2 tog, p6, p2 tog, k2, m1, k2 tog, k3, m1, p2 tog, m1, p2 tog, m1, p2 tog, p1, p2 tog, m1, p5.

Row 8: K6, m1, k2 tog, k2, m1, k2 tog, k7, m1, k2 tog, k2 tog, k4, k2 tog, k2, m1, k2 tog, k1.

Repeat rows 1–8 until desired length. Cast off.

Pattern 179

Cast on 30 sts.

Row 1: K.

Row 2: Sl 1, k18, (yon, k2 tog) twice, k1, (yon) twice, k1, (yon, k2 tog) twice, k1.

Row 3: Sl 1, k5, (k1, p1) twice in the double yon loop [making 4 sts from this loop], k24.

Row 4: Sl 1, k8, k2 tog, yon, k1, yon, sl 1, k1, psso, k6, (yon, k2 tog) twice, k5, (yon, k2 tog) twice, k1.

Row 5: Sl 1, k18, p2 tog tbl, yon, p3, yon, p2 tog, k8.

Row 6: Sl 1, k5, (k2 tog, yon, k1, yon, sl 1, k1, psso, k1) twice, k3, (yon, k2 tog) twice, k4, (yon, k2 tog) twice, k1.

Row 7: Sl 1, k15, p2 tog tbl, yon, p3, yon, p3 tog, yon, p3, yon, p2 tog, k5.

Row 8: Sl 1, k2, (k2 tog, yon, k1, yon, sl 1, k1, psso, k1) 3 times, k1, (yon, k2 tog) twice, k3, (yon, k2 tog) twice, k1.

Row 9: Sl 1, k12, p2 tog tbl, (yon, p3, yon, p3 tog) twice, yon, p3, yon, p2 tog, k2.

Row 10: Sl 1, k2, (yon, sl 1, k1, psso, k1, k2 tog, yon, k1) 3 times, (k2, [yon, k2 tog] twice) twice, k1.

Row 11: Sl 1, k14, (yon, p3 tog, yon, p3) twice, yon, p3 tog, yon, k4.

Row 12: Sl 1, k5, (yon, sl 1, k1, psso, k1, k2 tog, yon, k1) twice, k6, ([yon, k2 tog] twice, k1) twice.

Row 13: Sl 1, k17, yon, p3 tog, yon, p3, yon, p3 tog, yon, k7.

Row 14: Sl 1, k8, yon, sl 1, k1, psso, k1, k2 tog, yon, k11, (yon, k2 tog) 4 times, k1.

Row 15: Sl 1, k20, yon, p3 tog, yon, k10.

Row 16: Sl 1, k25, (yon, k2 tog) twice, k4.

Row 17: Sl 1, k4, pass first 4 sts on R.H. needle over the last st worked, k29.

Repeat rows 2–17 until desired length. Cast off.

Pattern 180

Cast on 24 sts.

Row 1: P.

Row 2: M1, sl 1, k1, psso, sl 1, k1, psso, m1, k1, (m1, k2 tog, k1) 4 times, m1, k4, m1, k2 tog, k1.

Row 3: Sl 1, p2, m1, p2 tog, p to end.

Row 4: M1, k1, k2 tog, m1, k3, (m1, sl 1, k1, psso, k1) 4 times, m1, sl 1, k1, psso, k2, m1, k2 tog, k1.

Row 5: Sl 1, p2, m1, p2 tog, p to end.

Row 6: M1, k1, k2 tog, m1, k5, (m1, sl 1, k1, psso, k1) 3 times, m1, sl 1, k1, psso, k4, m1, k2 tog, k1.

Row 7: Sl 1, p2, m1, p2 tog, p to end.

Row 8: M1, k1, k2 tog, m1, k7, (m1, sl 1, k1, psso, k1) 3 times, m1, sl 1, k1, psso, k3, m1, k2 tog, k1.

Row 9: Sl 1, p2, m1, p2 tog, p to end.

Row 10: M1, k1, k2 tog, m1, k2, k2 tog, m1, k1, m1, sl 1, k1, psso, k2, (m1, sl 1, k1, psso, k1) 3 times, m1, sl 1, k1, psso, k2, m1, k2 tog, k1.

Row 11: Sl 1, p2, m1, p2 tog, p to end.

Row 12: M1, k1, k2 tog, m1, k2, k2 tog, m1, k3, m1, sl 1, k1, psso, k2, (m1, sl 1, k1, psso, k1) twice, m1, sl 1, k1, psso, k4, m1, k2 tog, k1.

Row 13: Sl 1, p2, m1, p2 tog, p to end.

Row 14: M1, k1, k2 tog, m1, k2, k2 tog, m1, k5, m1, sl 1, k1, psso, k2, (m1, sl 1, k1, psso, k1) twice, m1, sl 1, k1, psso, k3, m1, k2 tog, k1.

Row 15: Sl 1, p2, m1, p2 tog, p to end.

Row 16: M1, k1, k2 tog, m1, k3, m1, k1, m1, sl 1, k1, psso, k3, k2 tog, m1, k1, m1, k3, (m1, sl 1, k1, psso, k1) twice, m1, sl 1, k1, psso, k2, m1, k2 tog, k1.

Row 17: Sl 1, p2, m1, p2 tog, p to end.

Row 18: M1, k1, k2 tog, m1, k2, k2 tog, m1, k3, m1, sl 1, k1, psso, k1, k2 tog, m1, k3, m1, sl 1, k1, psso, k2, m1, sl 1, k1, psso, k1, m1, sl 1, k1, psso, k4, m1, k2 tog, k1.

Row 19: Sl 1, p2, m1, p2 tog, p to end.

Row 20: M1, k1, k2 tog, m1, k2, k2 tog, m1, k5, m1, sl 1, k2 tog, psso, m1, k5, m1, sl 1, k1, psso, k2, m1, sl 1, k1, psso, k1, m1, sl 1, k1, psso, k3, m1, k2 tog, k1.

Row 21: Sl 1, p2, m1, p2 tog, p to end.

Row 22: M1, k1, k2 tog, m1, k2, k2 tog, m1, sl 1, k1, psso, k3, k2 tog, m1, k1, m1, sl 1, k1, psso, k3, k2 tog, m1, sl 1, k1, psso, k2, m1, sl 1, k1, psso, k1, m1, sl 1, k1, psso, k2, m1, k2 tog, k1. [35 sts on needle; this is the middle and widest row of the edging.]

Row 23: Sl 1, p2, m1, p2 tog, p to end.

Row 24: M1, sl 1, k1, psso, sl 1, k1, psso, m1, k2, sl 1, k1, psso, m1, sl 1, k1, psso, k1, k2 tog, m1, k3, m1, sl 1, k1, psso, k1, k2 tog, m1, k2 tog, k2, m1, k2 tog, k1, m1, k4, m1, k2 tog, k1.

Row 25: Sl 1, p2, m1, p2 tog, p to end.

Row 26: M1, sl 1, k1, psso, sl 1, k1, psso, m1, k2, sl 1, k1, psso, m1, sl 1, k2 tog, psso, m1, k5, m1, sl 1, k2 tog, psso, m1, k2 tog, k2, m1, k2 tog, k1, m1, k5, m1, k2 tog, k1.

Row 27: Sl 1, p2, m1, p2 tog, p to end.

Row 28: M1, sl 1, k1, psso, sl 1, k1, psso, m1, sl 1, k1, psso, sl 1, k1, psso, k1, m1, sl 1, k1, psso, k3, k2 tog, m1, k1, k2 tog, k2 tog, (m1, k2 tog, k1) twice, m1, k3, m1, k2 tog, k1.

Row 29: Sl 1, p2, m1, p2 tog, p to end.

Row 30: M1, sl 1, k1, psso, sl 1, k1, psso, m1, k2, sl 1, k1, psso, m1, sl 1, k1, psso, k1, k2 tog, m1, k2 tog, k2, (m1, k2 tog, k1) twice, m1, k4, m1, k2 tog, k1.

Row 31: Sl 1, p2, m1, p2 tog, p to end.

Row 32: M1, sl 1, k1, psso, sl 1, k1, psso, m1, k2, sl 1, k1, psso, m1, sl 1, k2 tog, psso, m1, k2 tog, k2, (m1, k2 tog, k1) twice, m1, k5, m1, k2 tog, k1.

Row 33: sl 1, p2, m1, p2 tog, p to end.

Row 34: M1, sl 1, k1, psso, sl 1, k1, psso, m1, k2, sl 1, k1, psso, k1, k2 tog, k2, (m1, k2 tog, k1) 3 times, m1, k3, m1, k2 tog, k1.

Row 35: Sl 1, p2, m1, p2 tog, p to end.

Row 36: M1, sl 1, k1, psso, sl 1, k1, psso, m1, sl 1, k1, psso, k3, k2 tog, (m1, k2 tog, k1) 3 times, m1, k4, m1, k2 tog, k1.

Row 37: Sl 1, p2, m1, p2 tog, p to end.

Row 38: M1, sl 1, k1, psso, sl 1, k1, psso, m1, sl 1, k1, psso, k1, k2 tog, (m1, k2 tog, k1) 3 times, m1, k5, m1, k2 tog, k1.

Row 39: Sl 1, p2, m1, p2 tog, p to end.

Row 40: M1, sl 1, k1, psso, sl 1, k1, psso, m1, sl 1, k2 tog, psso, (m1, k2 tog, k1) 4 times, m1, k3, m1, k2 tog, k1.

Row 41: Sl 1, p2, m1, p2 tog, p to end.

Repeat rows 2–41 until desired length. Cast off.

Pattern 181

Pattern 182

Cast on 22 sts.

Row 1: P.

Row 2: Sl 1, k2, m1, k2 tog, k2, (m1, k2 tog) twice, m1, k10, inc 1 k-wise in last st.

Row 3: P2, m1, p22.

Row 4: Sl 1, k2, k2 tog, m1, k3, (m1, k2 tog) twice, m1, k13.

Row 5: P2 tog, p1, m1, p1, m1, p22.

Row 6: Sl 1, k2, m1, k2 tog, k4, (m1, k2 tog) twice, m1, k14.

Row 7: P2 tog, p1, m1, p3, m1, p22.

Row 8: Sl 1, k2, k2 tog, m1, k5, (m1, k2 tog) twice, m1, k15.

Row 9: P2 tog, p1, m1, p5, m1, p22.

Row 10: Sl 1, k2, m1, k2 tog, k4, (k2 tog, m1) twice, k2 tog, k16.

Row 11: P2 tog, p1, m1, p7, m1, p20.

Row 12: Sl 1, k2, k2 tog, m1, k3, (k2 tog, m1) twice, k2 tog, k17.

Row 13: P2 tog, p1, m1, p9, m1, p18.

Row 14: Sl 1, k2, m1, k2 tog, k2, (k2 tog, m1) twice, k2 tog, k18.

Row 15: P1, (p2 tog, m1) 6 times, p1, m1, p16.

Row 16: Sl 1, k2, k2 tog, m1, k1, (k2 tog, m1) twice, k2 tog, k19.

Row 17: Cast off 8 sts, p21.

Repeat rows 2–17 until desired length. Cast off.

Cast on 36 sts.

Row 1: K.

Row 2: K.

Row 3: K1, m1, sl 1, k1, psso, p5, k3, p14, k3, m1, sl 1, k1, psso, p5, k1.

Row 4: K5, p1, *sl st just purled to L.H. needle, pass next st on L.H. needle over and sl the st back to R.H. needle*, m1, k1, p3, k7, (turn, sl 1, k6) 6 times, sl the 7 sts from R.H. needle onto dpn, hold to f of work, sl 7 sts from L.H. to R.H. needle, then sl the 7 sts from dpn onto R.H. needle [this forms zigzag], p3, k4, p1, repeat *—*, m1, k2.

Row 5: K1, p2, m1, sl 1, k1, psso, p3, k3, p14, k3, p2, m1, sl 1, k1, psso, p3, k1.

Row 6: K3, p1, repeat *—* row 4, m1, k3, p3, k14, p3, k2, p1, repeat *—* row 4, m1, k4.

Row 7: K1, p4, m1, sl 1, k1, psso, p1, k3, p7, (turn, k7, turn, sl 1, p6) 6 times, sl the 7 sts on R.H. needle onto dpn, hold to b of work, sl 7 sts from L.H. to R.H. needle, then sl the 7 sts on dpn onto R.H. needle [this forms zigzag], k3, p4, m1, sl 1, k1, psso, p1, k1.

Row 8: K1, p1, repeat *—* row 4, m1, k5, p3, k14, p4, repeat *—* row 4, m1, k6.

Repeat rows 3–8 until required length. Cast off thus: *p2 tog loosely, replace the st on L.H. needle*, repeat *—* until one st only remains. Fasten off.

Pattern 183

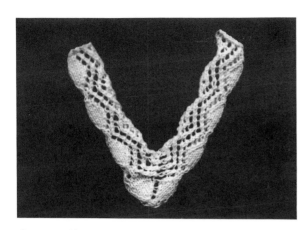

Cast on 11 sts.

Row 1: Sl 1, k1 tbl, m1, k1, m1, sl 1, k1, psso, m1, sl 1, k1, psso, m1, sl 1, k1, psso, k2.

Row 2: P.

Row 3: Sl 1, k1 tbl, m1, k3, m1, sl 1, k1, psso, m1, sl 1, k1, psso, m1, sl 1, k1, psso, k1.

Row 4: P.

Row 5: Sl 1, k1 tbl, m1, k5, m1, sl 1, k1, psso, m1, sl 1, k1, psso, k2.

Row 6: P.

Row 7: Sl 1, k1, tbl, m1, k7, m1, sl 1, k1, psso, m1, sl 1, k1, psso, k1.

Row 8: P.

Row 9: Sl 1, k1, psso, k1, m1, sl 1, k1, psso, k3, k2 tog, m1, k2 tog, m1, k3.

Row 10: P.

Row 11: Sl 1, k1, psso, k1, m1, sl 1, k1, psso, k1, k2 tog, m1, k2 tog, m1, k2 tog, m1, k2.

Row 12: P.

Row 13: Sl 1, k1, psso, k1, m1, sl 1, k2 tog, psso, m1, k2 tog, m1, k2 tog, m1, k3.

Row 14: P.

Row 15: Sl 1, k1, psso, k2, k2 tog, m1, k2 tog, m1, k2 tog, m1, k2.

Row 16: P.

Repeat rows 1–16 until desired length.

When a corner is required, work rows 1–14, then:

Corner

Row 17: Sl 1, k1, psso, k2, k2 tog, m1, k2 tog, m1, k2 tog, m1, k1, sl next st onto dpn.

Row 18: Sl 1, p9.

Row 19: Sl 1, k1 tbl, m1, k1, m1, sl 1, k1, psso, m1, sl 1, k1, psso, m1, sl 1, k1, psso, sl next st onto dpn.

Row 20: Sl 1, p9.

Row 21: Sl 1, k1 tbl, m1, k3, m1, sl 1, k1, psso, m1, sl 1, k1, psso, sl next st onto dpn.

Row 22: Sl 1, p9.

Row 23: Sl 1, k1 tbl, m1, k5, m1, sl 1, k1, psso, sl next st onto dpn.

Row 24: Sl 1, p9.

Row 25: Sl 1, k1 tbl, m1, k7, sl next st onto dpn.

Row 26: M1, p10.

Row 27: Sl 1, k1, psso, k1, m1, sl 1, k1, psso, k3, k2 tog, sl next st onto dpn.

Row 28: M1, p8.

Row 29: Sl 1, k1, psso, k1, m1, sl 1, k1, psso, k1, k2 tog, sl next st onto dpn.

Row 30: M1, p6.

Row 31: Sl 1, k1, psso, k1, m1, sl 1, k2 tog, psso, sl next st onto dpn.

Row 32: M1, p4.

Row 33: Sl 1, k1, psso, k2, sl next st onto dpn.

Row 34: Sl 1, p2.

Row 35: Sl 1, k1 tbl, m1, sl 1, *k1 tbl from dpn (the last stitch you slipped)*, psso.

Row 36: Sl 1, p3.

Row 37: Sl 1, k1 tbl, m1, k2, repeat *—* row 19.

Row 38: Sl 1, p5.

Row 39: Sl 1, k1 tbl, m1, k4, repeat *—* row 19.

Row 40: Sl 1, p7.

Row 41: Sl 1, k1 tbl, m1, k6, repeat *—* row 19.

Row 42: Sl 1, p9.

Row 43: Sl 1, k1, psso, k1, m1, sl 1, k1, psso, k3, k2 tog, m1, repeat *—* row 19.

Row 44: Sl 1, p9.

Row 45: Sl 1, k1, psso, k1, m1, sl 1, k1, psso, k1, k2 tog, m1, k2 tog, m1, repeat *—* row 19.

Row 46: Sl 1, p9.

Row 47: Sl 1, k1, psso, k1, m1, sl 1, k2 tog, psso, m1, k2 tog, m1, k2 tog, m1, repeat *—* row 19.

Row 48: Sl 1, p9.

Row 49: Sl 1, k1, psso, k2, k2 tog, m1, k2 tog, m1, k2 tog, m1, repeat *—* row 19.

Row 50: Sl 1, p9.

Row 51: Sl 1, k1 tbl, m1, k1, m1, sl 1, k1, psso, m1, sl 1, k1, psso, m1, sl 1, k1, psso, k1, repeat *—* row 19.

Row 52: Sl 1, p11.

Continue from row 3 repeating rows 1–16 until desired length. Cast off.

Pattern 184

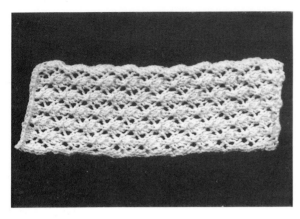

Cast on 21 sts.
Row 1: Sl 1, k1, m1, k1, sl 1, k2 tog, psso, k1, m1, k2.
Row 2: P.
Row 3: Sl 1, k2, m1, sl 1, k2 tog, psso, m1, k3.
Row 4: P.
Row 5: Sl 1, k2 tog, k1, m1, k1, m1, k1, sl 1, k2 tog, psso, k1.
Repeat rows 1-5 until desired length. Cast off.

Pattern 185

Semicircle
Cast on 66 sts.
Row 1: (Wrong side) k.
Row 2: P2 tog, p4, (*pick up the thread lying between st just worked and the next one and knit into it 5 times*, p6) 9 times, repeat *—*, p4, p2 tog.
Row 3: K5, (p5, k6) 9 times, p5, k5.

Row 4: P2 tog, p3, (sl 1, k1, psso, k1, k2 tog, p6) 9 times, sl 1, k1, psso, k1, k2 tog, p3, p2 tog.
Row 5: K4, (p3, k6) 9 times, p3, k4.
Row 6: P2 tog, p2, (sl 1, k2 tog, psso, p6) 9 times, sl 1, k2 tog, psso, p2, p2 tog.
Row 7: K2, (k2 tog, k5) 9 times, k2 tog, k3.
Rows 8-12: Repeat rows 2-6 with 1 triangular motif less.
Row 13: K2, (k2 tog, k5) 4 times, k7, (k2 tog, k5) 3 times, k2 tog, k3.
Row 14: P2 tog, p4, **(repeat *—* row 2, p6) twice, repeat *—* row 2**, p9, k1, p9, repeat **—**, p4, p2 tog.
Rows 15-19: Continue the 3 motifs placed at each side of centre, beginning and ending every other row with p2 tog. Also p2 tog, before and after the centre st. Always k the centre st on right side and wrong side of work until the semicircle is completed.
Row 20 onwards: Work in st. st, beginning and ending every other row with k2 tog. On centre 5 sts: k2 tog, k1, sl 1, k1, psso. When 3 sts remain, cast off.

Top of Semicircle
Pick up 58 sts along top of semicircle.
Row 1: P.
Row 2: K.
Row 3: P.
Row 4: *K2 tog, m1*, repeat *—* to end.
Row 5: P.
Row 6: K.
Row 7: K.
Row 8: P4, **repeat *—* row 2, p6**, repeat **—** [this starts a line of triangular motifs].
Rows 9-13: Continue straight forming motifs as in rows 3-7 of instructions for semicircle.
Row 14: K.
Row 15: P.
Row 16: *K2 tog, m1*, repeat *—* to end.
Row 17: P.
Row 18: K.
Row 19: P.
Cast off.

Edging
Cast on 6 sts.
Row 1: K.
Row 2: K.
Row 3: K.
Row 4: Sl 1, k3, pass 1st, 2nd & 3rd of these sts over the 4th st, k2.
Row 5: K.
Row 6: Cast on 3 sts, k to end.
Repeat rows 1-6 until desired length. Cast off.

Pattern 186

Cast on 34 sts.

Row 1: K.

Row 2: Sl 1, k3, yon, sl 1, k1, psso, k3, k2 tog, yon, p3, yon, sl 1, k1, psso, k3, yon, sl 1, k1, psso, (yon, k2 tog) 6 times, k1.

Row 3: Sl 1, k23, p5, k3, (k1, p1) in next st, k1.

Row 4: Sl 1, k5, yon, sl 1, k1, psso, k1, k2 tog, yon, p5, yon, sl 1, k1, psso, k3, (yon, k2 tog) 6 times, k2.

Row 5: Sl 1, k24, p3, k5, (k1, p1) in next st, k1.

Row 6: Sl 1, k7, yon, sl 1, k2 tog, psso, yon, p7, yon, sl 1, k1, psso, k3, (yon, k2 tog) 6 times, k1.

Row 7: Sl 1, k25, p1, k7, (k1, p1) in next st, k1.

Row 8: Sl 1, k6, k2 tog, yon, k3, yon, p2 tog, p3, p2 tog tbl, yon, k3, k2 tog, yon, k1 tbl, (yon, k2 tog) 5 times, k2.

Row 9: Sl 1, k24, p3, k6, k2 tog, k1.

Row 10: Sl 1, k4, k2 tog, yon, k5, yon, p2 tog, p1, p2 tog tbl, yon, k3, k2 tog, yon, k1 tbl, (yon, k2 tog) 6 times, k1.

Row 11: Sl 1, k23, p5, k4, k2 tog, k1.

Row 12: Sl 1, k2, k2 tog, yon, k7, yon, p3 tog, yon, k3, k2 tog, yon, k1 tbl, (yon, k2 tog) 6 times, k2.

Row 13: Sl 1, k21, p7, k2, k2 tog, k2.

Repeat rows 2-13 until desired length. Cast off.

Pattern 187

Cast on 36 sts. K2 edge sts each side, these are not referred to in pattern.

Row 1: *P2, k1*, repeat *—* to last 2 sts, p2.

Row 2: K2 *p1, k2*, repeat *—* to end.

Row 3: *P2, k1*, repeat *—* to last 2 sts, p2.

Row 4: K2, *p1, k2*, repeat *—* to end.

Row 5: *P2, k1*, repeat *—* to last 2 sts, p2.

Row 6: K2, *p1, k2*, repeat *—* to end.

Row 7: *P2, (k1) 3 times in next st, (k1 tbl) twice*, repeat *—* to last 2 sts, p2.

Rows 8-10: K the knit, and p the purl sts.

Row 11: *P2, sl 1, k2 tog, psso, repeat *—* to last 2 sts, p2.

Repeat rows 2-11 until desired length. Cast off.

Pattern 188

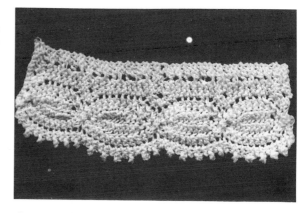

Cast on 18 sts.

Row 1: K.

Row 2: K5, k2 tog, k2, yon, k1, k2 tog, yon, k2 tog, k1, yon, k3.

Row 3: Sl 1, k2, yon, sl the 'yon' of previous row, k2, m1, k3, sl next 2 sts onto dpn, leave at f of work, k3, k2 from dpn, yon, k2 tog, k1.

Row 4: Cast on 2 sts, cast off 2 sts, k6, k2 tog, yon, k2 tog, k4, (k1, p1) into both 'yon' sts of previous row tog (as if they were a single st), k3.

Row 5: Sl 1, k1, k2 tog, yon, k2 tog, k10, yon, k2 tog, k1.

Row 6: K5, (yon, k1) twice, k2 tog, yon, k2 tog, k3, yon, drop loop of previous row, k3.

Row 7: Sl 1, k2, (k1, p1) into the 'yon' of previous row, k7, m1, k1, m1, k2, yon, k2 tog, k1.

Row 8: Cast on 2 sts, cast off 2 sts, k4, yon, k2, yon, k2 tog, k1, yon, (k1, k2 tog, yon, k2 tog) twice, k2.

Row 9: Sl 1, k2, yon, drop loop of previous row, k6, (yon, k2 tog, k1) 4 times.

Row 10: K5, (yon, k2 tog, k1) 3 times, yon, k2 tog, k2, (k1, p1) into yon of previous row, k3.

Row 11: Sl 1, k1, k2 tog, yon, k2 tog, k5, (yon, k2 tog, k1) 4 times.

Row 12: Cast on 2 sts, cast off 2 sts, k4, (yon, k2 tog, k1) 3 times, yon, k2 tog, k2, yon, drop loop of previous row, k3.

Row 13: Sl 1, k2, (k1, p1) into yon of previous row, k6, (yon, k2 tog, k1) 4 times.

Row 14: K5, (yon, k2 tog, k1) 4 times, k2 tog, yon, k2 tog, k2.

Row 15: Sl 1, k2, yon, drop loop of previous row, k6, (yon, k2 tog, k1) 4 times.

Row 16: Cast on 2 sts, cast off 2 sts, k4, (yon, k2 tog, k1) 3 times, yon, k2 tog, k2, (k1, p1) into yon of previous row, k3.

Row 17: Sl 1, k1, k2 tog, yon, k2 tog, k5, (yon, k2 tog, k1) 4 times.

Row 18: K5, (yon, k2 tog, k1) 3 times, yon, k2 tog, k2, yon, drop loop of previous row, k3.

Row 19: Sl 1, k2, (k1, p1) into yon of previous row, k6, yon, (k2 tog, k1) twice, (yon, k2 tog, k1) twice.

Row 20: Cast on 2 sts, cast off 2 sts, k4, yon, k2 tog, k1, k2 tog, yon, k2 tog, k1, yon, k3, k2 tog, yon, k2 tog, k2.

Row 21: Sl 1, k2, yon, drop the loop of previous row, k7, yon, k2 tog, k2, (yon, k2 tog, k1) twice.

Row 22: K5, yon, (k2 tog) twice, yon, k2 tog, k1, yon, k5, (k1, p1) into yon of previous row.

Row 23: Sl 1, k1, k2 tog, yon, k2 tog, k7, (k2 tog, k1) twice, yon, k2 tog, k1.

Row 24: K5, k2 tog, k2, yon, k1, k2 tog, yon, k2 tog, k1, yon, drop loop of previous row, k3.

Repeat rows 3–24 until desired length. Cast off.

Pattern 189

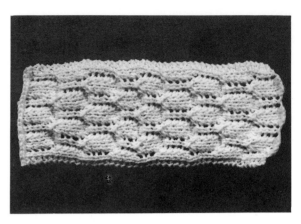

Cast on a multiple of 6 sts, plus 3 extra sts at beginning and 2 sts at the end of the row, for required width of edging.

Row 1: Sl 1, k2 *m1, sl 1, k1, psso, k1, k2 tog, m1, k1*, repeat *—* to last 2 sts, k2.

Row 2: Sl 1, k1, p to last 2 sts, k2.

Rows 3, 5 & 7: Repeat row 1.

Rows 4, 6 & 8: Repeat row 2.

Row 9: Sl 1, k3, *m1, sl 1, k2 tog, psso, m1, k3*, repeat *—* to last 4 sts, k4.

Row 10: Sl 1, k1, p to last 2 sts, k2.

Row 11: Sl 1, k2, k2 tog, *m1, k1, sl 1, k1, psso, k1, k2 tog*, repeat *—* to last 2 sts, k1.

Row 12: Sl 1, k1, p to last 2 sts, k2.

Rows 13, 15 & 17: Repeat row 11.

Rows 14, 16 & 18: Repeat row 12.

Row 19: Sl 1, k1, k2 tog, *m1, k3, m1, sl 1, k2 tog, psso*, repeat *—* to last 7 sts, m1, k3, m1, k2 tog, k2.

Row 20: Sl 1, k1, p to last 2 sts, k2.

Repeat rows 1–20 until desired length. Cast off after working row 8.

Pattern 190

*Pattern 191

Cast on 17 sts.

Row 1: K.

Row 2: K3, (yon, p2 tog) twice, yon, k1 tbl, k2 tog, p1, sl 1, k1, psso, k1 tbl, yon, k3.

Row 3: K3, p3, k1, p3, k2, (yon, p2 tog) twice, k1.

Row 4: K3, (yon, p2 tog) twice, yon, k1 tbl, k2 tog, p1, sl 1, k1, psso, k1 tbl, yon, k3.

Row 5: K3, p3, k1, p3, k2, (yon, p2 tog) twice, k1.

Row 6: K3, (yon, p2 tog) twice, yon, k1 tbl, yon, k2 tog, p1, sl 1, k1, psso, yon, k4.

Row 7: K4, p2, k1, p4, k2, (yon, p2 tog) twice, k1.

Row 8: K3, (yon, p2 tog) twice, yon, k1 tbl, k1, k1 tbl, yon, sl 1, k2 tog, psso, yon, k5.

Row 9: K5, p7, k2, (yon, p2 tog) twice, k1.

Row 10: K3, (yon, p2 tog) twice, yon, k1 tbl, k3, k1 tbl, yon, k7.

Row 11: Cast off 4 sts, k2, p7, k2, (yon, p2 tog) twice, k1.

Repeat rows 2-11 until desired length. Cast off.

Cast on any number of sts for required width of edging

Row 1: K.

Row 2: *Yrn (as if you were going to k a plain st) then twice around forefinger and needle, now knit the st*, repeat *—* to end.

Rows 3-7: K.

Repeat rows 2-7, making loops on only one side, until required length. Cast off.

Pattern 192

Cast of 54 sts.

Row 1: P2, yfwd, k4, sl 1, k1, psso, k6, k2 tog, k4, yfwd, p2, (k2, yfwd, sl 1, k1, psso) 8 times.

Row 2: (P2, yfwd, p2 tog,) 8 times, k2, p1, yfwd, p4, p2 tog, p4, p2 tog tbl, p4, yfwd, p1, k2.

Row 3: P2, k2, yfwd, k4, sl 1, k1, psso, k2, k2 tog, k4, yfwd, k2, p2, (k2, yfwd, sl 1, k1, psso) 8 times.
Row 4: (P2, yfwd, p2 tog) 8 times, k2, p3, yfwd, p4, p2 tog, p2 tog tbl, p4, yfwd, p3, k2.
Repeat rows 1–4 until desired length. Cast off.

Pattern 194

Pattern 193

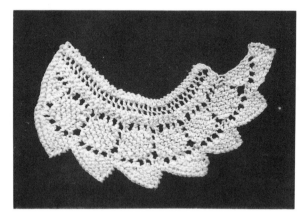

Cast on 16 sts.
Row 1: K.
Row 2: Sl 1, k2, m1, k2 tog, k1, m2, k7, m2, k3.
Row 3: Sl 1, k3, p1, k8, p1, k3, m1, k2 tog, k1.
Row 4: Sl 1, k2, m1, k2 tog, k1, m2, k2 tog, m2, k2 tog, k3, k2 tog, m2, k5.
Row 5: Sl 1, k5, p1, k6, p1, k2, p1, k3, m1, k2 tog, k1.
Row 6: Sl 1, k2, m1, k2 tog, k1, m2, k2 tog, k1, k2 tog, m2, k2 tog, k1, k2 tog, m2, k7.
Row 7: Sl 1, k7, p1, k4, p1, k4, p1, k3, m1, k2 tog, k1.
Row 8: Sl 1, k2, m1, k2 tog, k1, m2, k2 tog, k3, k2 tog, m2, sl 1, k2 tog, psso, m2, k9.
Row 9: Sl 1, k9, p1, k2, p1, k6, p1, k3, m1, k2 tog, k1.
Row 10: Sl 1, k2, m1, k2 tog, k22.
Row 11: Cast off 10 sts, k9, k2 tog, k2, m1, k2 tog, k1.
Repeat rows 2–11 until desired length. Cast off.

Cast on 3 sts.
Row 1: (Yfwd, k3).
Rows 2–32: Continue increasing like this, until you have 35 sts.
Row 33: K2 tog, k33.
Row 34: K2 tog, p31, k1.
Row 35: K2 tog, k31.
Row 36: K2 tog, k30.
Row 37: K2 tog, p28, k1.
Row 38: K2 tog, k28.
Row 39: K2 tog, k27.
Row 40: K2 tog, p25, k1.
Row 41: K2 tog, k25.
Row 42: K2 tog, k24.
Row 43: K2 tog, p22, k1.
Row 44: K2 tog, k22.
Row 45: K2 tog, k21.
Row 46: K2 tog, p19, k1.
Row 47: K2 tog, k19.
Row 48: K2 tog, k18.
Row 49: K2 tog, p16, k1.
Row 50: K2 tog, k16.
Row 51: K2 tog, k15.
Row 52: K2 tog, p13, k1.
Row 53: K2 tog, k13.
Row 54: K2 tog, k12.
Row 55: K2 tog, p10, k1.
Row 56: K2 tog, k10.
Row 57: K2 tog, k9.
Row 58: K2 tog, p7, k1.
Row 59: K2 tog, k7.
Row 60: K2 tog, k6.
Row 61: K2 tog, p4, k1.
Row 62: K2 tog, k4.
Row 63: K2 tog, k3.

Row 64: (K2 tog) twice.
Row 65: Cast off.
Repeat rows 1–65 four times, join the motifs to form squares.

Pattern 196

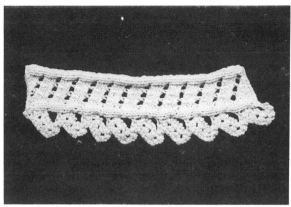

Pattern 195

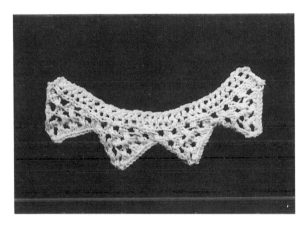

Cast on 7 sts.
Row 1: K.
Row 2: P1, m1, p2 tog, p1, m2, p2 tog, p1.
Row 3: K3, p1, k1, m1, p2 tog, p1.
Row 4: P1, m1, p2 tog, p5.
Row 5: K5, m1, p2 tog, p1..
Row 6: P1, m1, p2 tog, p1, m2, p2 tog, m2, p2 tog.
Row 7: K2, p1, k2, p1, k1, m1, p2 tog, p1.
Row 8: P1, m1, p2 tog, p7.
Row 9: K7, m1, p2 tog, p1.
Row 10: P1, m1, p2 tog, p1, (m2, p2 tog) 3 times.
Row 11: K2, p1, (m2, p2 tog) 3 times, k1, m1, p2 tog, p1.
Row 12: P1, m1, p2 tog, p10 dropping the second 'm2' st of previous row.
Row 13: K10, m1, p2 tog, p1.
Row 14: P1, m1, p2 tog, p2, (m2, p2 tog) 4 times.
Row 15: (K2, p1) 4 times, k2, m1, k2 tog, p1.
Row 16: P1, m1, p2 tog, p14.
Row 17: Cast off 10 sts, k3, m1, p2 tog, p1.
Repeat rows 2–17 until desired length. Cast off.

Cast on 14 sts.
Row 1: K.
Row 2: K3, m1, sl 1, k1, psso, p5, k2, m6, k2.
Row 3: K3, (p1, k1) twice, p3, k4, p1, *sl the st just purled back onto L.H. needle and pass the next st over it, then replace the st on R.H. needle*, m1, k1, p3.
Row 4: K3, p2, m1, sl 1, k1, psso, p3, k10.
Row 5: K8, p2, k2, repeat *—* row 3, m1, k3, p3.
Row 6: K3, p4, m1, sl 1, k1, psso, p1, k2 (m1, k2 tog) 4 times.
Row 7: K8, p2, repeat *—* row 3, m1, k5, p3.
Row 8: K3, m1, sl 1, k1, psso, p5, k10.
Row 9: Cast off 6 sts, k1, p2, k2, repeat *—* row 3, m1, k1, p3.
Row 10: K3, p2, m1, sl 1, k1, psso, p3, k2, m6, k2.
Row 11: K3, p1, k1, p1, k1, p3, k2, repeat *—* row 3, m1, k3, p3.
Row 12: K3, p4, m1, sl 1, k1, psso, p1, k10.
Row 13: K8, p2, repeat *—* row 3, m1, k5, p3.
Row 14: K3, m1, sl 1, k1, psso, p5, k2, (m1, k2 tog) 4 times.
Row 15: K8, p2, k4, repeat *—* row 3, m1, k1, p3.
Row 16: K3, p2, m1, sl 1, k1, psso, p3, k10.
Row 17: Cast off 6 sts, k1, p2, k2, repeat *—* row 3, m1, k3, p3.
Row 18: K3, p4, m1, sl 1, k1, psso, p1, k2, m6, k2.
Row 19: K3, p1, k1, p1, k1, p3, repeat *—* row 3, m1, k5, p3.
Row 20: K3, m1, sl 1, k1, psso, p5, k10.
Row 21: K8, p2, k4, repeat *—* row 3, m1, k1, p3.
Row 22: K3, p2, m1, sl 1, k1, psso, p3, k2, (m1, k2 tog) 4 times.
Row 23: K8, p2, k2, repeat *—* row 3, m1, k3, p3.
Row 24: K3, p4, m1, sl 1, k1, psso, p1, k10.

Row 25: Cast off 6 sts, k1, p2, repeat *—* row 3, m1, k5, p3.
Repeat rows 2–25 until desired length. Cast off.

Pattern 197

Cast on 31 sts.
Row 1: K.
Row 2: Sl 1, k1, k2 tog, m2, k2 tog, k1, m1, k2 tog, m1, (k2 tog) twice, m2, k2 tog, k1, m2, k2 tog, (m1, k2 tog) 6 times, k1.
Row 3: K15, p1, k3, p1, k8, p1, k3.
Row 4: Sl 1, k6, m1, k2 tog, m1, k2 tog, k5, m2, k2 tog, (m1, k2 tog) 6 times, m1, k2.
Row 5: Cast off 3 sts, k13, p1, k16.
Repeat rows 2–5 until required length. Cast off.

Pattern 198

Cast on 29 sts.
Row 1: P.
Row 2: K.
Row 3: P3, *(k2 tog putting yrn twice thus transferring 2 sts to R.H. needle) 5 times, p3*, repeat *—*.
Row 4: K3, *(k1, p1) 5 times [in the double sts of previous row], k3*, repeat *—*.
Row 5: P3, k1, (k2 tog, yrn) 4 times, p5, (k2 tog, yrn) 4 times, k1, p3.
Row 6: K4, (k1, p1) 4 times [in the double sts of previous row], k5, (k1, p1) 4 times [in the double sts of previous row], k4.
Row 7: P3, (k2 tog, yrn) 4 times, p7, (k2 tog, yrn) 4 times, p3.
Row 8: K3, (k1, p1) 4 times [in double sts of previous row], k7, (k1, p1) 4 times [in double sts of previous row], k3.
Row 9: P3, k1, (k2 tog, yrn) 3 times, k1, p3.
Row 10: K4, (k1, p1) 3 times, k9, (k1, p1) 3 times, k4.
Row 11: P3, (k2 tog putting yrn twice) 3 times, p11, (k2 tog, yrn) 3 times, p3.
Row 12: K3, (k1, p1) 3 times, k11, (k1, p1) 3 times, k3.
Row 13: P3, k1, (k2 tog, yrn) twice, p13, (k2 tog, yrn) twice, k1, p3.
Row 14: K5, p1, k1, p1, k14, p1, k1, p1, k4.
Row 15: P3, (k2 tog, yrn) twice, p15, (k2 tog, yrn) twice, p3.
Row 16: K4, p1, k1, p1, k16, p1, k1, p1, k3.
Row 17: P3, k1, k2 tog, yrn, p17, k2 tog, yrn, k1, p3.
Row 18: K5, p1, k18, p1, k4.
Row 19: P3, k2 tog, yrn, p19, k2 tog, yrn, p3.
Row 20: K4, p1, k20, p1, k3.
Repeat rows 1–20 until desired length. Cast off.

Pattern 199

Pattern 200

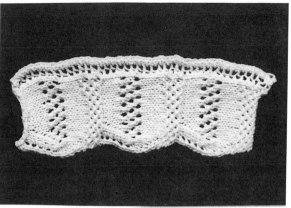

Cast on 37 sts.

Row 1: K1, k2 tog, m1, k5, (sl 1, k1, psso, m1, k1) 3 times, k2 tog, m1, k2, m1, sl 1, k1, psso, (k1, m1, sl 1, k1, psso) twice, k4, k2 tog, m1, k2.

Row 2: P.

Row 3: K2, m1, k2 tog, k3, sl 1, k1, psso, (m1, k1, sl 1, k1, psso) twice, m1, k3, m1, k2 tog, k2, m1, sl 1, k1, psso, k1, m1, sl 1, k1, psso, k1, m1, sl 1, k1, psso, k4, m1, k2 tog, k1.

Row 4: P.

Row 5: K1, k2 tog, m1, k3, sl 1, k1, psso, (m1, k1, sl 1, k1, psso) twice, m1, k3, k2 tog, m1, k4, m1, sl 1, k1, psso, k1, m1, sl 1, k1, psso, k1, m1, k2 tog, k2, k2 tog, m1, k2.

Row 6: P.

Row 7: K2, m1, k2 tog, k4, sl 1, k1, psso, (m1, k1, sl 1, k1, psso) twice, m1, k2, m1, k2 tog, (k1, m1, sl 1, k1, psso) 3 times, k5, m1, k2 tog, k1.

Row 8: P.

Row 9: K1, k2 tog, m1, k4, sl 1, k1, psso, (m1, k1, sl 1, k1, psso) twice, m1, k2, k2 tog, m1, k3, m1, sl 1, k1, psso (k1, m1, sl 1, k1, psso) twice, k3, k2 tog, m1, k2.

Row 10: P.

Row 11: K2, m1, k2 tog, k2, k2 tog, (m1, k1, sl 1, k1, psso) twice, m1, k4, m1, k2 tog, k3, m1, sl 1, k1, psso, k1, m1, sl 1, k1, psso, k1, m1, k2 tog, k3, m1, k2 tog, k1.

Row 12: P.

Repeat rows 1–12 until desired length. Cast off.

Cast on 20 sts.

Row 1: K3, m1, p2 tog (sl 1 p-wise, p1) 7 times, sl 1 p-wise.

Row 2: P17, m1, p2 tog, p1.

Row 3: K3, m1, k2 tog, p1 (sl 1 p-wise, p1) 7 times.

Row 4: P17, m1, p2 tog, p1.

Row 5: K3, m1, p2 tog, (sl 1 p-wise, p1) 7 times, sl 1 p-wise.

Row 6: P17, m1, p2 tog, p1.

Row 7: K3, m1, k2 tog, p1, (sl 1 p-wise, p1) 7 times.

Row 8: P17, m1, p2 tog, p1.

Row 9: K3, m1, k2 tog, k13, m1, k2.

Row 10: P18, m1, p2 tog, p1.

Row 11: K3, m1, k2 tog, k14, m1, k2.

Row 12: P19, m1, p2 tog, p1.

Row 13: K3, m1, k2 tog, k15, m1, k2.

Row 14: P20, m1, p2 tog, p1.

Row 15: K3, (m1, k2 tog) 8 times, k2, m1, k2.

Row 16: P21, m1, p2 tog, p1.

Row 17: K3, m1, k2 tog, k1, (m1, k2 tog) 7 times, k2 tog, m1, k2.

Row 18: P21, m1, p2 tog, p1.

Row 19: K3, (m1, k2 tog) 8 times, sl 1, k2 tog, psso, m1, k2.

Row 20: P20, m1, p2 tog, p1.

Row 21: K3, m1, k2 tog, k12, (k2 tog) twice, m1, k2.

Row 22: P19, m1, p2 tog, p1.

Row 23: K3, m1, k2 tog, k11, (k2 tog) twice, m1, k2.

Row 24: P18, m1, p2 tog, p1.

Row 25: K3, m1, k2 tog, k10, (k2 tog) twice, m1, k2.

Row 26: P17, m1, p2 tog, p1.

Repeat rows 1–26 until desired length. Cast off.

Bibliography

De Dillmont Thérèse, *Encyclopedia Of Needlework,* D.M.C. Publication, Mulhouse, France, 1924.

Klickman Flora, *The Modern Knitting Book,* published by Girls Own and Womans' Magazine, London, 1914.

Miall Agnes M., *Complete Needlecraft,* C. Pearson, London, 1934.

Mrs Leach's Fancy Work Basket, R.S. Cartwright, London, 1887.

Needlecraft Practical Journals, W. Briggs Co. Ltd, 34 Cannon St, Manchester, c.1911–1930.

Sibbald and Souter, *Dainty Work For Busy Fingers,* S.W. Partridge & Co. Ltd, London, 1915.

Thomas Mary, *Mary Thomas's Book Of Knitting Patterns*, Hodder & Stoughton Ltd, London, 1945.

Thomas Mary, *Mary Thomas's Knitting Book*, Hodder & Stoughton Ltd, London, 1985.

Weldon's Practical Knitter, series published by Weldon Ltd, The Strand, London, c.1890–1911.